Daily in His Presence

Andrew
MURRAY
with BRUCE WILKINSON

Multnomah® Publishers *Sisters, Oregon*

DAILY IN HIS PRESENCE
published by Multnomah Publishers, Inc.

Copyright in the United States, Canada, and Mexico is held by Exponential, Inc.
Copyright in the remaining territories is held by Lux verbi.BM.
© 2004 by Exponential, Inc.
International Standard Book Number: 1-59052-447-0

Cover design by The DesignWorks Group, Inc.
Cover image by George Ihring/istockphoto.com

Unless otherwise indicated, Scripture quotations are from:
The Holy Bible, New International Version © 1973, 1984 by International Bible
Society, used by permission of Zondervan Publishing House.

Other Scripture quotations are from:
The Holy Bible, King James Version (KJV).

Multnomah is a trademark of Multnomah Publishers, Inc.,
and is registered in the U.S. Patent and Trademark Office.
The colophon is a trademark of Multnomah Publishers, Inc.

Printed in the United States of America

For information:
MULTNOMAH PUBLISHERS, INC. • 601 N. LARCH ST. • SISTERS, OR 97759

Library of Congress Cataloging-in-Publication Data

Murray, Andrew, 1828-1917.
   Daily in His presence / Andrew Murray with Bruce Wilkinson.
      p. cm.
   Includes index.
   ISBN 1-59052-447-0
   1. Devotional calendars. 2. Christian life—Reformed authors.
3. Reformed Church—Prayer-books and devotions—English.
I. Wilkinson, Bruce. II. Title.
   BV4811.M796 2004
   242'.2—dc22

                                     2004019851

05 06 07 08 09 10—10 9 8 7 6 5 4 3 2

Contents

About This Book

Written over a period of twenty years, these devotions were composed by Dr. Andrew Murray to help his South African congregation experience "ongoing spiritual revival." The congregation consisted mostly of farmers who traveled a great distance to town only once every month to receive communion. So Dr. Murray compiled a series of thirty-day devotionals, each centered on a specific theme, in order to help the farmers to remain in the Word throughout the month.

In 1950, these devotionals were first collected and published in the Afrikaans language. Recently, a team comprising author Rev. Willie Botha, Pastor Roger Witter, and historian Dr. J. J. Joubert carefully adapted Murray's original text into modern English. Dr. Joubert is now busy completing a new biography of Andrew Murray.

In 2002, international bestselling author Bruce Wilkinson first visited the town of Wellington, South Africa, where Andrew Murray helped set ablaze one of the greatest spiritual revivals Africa has ever known. Dr. Wilkinson was fascinated by Murray's work and, in his studies, came to link up with Dr. Joubert and Lux Verbi, the longtime publishers of Murray's books in South Africa. Dr. Wilkinson would later help to develop the concept for this devotional, select the monthly themes, and write the monthly introductions, as well as approve the contemporization of Murray's writings.

This edition marks the first time this text has been made available in America.

Andrew Murray
Servant of God, Man of Revival

Bearing the name given to both his father and his grandfather, Andrew Murray was born in the small but attractive town of Graaff-Reinet in the Cape Province of South Africa on May 9, 1828. As the second son and second child of sixteen, he began his days in the pastoral home of the town's strong and flourishing Dutch church. His father, along with several other Scottish divines, had earlier responded to a need created by the reluctance of clergymen from the Netherlands to come to the Cape after its occupation by the British in 1860.

Thus, six years before the advent of his more famous prodigy, Andrew Murray Sr., having first spent some ten months studying the Dutch language in Utrecht, left his home and the church he pastored in Aberdeen to take up his new assignment as the ordained minister of the Graaff-Reinet congregation. It was here that the young Andrew received not only a godly father's reverence for the Scriptures, but also a profound respect for time spent in prayer, as imparted by his mother. This exceptional woman, born Maria Susanna Magdalena Stegmann, taught her children to read and to write and demonstrated to them the need and effect of prayer in the practicalities of daily life. Of Andrew's father, a friend would later describe him as, "a man with a warm heart and a courageous spirit, who loved hard work, and who had an unquenchable love for his Master and for the people whom he served."

The markedly spiritual tone of the Murray home may explain its choice as a refuge and stopover point for so many missionaries, including such well-known names as Moffat and Livingstone. The family's involvement with missionaries may also account for the fact that almost all of the Murray sons entered one form or another of Christian ministry, and the majority of the daughters married men of the cloth. In addition, some nineteen grandchildren went on to become missionaries, as did a further thirty of the following generation!

Early Days in Scotland and the Netherlands

Aged only ten and twelve years old respectively, Andrew and his elder brother, John, were, after much prayer and deliberation by the Murray family, sent to further their education in Aberdeen, Scotland. A remarkable aptitude and devotion to study saw both brothers graduating with Master of Arts degrees some seven years later.

In June 1845, Andrew and John left for Utrecht in the Netherlands, with the intention of studying the Dutch language, as well as theology. It was in Utrecht that Andrew truly submitted his life to God. In a letter to his father, he wrote, "I've been led to throw myself completely on Christ." From that day on a sharper, refined personal experience was destined to become part of all his future sermons. However, at the time, in what was a theological institution of predominantly liberal persuasion, Andrew was dismayed that he could not freely talk or write about his newfound experience and convictions.

In retrospect, however, the Murrays' exposure to the liberal theology of their day actually had a positive influence on their lives, as well as on those to whom they would later teach and minister. The rather unaccommodating situation in which the brothers found themselves forced them, after serious examination, to commit themselves unequivocally to a passionate propagation of the gospel of their Lord and Master.

The two brothers were ordained as ministers by The Hague Commission on Andrew's twentieth birthday in 1848. They returned to South Africa after a moving farewell from their own circle of student friends.

The First Years of Ministry

After eleven years abroad the brothers ascended their father's pulpit on their very first Sunday in Bloemfontein. In the morning the elder brother, John, with his clear power of thought, preached the sermon. That evening it was the turn of the younger brother, Andrew, who, with his seriousness and passion, exceeded the expectations of the congregation.

On May 6, 1849, three days before his becoming of age, Murray was inducted in Bloemfontein by his father. His pastoral responsibilities extended to Winburg, Smithfield, and Fauresmith—virtually the entire area between the Vaal and Orange Rivers. In addition, from the very beginning he had his eye on the neglected situation of expatriate church members in the Transvaal.

Journeys were invariably difficult and dangerous. Many roads were mere tracks in the veld, left behind by other travelers or traders. Bridges were few and pontoons were used, but travelers most frequently had to search for fords where it was easier to cross the rivers. The vastness of his place of work and the poor amenities on the long journeys by horse or ox-wagon exhausted the eager young clergyman in the beginning of his ministry, making his years in Bloemfontein extremely demanding. Distances were great and danger from wild animals was a daily occurrence.

Thus he ministered to some twelve thousand souls across a territory of fifty thousand square miles. But across the Vaal River another seven thousand immigrants were moving about without a clergyman, and Murray could only visit them during his vacations. Four long and exhaustive journeys to the people in Transvaal seriously impaired Murray's health. Still, from the very beginning he gave his all and was soon greatly respected and loved among the farming communities of the Transgariep.

Worcester and Revival

In 1856, eight years after arriving back in the land of his birth, Andrew Murray married a truly remarkable woman. Emma Rutherford came from a prominent and respected Cape family. She was educated and excelled in literature, music, painting, French, German, accountancy, and home craft—a background much of which was destined to lend support to the many books which Andrew later wrote. He immediately appointed her as a sounding board and critic of his sermons, as well as his secretary to cope with his correspondence, which was later to assume significant proportions. In addition, Emma played the organ and served as a Sunday school teacher. Furthermore, in consequence of his many travels, she was mainly responsible for the education of their eight children, with whom both she and Andrew shared a very close and special bond.

In 1860, four years into his marriage, Andrew Murray was called to Worcester, and although it was very difficult for him to break the bond with his Bloemfontein congregation, he accepted.

Murray's induction into the church at Worcester coincided with the great spiritual revivals that were taking place at the time in England, Scotland, Ireland, Wales, Sweden, and across the seas in America.

News of what God was doing soon reached South African shores, arousing among ministers and church members alike a longing for a similar outpouring of the Spirit of God. Several prayer meetings for revival commenced spontaneously. As a spirit of expectation began to take hold of the people, the attendance at church services and prayer meetings increased rapidly.

Over the eighteenth and nineteenth of April 1860, shortly before he assumed his duties as the minister of the Worcester congregation on Sunday, May 27, Murray attended and participated in an inter-church conference held in the town. It is generally agreed that it was this event that triggered the powerful revival that immediately fol-lowed, and moreover that it all began with a prayer that Murray delivered at that memorable gathering.

Almost immediately following the conference, revival broke out in the town of Montagu, some fifty miles southeast of Worcester, while in the congregation newly acquired by Murray, a mighty out-pouring took place among the youth of the church, which then spread to the rest of the congregation, as well as to prayer meetings which were being held at the time among the outlying farms.

Approximately four months later, the revival spread to the town of Wellington, which housed the congregation that a little more than a decade later was to become the center of Murray's ministry and achievements.

In the year following these events, revival fire spread to numer-ous other towns in the area, including Calvinia, Richmond, Graaff-Reinet, Murraysburg, and Beaufort-West, to name but a few, and thereafter beyond the Cape to towns such as Fauresmith and Kroonstad in the Orange Free State, Ladysmith in Natal, and Hartbeesfontein in the Transvaal.

These powerful revivals were accompanied by an intense out-break of unremitting prayer from young and old, rich and poor, white and black. Thousands turned to God in remorse and repentance. Frequently, entire congregations would break into simultaneous vocal prayer, often accompanied by fervent public confession of sin.

The results in many cases were of a lasting nature, with churches having to greatly extend their seating facilities to accommodate the large numbers of people being added to the family of God. For many churches it was a veritable resurrection from the dead. Homes where previously only idle chatter was to be heard became houses of prayer. Long-standing and respected church members suddenly sought deliverance from enslaving and often secret habits. Superficial Christian living gave way to an earnest seeking after holiness and sanctification. Denominational church reports over the ensuing five or six years reflected significant congregational growth, a marked increase of interest and investment in missionary endeavors, and a general spirit of love and unity prevailing among the believers.

Wellington and Missions

In 1864, Murray accepted a call to Cape Town, where he was inducted on November 11, 1864. There he gave special attention to the plight of the less fortunate and young people, and in 1865 the Young Men's Christian Association (YMCA) was founded under his guidance.

Although he ministered in Cape Town for almost eight years, Murray somehow seemed not to form close ties with the city, and on September 21, 1871, having accepted a call to Wellington, he was inducted into his fourth congregation, where he conducted his greatest work till his retirement in 1906. These years were the prime of Andrew's life. His clear insight and comprehension, as well as his astonishing enterprise, helped him to tackle projects under which people with fewer talents would have succumbed.

Murray played a major role in the training of missionaries in the land of his birth, as well as in supporting personnel who were involved with missionary work. And it was in Wellington that Murray found his real calling and his missionary zeal found its fullest outlet. In October 1877 the Missionary Institute in Wellington was opened to train missionaries and teachers of religious education. Murray and his willing congregation shouldered the burden of this institution until it received synodical support in 1903.

Murray entertained high expectations from especially the sons and daughters of his own people to become missionaries and teachers. His intense missionary zeal, which inspired the Wellington congregation, directly or indirectly led to the founding of at least five missionary organizations and an enterprising missions publication.

Along with his missionary vision, education shared an important place in Murray's heart and life, resulting in his leaving his congregation for months on end to proceed on fund-raising journeys, which provided him with an opportunity to visit former parishioners.

Andrew Murray as Author

One of the most prolific of Christian writers, Andrew Murray occupies a position that could perhaps be regarded as unique in terms of his ongoing popularity among contemporary readers. Few writers of his era can be said to enjoy the wide readership that Murray's works still command today. Though written in the classical style of a bygone Victorian era, the timelessness of his message concerning a deeper life and commitment to Christ has continued to ensure the reprinting of scores of his writings.

Between 1880 and his death, not a year passed in which Murray did not publish a book. His most fruitful year was 1895, when no less than sixteen of his works were published. He is perhaps best known and loved for his numerous shorter works consisting of thirty-one or fifty-two chapters, which were originally intended to be read every day of the month or per week by his many far-flung farming parishioners, whose church attendance was severely limited due to the great distances they had to travel.

Andrew Murray the Preacher

As a young boy, Murray was greatly influenced by the famous Scottish preacher, W. C. Burns and, like Burns, the young Murray's sermons became known for the employment of "naked and plain" language. As was the case with his early mentor, Murray's preaching was devoid of poetry or sentiment and exhibited the same passionate seriousness and lively conveyance of faith.

His performance in the pulpit was magnetic, and his seriousness moved people. Being bilingual, Murray could preach in South Africa, the Netherlands, Britain, or the United States with the greatest of ease. Yet he never saw himself as an orator, only as a servant of the gospel.

In 1893, Murray sustained a permanent back injury in a horse cart accident in Natal. This changed his previously buoyant, upright figure to a more bent, nearly crippled appearance. He later resorted to sitting while preaching, a practice which did nothing to impede the seriousness of his message, which was frequently punctuated by a pounding of his Bible and the cushion upon which he sat.

Of that period of Murray's ministry, a Presbyterian minister who saw him preaching at the Keswick Convention in 1895, witnessed, "The sober, venerable reverend disappeared and an old Hebrew prophet stood in front of us."

H. V. Taylor wrote of Murray in *The British Weekly* of December 6, 1894:

> When preaching or conducting a service, his whole being is thrown into the task, and he glows with a fervency of spirit which seems impossible for human flesh to sustain. At times he startles and overwhelms the listeners. Earnestness and power of the electric sort stream from him and affect alike the large audience or the quiet circle gathered round him. In his slight, spent frame of middle height, he carries in repose a volcanic energy which, when he is roused, bursts its barriers and sweeps all before it. Then his form quivers and dilates, the lips tremble, the features work, and the eyes spasmodically open and close, as from the white-hot furnace of his spirit he pours the molten torrent of his unstudied eloquence."

Murray's own father once said to him, "William is my beloved 'John,' but you, Andrew, are Boanerges, the son of thunder."

Murray the Missionary and Evangelist

The most active time of Murray's extremely busy career in Wellington was from 1879 to 1891. During that time he undertook no less than seven evangelistic tours to all parts of South Africa, some of which lasted for weeks, others several months. Before and during his journeys he wrote down even the smallest planning details and continually strove to keep to his predetermined plans. Therefore, even the routes, distances, resting places, and the number and duration of meetings were recorded before he undertook the journeys. In addition, he particularly saw to it that very thorough spiritual and psychological preparation was done. It was his practice to send ahead packages of his latest books, in order to prepare the hearts of those to whom he would be ministering.

There can be little doubt that events overseas had an effect on much of Murray's life and ministry. This is particularly true as regards the news that reached South Africa of how the American evangelists Dwight L. Moody and Ira D. Sankey's revival services in Britain had set the whole world in uproar. Stirred by the reports of what God was doing overseas, Murray was keen to travel the country to bring the gospel to the countless numbers of its people who had yet to enter the kingdom of God.

In 1879, when about to undertake the first of seven large evangelistic tours, Murray wrote in *De Kerkbode* the reasons behind his undertaking, and mentioned the conditions that could lead to results. It was not some new gospel that he would be preaching, but simply the old, yet ever new message of great joy. "At these special services," he said, "a person could, by means of the continual repetition of the calling to repentance and faith, be led to a point where he will have to decide for himself what he will do." He made repeated mention of the need for good preparation and the cooperation of all the faithful.

The spiritual results of that series of services were both substantial and permanent. A typical congregation in the interior reported that the "complaining, doubtful language of many was changed into the thankful language of the assurance of faith, and we walk the road to Zion with new courage."

Away from home, Andrew Murray was, and still is, internationally regarded as an esteemed and respected Christian leader of his time. In addition to his many activities and achievements in South Africa, he traveled extensively, visiting Europe five times. Several of his approximately two hundred and fifty English and Dutch publications have been translated into at least fifteen languages, including French, German, Spanish, modern Greek, Danish, Swedish, Japanese, and Russian, as well as three different Indian languages and several forms of Chinese.

His Final Days

The year 1905 was a dark year for Murray and his family. Mrs Murray died suddenly on January 2, 1905. Murray's health also took a turn for the worse. On December 25 he applied to the church council to retire. It was granted and he was released from his duties on February 20, 1906. The minutes of the meeting that effected his retirement include the following:

> We record that we cannot express in words what the Rev. Murray has meant for this congregation. His life and example in our midst for so many years was worthy of a servant of the gospel and a man of God. His preaching of the Word occurred with much blessing and power, and it can be eminently mentioned that it was Christ's preaching…and it is with deep emotion that we testify of the severance of such a tender, sincere and important bond of so many years."

In August 1916, Andrew Murray contracted a cold that soon developed into pneumonia. And on January 18, 1917, the old prophet breathed his last. Two days later he was buried in front of the church he had so faithfully and lovingly served.

The town council of Wellington accepted the following motion at its meeting on February 6, 1917:

This Council on behalf of the whole community of Wellington wish to place on record their deep appreciation of the great services rendered by Dr. Andrew Murray, not only to the whole of South Africa, but specially to Wellington in what he did in the cause of Education, of which the Huguenot Seminary and Ladies' College will ever remain as living monuments to his memory.

A long obituary in *The Paarl Post* of January 20 started as follows:

Father Andrew Murray is no more. Last Thursday, towards the evening, when the birds returned to their nests, his soul flew to the place of rest and peace. His career has ended and his work, for which God had placed him on earth, is accomplished.

The Secret of Adoration

Why are so many Christians reluctant to spend time in prayer? If, on the human level, spending time in the company of a parent is normally something quite natural and enjoyable for a child, what is it that hinders God's children from doing the same with their heavenly Father?

One answer could be that we are too focused on our human limitations, on our own meekness and sinfulness, and not enough on God's greatness, holiness, love, and omnipotence. The thoughts and feelings that fill our hearts and minds influence our prayers.

If we dwell upon our own needs and desires, our own efforts, and our own faith, we shall soon find that there is no real power in our prayers. It is essential that we see prayer in the light of *God*: the deep interest He takes in us, the great love with which He desires to answer prayer, the omnipotence of His power, and the magnitude of His strengthening grace.

As with all else, in prayer God must be first. Prayer, to be effective, needs to first be approached in the light of heaven and the infinite glory of the living God. It is when, by this marvelous grace, we have been lifted up into His fellowship and love that He bestows upon us the blessings we need. The first thing, then, must be to bow in lowly reverence before God, offering Him our adoration and worship.

We need to take time to adore God and to secure some sense of His presence. Give God time to reveal Himself to you. Then adore Him. God is in the temple: Let all who appear before Him do so in awe. Prostrate yourself before Him with deepest reverence. Own Him alone as your God and Savior, and praise His name forever.

True Worship

Worship God!
REVELATION 22:9

What might be the reason that prayer is not for us a greater joy and delight? How can we bring down the power and the blessing on those for whom we pray?

The primary answer is undoubtedly that our experience of the presence of God is too limited. When we pray, we do not seek after His presence with all our hearts. We think mostly of *our* need, *our* weakness, *our* desire, *our* prayer. We forget that in every prayer *God* must be first and foremost. To seek Him, to find Him, to linger in His presence, is the approach that gives prayer its inspiration.

How then can you acquire an intimate experience of the presence of God in your communion with Him? The answer is quite simple: Believe with your whole heart that He offers Himself as the listener. Give God the opportunity to make Himself known to you when you approach Him in prayer. You will never discover this, however, if you do not take time to have genuine fellowship with God. The power of prayer does not lie in the number or earnestness of the words you use, but in a living faith that God Himself accepts both you and your prayer into His loving heart.

Lord, lead me into a true experience of Your presence. Teach me to adore You with all my heart.

It is the goal of this month's readings to help you to meet with God every time you pray. Each day you will be given one or more texts, with which you can bow before God in adoration, waiting for Him to lead you into a real experience of their truth and power. Therefore, begin the day with the desire, "My soul thirsts for God, for the living God. When can I go and meet with God?" (Psalm 42:2).

God Is Spirit

God is spirit, and his worshipers must
worship in spirit and in truth.
JOHN 4:24

When God created Adam and breathed his spirit into him, Adam became a living soul. When Adam disobeyed God, he became a slave of the body and the lusts of the flesh. Utter darkness pervaded his spirit and, thereafter, the spirit of the entire human race.

In the new birth it is the spirit of a person that is renewed. As that newborn life enters into fellowship with God, the spirit—which is our deepest inward part—is that which surrenders to the Spirit of God. As the psalmist says, "You teach me wisdom in the inmost place" (Psalm 51:6). And God Himself declares, "I will put my law in their minds and write it on their hearts" (Jeremiah 31:33).

God is spirit, holy and glorious. He gave us a spirit with one objective: that we might have fellowship with Him. Sin, however, has darkened and all but extinguished this ability. There is no other way whereby it can be restored than by waiting upon the working of the Holy Spirit in stillness before God. He will work in your spirit, in your inner being, a level far deeper than that of your thoughts and emotions, as He teaches you to worship Him in Spirit and in truth.

Jesus explained to the woman at the well in Samaria, "The true worshipers...worship the Father in spirit and truth. They are the kind of worshipers the Father seeks" (John 4:23–24). In your quiet hour, become still and give yourself completely to the working of the Spirit.

Thank You, Lord,
that in Your mercy
You lovingly write
on the tablets of
my heart. I wait
on You, Lord, to
complete the good
that You have
begun in me.

Intercession and Adoration

Worship the LORD in the splendor of his holiness.
PSALM 96:9

The better we know God, the more wonderful becomes our insight into the power of intercession. We begin to understand that it is the great means by which we can take part in the carrying out of God's purpose.

God has entrusted the redemption in Christ to His people to make known and communicate to others. In all of this, intercession is the primary essential element, because it is the way in which we enter into dynamic fellowship with Christ and receive the power of the Spirit for service.

It is quite simple to see why God would have it so: He desires to renew us in His image. And there is no other way to do this than to make His desires and attitudes our own, so that we become more like Him who "always lives to intercede" (Hebrews 7:25).

Lord, I bow before You in adoration because You are my God. Lead me into a deeper adoration and more powerful intercession.

The more you come to understand the truth, the more you will sense your need to truly experience God's presence in humble adoration. The more time you spend in God's presence, making His thoughts and will your own, the stronger your faith will grow that God will use your prayers in the carrying out of His plan of redemption.

Intercession will lead you to a realization of your need to enter into deeper adoration. Adoration will give new power for intercession. These two matters are inseparable.

The Desire for God

My soul yearns for you in the night.
ISAIAH 26:9

What is the most worthwhile thing humankind can experience on earth? Nothing less than God Himself!

And what is the first and most important thing to be done each day? It is nothing less than to seek, to know, to love, and to praise God. As glorious as God is, so is the glory that begins to work in the hearts and lives of those who give themselves to live for God.

It is a great step forward in the life of a Christian when he or she truly sees this and regards their daily fellowship with God as the most important aspect of their existence.

Take time and ask yourself whether this is indeed not the most important thing around which your life should revolve—to know God and to love Him with your whole heart. This is what God desires above all else; and it is that which, in answer to your prayer, He will enable you to do.

So begin this and every day of the year with the impassioned prayer of David: "O God, you are my God, earnestly I seek you; my soul thirsts for you...in a dry and weary land" (Psalm 63:1).

Repeat these words in reverence and childlike longing until their spirit and power enter your heart. Then wait upon God till you realize how great a blessing it is thus to meet with Him. As you persevere in this, you will learn to expect the presence of God to surround you throughout the day.

Lord, my God, I confess that I know little of seeking You for Your own sake first. Make me to hunger and thirst after You, and help me to wait patiently for You.

Quiet Adoration

My soul finds rest in God alone; my salvation comes from him.
PSALM 62:1

Who would dispute the fact that when a human being in his or her insignificance meets with God in His glory, that which God has to say must have infinitely more worth than what that person has to say? And yet we so often fill our quiet times in the presence of God with our own thoughts and needs instead of giving Him time to speak to us. Moreover, our prayers are frequently indefinite and vague. We learn a great lesson when we come to understand that the deliberate quieting of our souls and minds before God is the secret of true adoration.

It is when we bow before God, recognizing His majesty and His holiness, His power and His love, and seek to give Him the honor and the reverence and the worship that are His due, that our hearts awaken to the nearness of God and the working of His power. It is when we bow low in our nothingness and lift up our thoughts to realize His presence as He gives Himself to us in Christ Jesus that we find the greatest possible blessing in prayer.

Lord, teach me to be quiet before You. My expectations are from You.

Do not for a moment think of the time as being lost. Persevere in your adoration, even if at first it seems difficult or fruitless. Be assured, it will lead to real fellowship with God. The assurance that He is listening to you in love and working in you with power will come.

As time goes by, you will become increasingly aware of His presence throughout the day. People will begin to sense that you have been with God. It will make you strong to witness for Him. Someone once said, "No one can influence another for good, beyond the amount that there is of God in him."

The Light of God's Presence

The LORD is my light.
PSALM 27:1

Each morning the sun rises and we walk in its light as we joyfully go about our daily work. The light of the sun shines on us all day, whether we are conscious of it or not. Each morning the light of God also shines upon His children.

When there is a shipwreck at night, the crew anxiously watches for the dawn. They sigh, "When will the day break?" This is also how the Christian must wait on God. As the psalmist says, "My soul waits for the Lord more than watchmen wait for the morning" (Psalm 130:6). Wait, until you become aware that the light of His countenance and His blessing is resting on you.

It is the heartfelt wish of our Father in heaven that His children remain in His light throughout the day. As much as we need the light of the sun by day, we need the light of God every moment of our lives.

Even when there are clouds, we still have the sun. So the light of God also shines upon His children even in difficult times. As surely as we know that the sun will rise, we can depend on the light of God. Ensure that you receive it in the morning— then you can count on it to remain with you all day long.

Lord, thank you for the light that comes from you. Help me to be the extension of that light to all those around me today.

Allow yourself time to receive the light of God in your life and you will be able to join the psalmist in saying, "The LORD is my light and my salvation" (Psalm 27:1).

Faith in God

"Have faith in God," Jesus answered.

MARK 11:22

As the eye is the organ by which we see the light of day, so faith is the power by which we see the light of God and walk in it.

Humankind was made for God. Our whole being was made in His likeness, formed according to the divine pattern. We are made to seek Him, to find Him, to become like Him, and so reflecting His glory, to be in the fullest sense the place where He lives. And faith is the eye that, turning away from the world and self, looks up to God and sees light.

How often do we try to arouse feelings about God which are actually just vague, shadowy impressions. We do not turn to the real God.

If we but realized it, He reveals Himself in the depth of our being.

Without faith it is impossible to please or know God. During your quiet time, pray to your Father who dwells in the secret place. If you wait upon and adore Him, He will reveal Himself as surely as light cannot do otherwise than shine.

Lord, make me strong in faith. Empower me to contemplate the greatness of Your glory, power, and love.

Your one desire must be to take time to be still before God, believing that He longs to make Himself known to you. In faith, allow yourself to think great thoughts concerning the magnitude of God's glory, the power by which He reveals Himself to us, and the depths of the love with which He longs to possess us.

Practicing your faith in this manner will become a habit that enables you to always enjoy God's presence and the experience of His saving power.

Alone with God

Jesus…withdrew again to a mountain.
JOHN 6:15

Humankind needs God. God made us for His own possession, to find our life and happiness in Him alone.

As sinful beings, we have been subject to the desires of the human nature and the world. We have been brought under the power of the visible and temporal. Our restoration in Christ is meant to bring us back into the Father's presence, love, and fellowship. We have been saved to love and delight in the presence of God.

We need to be alone with God. Even Christ Himself, during His time on earth, needed this. He could not live the life of the Son of God here in an earthly form without at times isolating Himself to be alone with the Father. How much more you and I need it!

When Jesus instructed us to enter our inner sanctuary, to shut the door, and spend time alone with the Father, He also promised that God would hear our prayers and answer them.

Alone with God. That is the secret of true prayer—of a living, close intimacy with God, and of power for service. Without time spent alone with the Father, there can be no true, deep conversion, no growing devotedness to God, no powerful equipping from the Holy Spirit, and no continued peace or joy.

It is an inestimable privilege to begin each day in secret prayer. Let it be the one thing you set your heart upon: to seek, find, and meet with God.

Lord, teach me to put my priorities in order so that I take time to enter Your secret place. It is the one thing I need more than anything else.

Entirely Committed to God

Whom have I in heaven but you?
And earth has nothing I desire besides you.
PSALM 73:25

Because God alone is God, and the only one who is truly adorable, He has the right to claim us wholly for Himself. Without an appropriate surrender on our part, He cannot manifest his power.

In the Old Testament we read that God's servants Abraham, Moses, Elijah, and David gave themselves wholly to God, without reservation, so that He could accomplish His plans through them. It is only the fully surrendered heart that can fully trust God for all that He has promised.

Life teaches us that if anyone desires to carry out some big task, he must commit himself to it wholeheartedly. This is very true of the love of a mother for her child: She gives herself entirely to the child she loves. May God Almighty then not claim us completely for Himself? And should we not therefore declare that there is nothing on earth or in heaven that means more to us than He? As fully as God gives Himself to us, so fully does He desire that we give ourselves to Him.

Lord, I claim to love You with all my heart, soul, and mind. Add to my love where I still fall short.

Meditate on these things in your inner sanctuary, alone before God. Ask Him to establish in you that which pleases Him.

Entirely committed to God! What a privilege that is! How wonderful the grace that calls us to it! How blessed the separation from men, and work, and all that might draw us away from God. Totally dedicated to God! How sweet the discovery of all that it means, and all that God gives us with it!

The Knowledge of God

Now this is eternal life: that they may know you,
the only true God, and Jesus Christ, whom you have sent.
JOHN 17:3

The knowledge of God is essential for the spiritual life. It is *life eternal*. The knowledge spoken of here is not intellectual knowledge received from others, nor the product of our own thinking, but a living knowledge wherein God makes Himself known to us.

How is it that we so seldom experience the life-giving power of *truly knowing* God? Because we do not give God time to reveal Himself to us. When we pray, we think that we know well enough how to speak to God. We forget that one of the most important principles of prayer is to be silent before Him so that He may reveal Himself. God desires to manifest His presence by causing it to rest upon us and work within us. To know God as a personal and loving God is to know real life.

Brother Lawrence, who had the desire to know God, can be quoted as an example. Various prayer books were given to the monk, but he replied that it would not help to pray if he did not know the God to whom he was speaking. And he believed that God *would* reveal Himself. He spent long hours in quiet adoration in order to become conscious of God's presence, nearness, and sustaining power.

Lord, teach me more about Yourself. Your presence is precious to me.

That is the secret. As the rising sun holds the promise of light for the rest of the day, so your quiet time spent waiting on God will be your promise of His presence and power throughout your day.

God the Father

Baptizing them in the name of the Father
and of the Son and of the Holy Spirit.
MATTHEW 28:19

The truth of the Trinity has a deeply devotional aspect to it.

When we think of *God*, we think of the great distance that separates Him in His holiness from humankind in its sinfulness, and we bow before Him in deep reverence and respect.

When we consider the *Son*, we recall the incomprehensible wonder of Him who was born of a woman descended from Adam, who died a cursed death, and who is inextricably bound to us for eternity.

And when we consider the *Holy Spirit*, we are reminded of the wonder of God within us—He who makes us His eternal temple.

When Christ taught us to address God as "our Father," He added, "hallowed be your name." As God is holy, so we too must be holy. And there is no other way to become more like Him than to honor Him and draw near to Him through prayer.

Father, thank You that I may talk to You and may welcome You into my inner sanctuary. Thank You that I may call You "my Father."

How often we say God's name without giving a thought to the indescribable privilege we enjoy being in a relationship with Him. The time we take to be with Him in our inner sanctuary will become the gateway to heaven. We ought, therefore, to bow low before Him and adore His name as holy.

It is an indescribable privilege to speak to God as "my Father" and have the assurance that He sees and hears and will reward us openly.

God the Son

*Grace and peace to you from God our Father
and from the Lord Jesus Christ.*
ROMANS 1:7

In each of his thirteen letters, Paul wrote, "Grace and peace to you, from God our Father and from the Lord Jesus Christ." The apostle had such a clear perception of the inseparable unity of the Father and the Son in the work of grace that he referred to both in each of his greetings.

There may be times in the Christian life when one is inclined to think chiefly of God the Father and address all prayers to Him. Later on, we come to realize that it is only through faith in Christ and in living in His presence that we can have a lasting relationship with God.

John saw the Lamb in the center of the throne (see Revelation 5:6). Of all the worshiping multitudes, none could see God without first recognizing the Lamb of God. And none could see Christ without seeing the glory of both as inseparably one.

To know and adore God, you have to seek and adore Him through Christ. And if you seek Christ, you must seek and adore Him in God. Then you will understand what it means to have your life hidden with Christ in God and you will experience the fellowship and adoration of Christ as indispensable to the full knowledge of the love and holiness of God.

Take time to meditate and believe, to expect all from God the Father who sits on the throne and from Jesus Christ the Lamb in the center of the throne.

Lord Jesus, I worship You as my Redeemer. Thank You for pouring Your grace out upon my life, and for opening the way for me to the Father.

God the Holy Spirit

For through him we both have
access to the Father by one Spirit.
EPHESIANS 2:18

In our fellowship with God within our inner sanctuary, we must guard against approaching God and Christ either with our emotions or with our intellect. The Holy Spirit has been given to us for the express purpose that we might have access to the Father through the Son. Therefore, we must wait for the Spirit's instruction.

On the last evening before His crucifixion, Christ imparted the truth to His disciples. He gave them the assurance that whatever they asked the Father for in His name, it would be given to them.

In receiving the gift of the Holy Spirit, the disciples learned how to pray. The Spirit makes the fellowship with the Father and the Son a reality. Believe that He is working this in you. In your inner sanctuary, give yourself wholeheartedly to His guidance, both for worship and for intercession.

Holy Spirit, thank You for Your guidance. Strengthen me so that I may learn to know You and the Father and the Son better.

Before Jesus ascended into heaven, the Holy Spirit was given to the disciples to prepare them for the ten days of prayer. From this we can learn three things:

First, that we must pray in the confidence that the Holy Spirit lives within us and must yield to His leading. Set aside time for this.

Second, we must believe that those "greater works" of the Holy Spirit for the strengthening of spiritual life will be given if we pray.

Third, we must believe that, together with all God's children, we may ask for the mighty working of the Spirit of God in His church.

In the Secret Place with God

But when you pray, go into your room, close the door and pray to your Father, who is unseen. Then your Father, who sees what is done in secret, will reward you.
MATTHEW 6:6

Christ longed for His disciples to know God as their Father and have fellowship with Him within the secret place. In His own life, Jesus considered such communion with His Father to be indispensable and found in it great happiness. Thus He longs that we should understand that we cannot be dedicated disciples without daily communion with the Father who eagerly waits for us in secret.

God hides Himself from the world and all that is of the world. He desires to draw us away from the world and our self-absorption. He offers us the wonder of an intimate relationship with Him. If only God's children would take the privilege to heart!

Believers of the Old Testament enjoyed this experience. David often wrote poetry and sang of the Lord being a secret place of refuge for him. How much more should Christians in the New Covenant value this intimate relationship with their Father. We need to commune with our heavenly Father regularly, day by day, that our spiritual life might be restored and renewed.

We have died with Christ and are made one with Him in His resurrection—one plant, one tree. As the roots of a tree are hidden underground, so the roots of our daily lives are hidden deep in God. Take time, therefore, to ponder these words of David: "How great is your goodness...in the sight of men on those who take refuge in you" (Psalm 31:19).

Thank You, Lord, for those times I spend with You in the secret place of prayer, where I can recover, be renewed, and be encouraged.

Half an Hour of Silence

When he opened the seventh seal,
there was silence in heaven for about half an hour.
REVELATION 8:1

Before the first angel sounded the trumpet, there was a half-hour of silence in heaven for the prayers of the saints to be laid before God. In like fashion, the children of God still have the need for silence and separation to bring their prayers before God and be strengthened for their daily work.

One does, of course, hear the objection that there is not sufficient time for prayer. And often the statement is made that even when time is found or made for it, real communion with God is seldom experienced. Christ, however, tells us to close our door and pray to our Father in secret.

Do not think that you will not know how to employ the time spent. Just believe that if you begin and are faithful to bow in silence and expectation before Him, God will reveal Himself to you.

You could begin by reading a portion of Scripture, allowing God's Word to speak to you. Take Psalm 61 or 62, for example, and speak the words therein to God. Then begin to pray. Intercede for your own household and children, for your community, for your church and minister, for schools and missions. Above all, meet with God.

God desires to bless you. Would it not be worthwhile to give up half an hour to be alone with God? If you persevere, you will, after a while, find that the half-hour you initially found so difficult has become the most blessed part of your day.

Lord, thank You that You wish to speak to a sinner like me. My expectation is from You. Let my quiet time this year be precious to me, even when my program is very busy.

The Majesty of God

For you are great and do marvelous deeds;
you alone are God.
PSALM 86:10

Before anyone starts with an important task, he will invariably take time to consider the magnitude of his undertaking. Scientists who study nature require years of intensive research before they are able to gain a reasonable understanding of the vastness of the universe.

Ought we not then to take time to get to know our great and wonderful God, so that we might give Him the adoration that is His due?

Yet how superficial our knowledge of His greatness tends to be! We do not set aside enough time to bow before Him in adoration, with the result that we fail to gain a real appreciation of His majesty and glory.

Meditate on the following texts until you are filled with a sense of God and His glory: Psalm 95:3, 6; 145:3–7; Jeremiah 32:17–19.

It is not easy to grasp the full meaning of these texts. Therefore, you must give time for the words to sink in and stir your heart until you feel compelled to bow in speechless adoration before God.

A genuine comprehension of God's greatness takes time. But if you honor God as He should be honored, and if your faith grows strong in the knowledge of His greatness and power, you will find yourself drawn to linger in the inner sanctuary where you will bow in humble worship before a great and mighty God.

Lord God, my
words are too
inadequate to
worship You as I
should. Thank You
that You are
my Father.

A Committed Heart

For the eyes of the LORD range throughout the earth
to strengthen those whose hearts are fully committed to him.
2 CHRONICLES 16:9

In our temporal lives, we know how important it is to put our heart into our daily work and practical activities. In the spiritual domain it is equally important. God commands that we love Him with our whole heart, soul, and strength. "You will seek me and find me when you seek me with all your heart" (Jeremiah 29:13).

Yet it is amazing that earnest Christians, who are dedicated to their secular work, are content to give God half-hearted service. It does not seem to dawn upon them that the same committed approach toward the things of God is required.

God furthermore encourages us to wait humbly upon Him with a sincere heart. He assures us that His eye will be upon us, and that He will demonstrate His power in us and in our work.

Lord, there are so many things I do with enthusiasm. Forgive me that my devotional life is at times a mere duty that I perform half-heartedly. Teach me perseverance and strengthen me to wait upon You in expectation.

Therefore, first thing in the morning, commit yourself to God wholeheartedly. Pray to Him unreservedly with a committed heart and expect in faith that His power will be shown in and through you. It requires first that you still your heart and mind before God until you are aware that He is at work in you. He promises to shelter you in the day of trouble and set you "high upon a rock" (Psalm 27:5).

The Omnipotence of God

I am God Almighty.
GENESIS 17:1

When Abraham heard these words, he fell on his face. God spoke to him and filled his heart with faith in what God would do for him.

Have you ever bowed in deep humility before God until you felt that you were in living contact with the Almighty? Until your heart has been filled with the conviction that God is at work in you, and that He will complete that work?

The psalms contain many examples of how Old Testament believers rejoiced in God and His power. "I love you, O LORD, my strength" (18:1). "The LORD is the stronghold of my life" (27:1). You "made me bold and stout-hearted" (138:3). Take the time to appropriate these words and to adore God as the Almighty One, your strength.

Lord, almighty God, I want to say along with David, "I love you, O LORD, my strength."

Christ taught us that redemption is the work of God, and beyond human ability. When the disciples asked who could then be saved, Christ replied, "With man this is impossible, but with God all things are possible" (Matthew 19:26). If we firmly believe this, we shall have the courage to believe that God is working in us all that He desires.

Paul's prayer for the Ephesians was that the Spirit of God would enable them to realize what great power He exercises for those who believe (see Ephesians 1:19). When you fully believe that the mighty power of God is unceasingly at work in you, you will joyfully say, "God is the strength of my heart" (Psalm 73:26). Many Christians do not realize that almighty God has committed Himself to work in them every moment of every day. That is the secret of the true life of faith.

The Fear of the Lord

Blessed are all who fear the LORD, who walk in his ways.
Thus is the man blessed who fears the LORD.
PSALM 128:1, 4

The fear of God. These words characterize the religion of the Old Testament and the foundation that was laid for the more abundant life of the New. Reverence and respect for God still mark the life of the true child of God. They provide that essential quality of life that makes a true impression on those around us. It is one of the great promises of the New Covenant as given in Jeremiah: "I will inspire them to fear me" (32:40).

The early church experienced the twin concepts of godly fear and its accompanying blessedness: The church "enjoyed a time of peace. It was strengthened; and encouraged by the Holy Spirit, it grew in numbers, living in the fear of the Lord" (Acts 9:31). And Paul gives fear a high place in the Christian life, writing in terms such as "perfecting holiness out of reverence for God" (2 Corinthians 7:1).

Lord, grant me grace to serve You with godly fear.

It has often been said that the lack of the fear of God is one of the most significant reasons why the church of today compares so unfavorably with the church of earlier times. Texts such as the one at the head of today's devotion need to be brought to our attention again, for we lack the awareness of the need for a holy fear of God, and we know little of the blessedness of life that it brings. The secret of such blessedness is to be found in genuine awe and reverence for God. And it is indeed in the inner sanctuary of adoration that such a grace is cultivated.

God Unfathomable

How great is God—beyond our understanding!
The number of his years is past finding out.
JOB 36:26

The greatness of God's being and glory, though beyond our understanding, is a reality that we give too little consideration. As high as the heavens are above the earth, so far beyond our comprehension are the thoughts and ways of God. A deep appreciation of this is of the utmost importance in the spiritual life.

We need to look up to God with deep humility and holy reverence, and then with childlike simplicity to accept the teaching of the Holy Spirit. His greatness, power, wisdom, holiness, grace, love—all are far above that which we can grasp or understand.

The Word declares, "Oh, the depth of the riches...the wisdom and knowledge of God! How unsearchable his judgments, and his paths beyond tracing out" (Romans 11:33).

Our hearts are meant to respond, "Indeed, how wonderful, Lord, are all Your thoughts! How deep are Your purposes!" Our meditations upon what God is ought always to fill us with a holy reverence and deep longing to know and honor Him.

When you worship God, therefore, cry out, "How great is the glory of the Lord who is my God and Father!" Confess with shame how little you have tried to get to know Him, or how reluctant you have been to wait upon Him to make Himself known to you. Then start believing that the incomprehensible and wonderful God will begin to work in your heart and life, enabling you to know, to love, and to serve Him better.

Lord, teach me to be still and know that You are God, exalted high above all people, exalted high above the earth.

The Holiness of God
Old Testament

I am the LORD your God; consecrate yourselves and be holy, because I am holy.
I am the LORD who brought you up out of Egypt to be your God;
therefore be holy, because I am holy.

LEVITICUS 11:44–45

The holiness of God is repeatedly emphasized in the book of Leviticus. Israel had to understand that as holiness is the outstanding characteristic of God, so it should be the marked characteristic of His people. Those who would truly know God, would meet Him in the inner sanctuary, must above all desire to be like Him. The priests who were to have access to God had to be set apart for a life of holiness.

This was to be true also of the prophets who spoke on God's behalf. Isaiah describes how he saw the Lord seated on the throne, as the seraphim sang, "Holy, holy, holy is the LORD Almighty!" In response, Isaiah cried out, "Woe to me…I am ruined! For I am a man of unclean lips, and I live among a people of unclean lips" (Isaiah 6:3, 5). These are the words of a broken and repentant heart.

Thank You, Lord,

that I may

worship You

in Your holiness.

Let the beauty of

Your holiness

dwell in me.

Be still and take time to worship God in His might and holiness, and marvel at the condescension with which He offers to dwell with us and in us. "For this is what the high and lofty One says— he who lives forever, whose name is holy: 'I live in a high and holy place, but also with him who is contrite and lowly in spirit, to revive the spirit of the lowly and to revive the heart of the contrite'" (Isaiah 57:15).

If you would truly meet with your Father in your secret place, bow low and worship Him in the glory of His holiness. Give Him time to make Himself known to you.

The Holiness of God
New Testament

Holy Father, protect them by the power of your name—the name you gave me—so that they may be one as we are one. Sanctify them by the truth. For them I sanctify myself, that they too may be truly sanctified.
JOHN 17:11, 17, 19

Christ lives eternally as our intercessor, praying the great prayer. We are to expect and appropriate the answer.

Paul writes to the Thessalonians, "Night and day we pray most earnestly [that] you will be blameless and holy. May God himself, the God of peace, sanctify you through and through. May your whole spirit, soul and body be kept blameless at the coming of our Lord Jesus Christ. The one who calls you is faithful and he will do it" (see 1 Thessalonians 3:10,13; 5:23–24).

Ponder these words of Scripture, and in your place of prayer use them as a supplication to God: "Lord, strengthen my heart that I may be blameless and filled with Your holiness. You are faithful and will do it."

What a privilege to spend time secluded with God and to allow the Spirit to reveal to you something of His holiness. In the New Testament we discover that the holiness of Christ is imparted to His people through the sanctifying work of the Spirit.

If we could but grasp the blessing contained in these words: "Be holy, because I am holy" (Leviticus 11:45). For this purpose the God of holiness revealed Himself through the Son and the Holy Spirit.

Let us, therefore, use the word *holy* with great reverence and with a sincere desire to become more like God.

Lord, strengthen my heart that it may become holy and blameless. You are faithful; You will do it.

Sin

Christ Jesus came into the world to save sinners—of whom I am the worst.
But for that very reason I was shown mercy.
1 TIMOTHY 1:15–16

Never forget as you enter your inner sanctuary that your whole relationship with God depends on what you think of sin and of yourself as a redeemed sinner.

It was because of sin that God did not spare His own Son. It was sin that nailed Jesus to the cross, and revealed the depth and the power of the love with which He loved. Our salvation as sinners will sound through our praise for all eternity.

Never forget that it was sin that led to your experience of salvation in Jesus Christ, and that each day He greatly desires to deliver and keep you from its power and transform you into His likeness. It is the thought of sin that will keep you low at His feet and provide depth to your adoration. It is the thought of sin always surrounding and tempting you that will give fervency to your prayers and compel you toward the faith that protects you in Christ.

It is the thought of sin that makes Christ so precious, keeps us dependent on His grace every moment, and inspires us to lay claim to being more than conquerors through Him who loved us. It is the thought of sin that calls us to thank God with a broken and humble heart.

It is in our inner sanctuary, in quiet communion with God, that sin can be conquered. There the holiness of Christ can be imparted and the Spirit of holiness can take possession of our lives.

Thank You, Father, that the blood of the Lamb cleanses me of all my sin. May I learn to abide in You, so that I can be free of its power.

The Mercy of God

Give thanks to the LORD, for he is good.
His love endures forever.
PSALM 136:1

Psalm 136 is devoted entirely to the praise of God's merciful love. "His love ['mercy' in the King James Version] endures forever" is the repeated refrain. Our hearts should be full of this wonderful assurance. The eternal, unchanging mercy of God is cause for unceasing thanksgiving.

Earlier, the same thought is expressed in the psalmist's exhortation to praise the Lord "who crowns you with love and compassion" (Psalm 103:4). Of all God's attributes, loving mercy is the crown. "The LORD is compassionate and gracious, slow to anger, abounding in love" (v. 8). As wonderful as the greatness of God is, so unending is His mercy. "For as high as the heavens are above the earth, so great is his love for those who fear him" (v. 11). What an overwhelming thought! *The love of the Lord is unchangeable toward those who serve Him.*

How often have we not read these words without really thinking of their immeasurable greatness! Be still and meditate on them until your heart responds thus: "Your love, O LORD, reaches to the heavens, your faithfulness to the skies. Your righteousness is like the mighty mountains, your justice like the great deep" (Psalm 36:5–6).

Take time to thank God for all the loving mercy with which He crowns your life. For His love is "better than life" (Psalm 63:3).

Lord, I thank You for Your merciful love that You have demonstrated to me in so many ways. Help me to place my trust in Your faithfulness each day.

The Word of God

The word of God is living and active.
HEBREWS 4:12

The Word of God and prayer are, together, indispensable for communion with God. In His Word, God speaks to me; in prayer, I speak to God.

The Word teaches me about the God to whom I pray, and how He would have me pray. It gives me wonderful promises to encourage me in prayer.

The Word comes from God's heart, and carries His thoughts and His love to my heart. And the Word returns from my heart into His. Prayer is thus the means of fellowship between God's heart and mine.

The Word teaches me God's will—His promises as to what He will do for me, and His commands as to what He would have me be and do for Him.

Cause me, Lord, to delight in Your Word and to meditate upon it day and night.

The more I pray, the more I feel need of the Word and find joy in it. The more I read God's Word, the more I have to pray about, and the more power I have in prayer. One great cause of prayerlessness is that we read God's Word too little, too superficially, or in the pale light of human wisdom.

It is the Holy Spirit through whom the Word has been spoken. And it is He who is also the Spirit of prayer. Thus it is that He will teach us both how to receive the Word and how to pray.

How blessed the inner chamber would be, and what a power and inspiration in our worship, if we would only learn to receive God's Word as words that He speaks to us personally. It is a message full of life-giving power to make us strong, that we might expect and receive great things from God. Above all, it will bring us the daily-blessed fellowship with Him as the living God.

The Psalms

How sweet are your words to my taste,
sweeter than honey to my mouth!
PSALM 119:103

Of the sixty-six books in the Bible, the book of Psalms is given us especially for worship. The other books are, for the most part, historical, doctrinal, or practical. But the psalms take us into the sanctuary of God's presence to experience the riches of fellowship with Him. If you truly desire, each morning, to meet with God and worship Him in Spirit and in truth, then let your heart be filled with the Word of God expressed in the psalms.

As you read the psalms, underline the words *Lord* or *God* wherever they occur, and also the pronouns referring to God: *You, He,* and *I.* This will assist you in connecting the content of the psalm with God, who is the object of all prayer. Once you have taken the trouble to mark the names of God, you will find that more than one difficult psalm becomes clearer. The underlined words will help you to make God your focal point and lead you to a new adoration of Him. Employ them as you address Him in worship. Your faith will be strengthened once again as you realize that God is your strength and help in all the circumstances of your life.

Thank You, Lord, that You teach me through Your Word how to pray and to worship You.

Just as the psalms were used by the Holy Spirit to teach the Old Testament people of God how to pray, they will, by the power of the Spirit, teach us how to abide in God's presence. Take Psalm 119. Underline all the words used to address God. Meditate on the thought that the God of the psalm is the same God who, in Christ, has placed His law in our hearts and empowers us to walk in love and obedience to Him.

The Glory of God

*God, who said, "Let light shine out of darkness,"
made his light shine in our hearts to give us the light of the
knowledge of the glory of God in the face of Christ.*
2 CORINTHIANS 4:6

God Himself must reveal His glory to us; only then will we know how to truly glorify Him. Nothing in nature reflects the glory of God as do the starry heavens. Telescopes, which are becoming increasingly more powerful, tell of the wonders of God's universe. And by means of photography, new dimensions of that glory are being revealed.

What a lesson this is for those who desire to see the glory of God in His Word! Put aside your own efforts and thoughts. Let your heart be as a camera that waits for God's glory to be revealed and imprinted upon its film. The lens must be prepared and clean; so let your heart be prepared and cleansed by God's Spirit. The camera must be kept still; so let your heart be still before God. The film must also sometimes be exposed for hours to capture the wonders of Creation; so let your heart, too, take time to wait silently before God that He might reveal His glory.

*Thank You, Lord,
that I may
worship You
in Your holiness.
Let the beauty of
Your holiness
dwell in me.*

In such times of silent waiting before Him, God will place His thoughts in your heart so they become a great blessing to you and to others. He will create within you desires and dispositions that will be as rays of His glory shining in you.

Put it to the test this morning. Offer yourself to Him in sincere humility, and believe that God, in His holy love, will make Himself known to you.

The Holy Trinity

God's elect…have been chosen…
for obedience to Jesus Christ and sprinkling by his blood.
1 PETER 1:1–2

We have thus far concentrated on the adoration of God the Father, and how necessary it is to give sufficient time each day to worship. But it must also be borne in mind that to enter into fellowship with God, the presence and power of the Son and the Spirit are also needed.

How wide a field this opens for us in the inner sanctuary! It may take us some time before we become truly aware of our need for the presence and working of Jesus Christ each time we approach to worship God. We do not immediately realize that our fellowship with the Father is always dependent upon the active and personal work of Jesus Christ. It takes time to fully understand what confidence we can have in the work He is doing for us and in us, and with what holy and intimate love He makes His presence real to us.

So, too, the Holy Spirit works powerfully in the depths of our hearts. Only through His activity can we know what and how to pray, and above all, have the assurance that our prayers have been heard.

True fellowship with God in Christ through the Holy Spirit requires time—enough time. The reward, however, is the ability to become increasingly aware of God's presence throughout every day.

Lord, lead me into an ever-deepening awareness of the presence of the triune God, as I learn the secret of unhurried time spent in Your sanctuary.

The Love of God

God is love. Whoever lives in love lives in God, and God in him.
1 JOHN 4:16

The best and most wonderful word in heaven is *love*. For God is love. Therefore, the best and most wonderful word in our inner sanctuary must be *love*.

What is love? Love finds its joy in giving everything it has to make the loved one happy. And the heavenly Father, who meets with you in your inner sanctuary, has as His objective to fill your heart with His love.

All the other qualities of God have their greatest joy in love. The true and full blessing of the inner sanctuary is nothing less than a life in the abundance of God's love.

Your first and foremost thought in the inner sanctuary, therefore, should be faith in the love of God. Therefore, as you pray, believe in the love of God.

Lord, I pray that You will continue to pour Your love into my heart so that I can love and serve You and my neighbor.

Take time to meditate in quietness on the revelation of God's love in Christ, until you are filled with a spirit of worship, wonder, and longing. God has poured out His love into our hearts by the Holy Spirit, whom He has given us (see Romans 5:5).

Let us remember with regret how little we have believed in, or sought after, His love. While you pray, hold fast to the assurance: *I firmly believe that my heavenly Father longs to reveal His love to me. I am absolutely convinced of the truth: He can, and will, do it.*

Waiting upon God

O Israel, put your hope in the LORD both now and forevermore.
PSALM 131:3

Waiting upon God—in the expression we find one of the deepest truths in God's Word regarding the attitude we need to adopt in our communion with Him.

Waiting upon God. To think that He makes Himself known to us; that He wants to teach us; that He will keep His promises to us; that in all things He remains the everlasting God! This is the way in which we should begin each day, in quiet meditation, offering our heartfelt longings and desires to our Father. Indeed, this should be our attitude throughout the day while we are busy with the day's activities.

Waiting upon God. In striving towards obedience and holiness, in our struggles against sin and self—in all these things there should be a waiting upon God, to receive what He would supply, to see what He would do, and to allow Him to be almighty God in our lives.

Meditate upon these things and they will help you to truly appreciate the precious promises of God's Word. The deep root of all scriptural truth is this: *absolute dependence upon God.* As we practice that attitude, it will become more natural and achievable for you to wait upon God.

Lord, at times I am in such a hurry. Teach me to wait on You in quiet trust.

Perhaps the month's readings have helped you in your adoration of God. Or maybe they have led you to realize how little you know of it. Whichever it may be, give thanks to Him. "I wait for the LORD, my soul waits, and in his word I put my hope" (Psalm 130:5).

The Praise of God

Sing joyfully to the LORD, you righteous;
it is fitting for the upright to praise him.

PSALM 33:1

Praise will always be a part of adoration. Adoration, when it has entered God's presence, will always lead to the praise of His name.

After their deliverance from the bondage of the Egyptians, the children of Israel praised God: "Who…is like you, O LORD? Who is like you—majestic in holiness, awesome in glory, working wonders?" (Exodus 15:11).

In the psalms, one can see the important role which praise ought to play in the spiritual life. The psalms include more than sixty songs of praise. They occur more frequently toward the end of the book, the last group of which all begin and end with the words "Praise the LORD!" The very last, Psalm 150, repeats the phrase "praise him" twice in each of five successive verses and ends thus: "Let everything that has breath praise the LORD. Praise the LORD."

Lord, I pray that my life may be a steady stream of praise.

The coming of Christ into the world was greeted with songs of praise from the mouths of Mary, Zechariah, and Simon.

In Revelation, we also hear the song of Moses, priest of God, which becomes the song of the Lamb: "Great and marvelous are your deeds, Lord God Almighty. Just and true are your ways, King of the ages. Who will not fear you, O Lord, and bring glory to your name? For you alone are holy!" (Revelation 15:3–4). And, on four occasions in the nineteenth chapter, the great multitude shouts, "Hallelujah! Our Lord God Almighty reigns."

May your inner sanctuary, and your quiet times with God, always bring your heart to sing His praises.

The Secret of a New Life in Christ

In Galatians 2:20, Paul gives a glorious personal confession of faith. I want to emphasize, in particular, two phrases he uses, "for me" and "in me," for therein lies the twofold secret of the Christian life. Of the first Paul says, "I live by faith in the Son of God, who loved me and gave himself *for me*." Of the other he says, "I no longer live, but Christ lives *in me*."

"For me" points to the foundation of our faith: Christ bore our sins for us. While "in me" speaks of our life source: Christ living in us. Most believers today get no further than "for me." They understand little or nothing of the fact that the believer lives by the life of Christ. Our Lord referred to this when He spoke of our remaining in Him and He in us. "On that day," He said, "you will realize that I am in my Father, and you are in me, and I am in you" (John 14:20).

Our faith must always remain in the fact that Christ was crucified *for us* in order that He might remain *in us* as our source of life. The Christian who thinks that *Christ for me* is enough ends up living an impoverished spiritual life, for that which Jesus ultimately promises is *Christ in me*. It is only by His remaining in us that we shall live to the glory of the Father.

The message of *Christ our life* is a glorious one—namely, that as the Son of God once led a human life here on earth, He now desires to live in every believer.

May God the Father teach us by His Spirit daily, in our quiet time, to fellowship with our Lord Jesus, so that with Paul we may say, "I no longer live, but Christ lives in me." Christ is our life.

God's Plan of Salvation

When Christ, who is your life, appears,
then you also will appear with him in glory.
COLOSSIANS 3:4

After Adam had sinned and brought death upon himself and his descendants, God gave the promise of a second Adam—the Son of God, who would break the power of Satan and sin.

Paul, in Romans 5:14, tells us that the first Adam was "a pattern of the one to come." The first Adam brought the curse of sin and death on his descendants. As a consequence a sinful nature has ruled in every one of those who came after him. However, the *second* Adam, by His death, delivered us from the power of sin and death, and now lives in each of His redeemed children as their life.

We are too apt to think of Christ as simply reigning in heaven and, from there, living through us. However, Jesus taught that, just as His Father dwelt and worked in Him here on earth, after His resurrection He would live and work in us. The full gospel is contained in these words: *Christ lives in me.*

Lord, I believe that You are living in me. I praise You for this wonderful privilege.

Many Christians forget this. Though they believe that Christ died on the cross and now lives in heaven for them, they do not really believe that Christ also now lives in them. The primary reason for the powerlessness of the church lies in the fact that Christians no longer have, nor exult in, the knowledge that almighty God, in the person of His Son, Jesus Christ, has taken up residence within them. Real and lasting revival in the church of Christ depends on our knowing, explaining, and testifying to this truth. Then we shall know what it is to submit ourselves wholly to Christ, to always remain in Him, and have His work accomplished through us.

The Twofold Life

I have come that they may have life,
and have it to the full.
JOHN 10:10

Everyone can understand the difference between a life that is weak and sickly and one that is full of vitality. This is what Paul had in mind when he spoke of the lives of the Corinthians as being carnal and not spiritual. Like infants who cannot eat solid food, they could not understand the deeper truths of the gospel (see 1 Corinthians 3).

Many Christians never progress beyond the basic principles of the gospel; others—the minority—demonstrate the abundant riches of God's grace. We find this lopsided dichotomy throughout the history of the church. Today, too, the number of believers who live wholeheartedly for God and display such abundance is alarmingly small.

The preacher's task should be to preach of the fullness of grace through Jesus Christ. Christians need to become aware of how impoverished their spiritual lives are, and be encouraged to believe that a life of abundance in the fullness of the Spirit is meant for them.

Thank You that Your Spirit seeks to enable me to have abundant life every day.

I would urge you to ask yourself whether you are living in the abundance of life that Jesus came to give you. If you are, it will be evidenced in your love for your Redeemer, by much bearing of spiritual fruit to the honor of God, and by winning others for God's kingdom. If this is not the case, pray that God will give you such abundance. Seek Christ that He may become very precious to you, and allow your daily communion with Him to become indispensable. He will lead you into an abundant life lived in the power of the Spirit for His glory.

Abundant Life

But where sin increased, grace increased all the more,
so that…grace might reign through righteousness to bring eternal life.
ROMANS 5:20–21

This great truth is seldom fully grasped. That sin increases, we know only too well. But do we believe that grace increases all the more, enabling us to overcome sin? It is absolutely essential that you grasp this truth if you want to live a life of abundance in Christ.

In 2 Corinthians 9:8, Paul particularly uses the words *all* and *every*, denoting abundance: "God is able to make *all* grace abound to you, so that in *all* things at *all* times, having *all* that you need, you will abound in *every* good work." Ask yourself, *Is the all-abounding life for me?* Your answer should be, *If God is faithful, it is possible for me!*

Another example of God's abundance is found in Paul's prayer in Colossians 1:9–11: "We have not stopped praying for you and asking God to fill you with the knowledge of his will through all spiritual wisdom and understanding. And we pray this in order that you may live a life worthy of the Lord and may please him in *every* way: bearing fruit in *every* good work…strengthened with *all* power according to his glorious might."

Thank You, Lord,
that the power
and bounty of
Your grace is
far greater than
the power of sin
in my life.

These words, given by the Holy Spirit, are almost beyond our grasp. Take them to God so that He can, through His Spirit, cause them to come alive in your heart. In this way your faith will grow firm and joyous. With God's gift of abundant mercy—much greater than the sin that overwhelms you—you can firmly believe that a life of abundance can be yours.

Christ Lives in Me

I have been crucified with Christ and
I no longer live, but Christ lives in me.
GALATIANS 2:20

In these words, Paul expresses three great thoughts.

The first of these finds expression in the words "I have been crucified with Christ." When Christ died upon the cross, all of God's
people were identified with Him and included in that death. As we all
died in Adam and inherited his sinful nature, so we all have been crucified together with Christ. Moreover, the power of His death now
works in us daily. In Christ we have died to sin, so that we can live to
God. Our union with Christ is total and dynamic, in that the power
of His death and His life are both active in us.

Paul's second thought is, "I no longer live." Having participated
in Christ's death, he was able to say that. This is also the truth for
every believer. My life has been given up to death
on the cross of Christ. By faith, I see my old life,
lived under the sentence of death, as now ended.
While it may still reside and be able to operate
within my sinful human nature, I have been set
free in Christ, so that I am no longer obliged to
serve sin.

The third thought expressed here by Paul is,
"Christ lives in me." Herein lies the secret of living
a Christlike life. Christ was not only crucified for
me. Nor does He live in heaven only to intercede
for me. *He actually lives in me!* As His Father lived
and worked in Him, so Christ now lives and works in us.

Thank You, Lord
Jesus, that I have
a share in Your
death and
resurrection.

Take time to meditate on this. Allow the Holy Spirit to cause
these words to live within you, and to gloriously manifest Christ in
you.

The Life of Faith

The life I live in the body, I live by faith in the Son of God,
who loved me and gave himself for me.
GALATIANS 2:20

These words were Paul's answer to the objection "If, as you say, 'Christ lives in me,' what happens to my free will?" In other words, if Christ assumes responsibility for our lives, what remains for us to do?

Paul's words hold the secret of the true life of faith. Paul prays for the Christians in Ephesus that Christ may dwell in their hearts by faith (see Ephesians 3:14–19). Here we see the great work that faith accomplishes for us and in us, moment by moment, in order to allow the living God to work His will in us. Christ will accomplish the work. In His divinity, the Lord Jesus is positioned to fill all things, to be the all in all. This certainly includes the lives of God's children.

Christ's own words to His disciples explain this best. Just as the Father lived and worked in Him, so Jesus lives and works in us. The Son expressed the Father. We are to express Christ. The Father worked in the Son, and the Son gave expression to that which the Father brought about in Him. Christ works in us and enables us to carry on His work. This is His gift to us.

Thank You, Father, that You love me and gave Your Son for me. Thank You that we are inseparably bound together.

All that I need do is strengthen my faith in the certainty that He loved me and gave Himself for me—He and I are eternally and inseparably one.

To consider these important words, times of meditation and adoration are necessary so that the Spirit of God may reveal to you how completely He will fill your being and finish the work in you.

The Spirit with Us Forever

He will give you another Counselor to be with you forever.
He lives with you and will be in you.
JOHN 14:16–17

The promise given to us that the presence of the Lord Jesus will remain with us is often referred to and thought upon. He explicitly said that we are to remain in Him, and that He will remain in us (see John 15:4).

In today's verse, Christ speaks of His being in us, and we in Him, in the sense of the indwelling and work of the Holy Spirit. A careful consideration of His words reveals that His life in us is inextricably linked with the indwelling of the Holy Spirit within us. It is therefore of the utmost importance that we correctly grasp the reality of the Holy Spirit who is always present in us

Christ in us becomes a reality only when we perceive and open up to the Holy Spirit's presence within us. As the Comforter encouraged the disciples after Jesus' ascension into heaven, He now desires to encourage *us* each hour of the day. It is through the Holy Spirit that we have Christ in our hearts—a mighty living force stirring, enlightening, and filling us.

The conviction of faith can be yours when, through Christ, you seek the presence of God each day and by this means receive new power to influence and bless others. Therefore, begin the day with the triune God. Take time to worship God in Christ. Take time to yield yourself to the Holy Spirit, and to depend on Him to complete the important work of making the living presence of Christ in you a reality.

Thank You, Lord, that Your Spirit encourages me to seek Your presence. Thank You that You are my source of power. I worship You in Your glory.

Christic and the Spirit

"Whoever believes in me...streams of living
water will flow from within him."
By this he meant the Spirit, whom those who believed in him,
were later to receive.
JOHN 7:38–39

Each person of the Holy Trinity gives honor to the others. The Father honors the Son, the Son honors the Spirit, the Spirit honors the Son. In our text for today, Christ calls us to believe in Him, confident that the Holy Spirit will work powerfully in us according to the measure of our faith in Christ. Further on in his Gospel, John records Jesus as saying, "When he, the Spirit of truth, comes...he will not speak on his own; he will speak only what he hears. He will bring glory to me by taking from what is mine and making it known to you" (John 16:13–14).

Lord, bind me ever closer to the Spirit that lives in me, so that I will always know for certain that Christ is at work within me.

Here we learn the important lesson that we must not expect the Holy Spirit to constantly give us signs of His own presence: He will always seek to fix our attention upon Christ. The surest way to remain filled with the Spirit is to focus our attention on Christ.

Begin every morning in the presence of God and there commit yourself to Christ, trusting Him to accomplish His work in you. Thank the Father for the gift of the Holy Spirit, which enables you to remain in the love of Christ. Believe with all your heart that the triune God is at work in you. These truths will be revealed to you increasingly as you commit yourself to the Son and to the Spirit of God.

The Spirit and Christ

*He will bring glory to me by taking from what is mine
and making it known to you.*
JOHN 16:14

We have seen that Christ promised that the Holy Spirit would flow as living water from those who believe in Him. Today we have the other side of the same truth: The Holy Spirit flows from Christ, reveals Christ, and imparts Christ.

Do you desire the Spirit? Have faith in Christ who gives the Spirit. Do you desire Christ? Trust the Spirit to reveal Christ to you. The Spirit is sent from Christ glorified in heaven to impart Christ glorified to us upon the earth.

The fullness of the Godhead dwelt in Christ in order that the life of the Godhead might dwell in us. All this is in Christ. Our entire life exists in union with Christ. As the branch is in the vine, so we are in Christ and He in us. Each new day we must begin with this conviction: *Christ lives in me and the Holy Spirit will make this a reality for me.* Count on the quiet, unseen working of the Holy Spirit in your heart.

This truth is so profound and so divine that it is almost beyond our grasp. Yet the Holy Spirit, who is God, will reveal it to us. Cling to Christ in childlike faith and trust that the Holy Spirit is at work in you in order that Christ living in you can be a reality.

In childlike faith, fix your heart upon Christ on the cross and upon Christ on the throne. As you do this, the Holy Spirit will reveal Christ to you and in you. You will be able to confidently say, "Christ lives in me! Christ is my life!"

*Spirit of God,
I cling to Christ
and His
worthiness,
so that I may
increasingly
reflect His image.*

Carnal or Spiritual?

*Brothers, I could not address you as spiritual
but as worldly—mere infants in Christ.*

1 CORINTHIANS 3:1

The difference that Paul points out between two kinds of Christians is of great importance. At the new birth we received the Holy Spirit, yet our fallen human nature has remained altogether carnal. Since that time there has been a struggle between the sinful nature and the Spirit. If we allow the Spirit to conquer, His power within us increases, so that we grow as spiritual beings. The carnal nature, however, continues to harbor nothing good. Therefore, we need to learn that our sinful nature has been crucified, and that we are free to grow in Christ.

If we do not realize that we have died with Christ, or we fail to submit to the work of the Holy Spirit, our carnal nature will gain the upper hand, causing us to remain spiritual babies. We may then, in our own strength, try to do better. The result, however, is that what began in the Spirit becomes a purely carnal attempt to be holy; ultimately, the sinful nature will triumph, leaving us powerless to resist.

This is the sad condition of the church. The majority of her members remain carnal, constantly falling victim to the sinful nature. Such Christians have little insight into spiritual truth, enjoy meager daily fellowship with God, and fail to lay hold of His promises. We should earnestly ask God to help us distinguish between the carnal and the spiritual, and to enable us to yield ourselves completely to the guidance of His Spirit.

*Lord God, reveal
to me, by the
working of Your
Spirit, where I still
live and speak as
a carnal person.*

Go on to Maturity

*Solid food is for the mature, who by constant use have
trained themselves to distinguish good from evil.
Therefore let us leave the elementary teachings
about Christ and go on to maturity.*

HEBREWS 5:14–6:1

In the letter to the Hebrews, we discover that the recipients had long been Christians, who by then ought to have been teaching others. Instead, they were still like infants, needing to be fed milk (see Hebrews 5:12–14). The writer attempts to rouse them to go beyond the elementary teachings about Christ, "not laying again the foundation of repentance." They were to go on to maturity, to the status of spiritual adults, and to more profound truths concerning Christ's priesthood and the fullness of their salvation.

Because Jesus lives forever, He has a permanent priesthood. Therefore, He is able to save completely those who come to God through Him, because He ever lives to intercede for them (see Hebrews 7:24–25). This is the solid food of which the writer speaks. He goes on to tell of Christ appearing before God for us and, later, of our privilege to enter into the Holy Place to live in fellowship with God (see 10:19–20).

It is only when the Christian ceases to remain at the elementary teachings about Christ that he or she will grow and be strengthened in grace and truly live in fellowship with Christ.

*Lord Jesus, I want
so much to
progress and grow
in my commitment.
Help me go on to
maturity.*

This is what God desires and what the Son of God wants to do for you. Yield yourself fully to Christ and find in Him the hidden life. Then you will grow in grace and win others for Christ. Nothing short of conformity to Christ—a life wholly dedicated to God—should satisfy you.

The Building and Its Foundation

Let us...go on to maturity, not laying again the foundation of repentance from acts that lead to death, and of faith in God.
HEBREWS 6:1

Paul laid the foundation of the house of God in the doctrine of justification by faith in Jesus Christ. This is the firm ground upon which a lost sinner finds his eternal salvation (see Romans 5:1–2).

What house is built upon the foundation? In Romans 5:12–18, Paul tells us that justification and peace with God are only the beginning. He goes on to show that just as the result of the first Adam's disobedience was condemnation for all, so also the result of the obedience of the second Adam, Jesus Christ, brought justification and abundant grace to life. That is the life built on this foundation.

Lord, I want to progress along the road of faith. I desire to go beyond laying the foundation. I am seeking joy and victory in the Spirit.

Paul then goes on to point out that, in Christ, just as we have died to sin through His death, we are united to Him in His resurrection. If we died with Christ, we can be sure we are dead to sin but alive to God through Jesus Christ.

It is in our identification with the crucified and risen Christ that we are set free from the power of sin. Through the power of the Spirit, Christ releases us from the power of sin. The life in Christ is the house that must be built upon the foundation of justification.

Too often people are satisfied if just the foundation is there. Our spiritual experience should extend beyond that. We must experience Christ as our life, that we have died and risen again with Him. That alone will enable us to live a life of joy, holiness, and victory in the Holy Spirit.

The Reformation

*For no one can lay any foundation other than
the one already laid, which is Jesus Christ.*
1 CORINTHIANS 3:11

Over the centuries, the church departed from the true foundation laid by the Lord and His apostles. In place of justification through faith in Jesus Christ, the church took upon itself the right to forgive sins. Forgiveness could be obtained only through a priest, and in many cases this involved the payment of money.

The great work of Luther and Calvin was to lay anew the foundation of Jesus Christ to the comfort of thousands of souls. The Reformation was not accomplished in a day or two. It took fifty years to establish, and even after that, there were many priests whose conversion did not include the power of a holy life. Calvin himself said that the Reformation was a doctrinal restoration rather than something lived out in the lives of people. He felt a serious need in the people to be taught anew the ways of righteousness.

The Reformation is sometimes seen as a return to the original Pentecost, but it was by no means that. There was much dissension and argument among the reformers, instead of brotherly love, separation from the world, and earnestness in proclaiming Jesus Christ. They depended too much on the protection of statesmen who were sympathetic to the Reformation. Preaching was still the work of ordained priests only, in contrast to the witnessing for Christ that marked the early church, where every believer was constrained by the love of Christ.

*Lord Jesus, You
are the only way,
the truth,
and the life.
Let my
lifestyle reflect
my convictions.*

We can, however, never thank God enough for the Reformation when Jesus was proclaimed anew our righteousness, our peace with God.

The Walk in Christ

So then, just as you received Christ Jesus as Lord,
continue to live in him, rooted and built up in him,
strengthened in the faith as you were taught,
and overflowing with thankfulness.

COLOSSIANS 2:6–7

Two kinds of life are described here. The first is to be found in the words "you received Christ Jesus." This includes conversion, forgiveness of sin through the blood of Christ, and acceptance as a child of God. The second involves our walk in Christ and is found in the words "rooted...in him." The image is one of a tree that takes life from the soil in order to bear fruit. It speaks of the Christian who reveals by his or her walk and conversation a life of one daily living and abiding in Christ.

Lord, teach me to live in Your presence every day, so that I can bear more fruit in order to glorify You.

In the Confessions of Faith drawn up by the Reformers, prominence was given to conversion and the acceptance of Christ. *Justification* and *justified* were words in frequent use. The word *sanctification*, however, was rarely heard. Little mention was made of our life being rooted in Christ, or of Christ living in us. The Heidelberg Catechism explained the Ten Commandments, but the commandments of Christ in Matthew 5 and John 13–16 were seldom referred to.

Let us thank God for the reformers who laid again the foundation of a crucified Savior. At the same time, let us go on to maturity, to a constant walk in Christ. As Enoch walked with God, let us become established in the Faith and abound therein.

The Mediator of a New Covenant

You have come to…Jesus the mediator of a new covenant,
and to the sprinkled blood that speaks a better word than the blood of Abel.
HEBREWS 12:23–24

A mediator is responsible for both parties fulfilling the obligations of a covenant. Jesus is our surety that God will fulfill His promises; He is also the surety that we, on our part, will faithfully do what God requires of us. Jesus will enable us to fulfill the terms of the Covenant.

It was as Mediator, on the night of the Last Supper, that Jesus gave His disciples the great promise of the New Covenant: the gift of the Holy Spirit, foretold earlier by Ezekiel.

He also undertook to fulfill the promise, "I will put my Spirit in you and move you to follow my decrees and be careful to keep my laws" (Ezekiel 36:27). It was in fulfillment of this promise that He told His disciples, "I will ask the Father, and he will give you another Counselor to be with you forever" (John 14:16). This promise is of great importance if we are to fulfill the requirement of God's holiness that we be obedient to Him in all things. It was in this context that Christ had given the promise of the Holy Spirit's coming: "If you love me, you will obey my commandments" (John 14:15).

Thank You, Lord, that You equip me to do all that You ask. Teach me to live in obedience and devotion to You.

It is clear from Christ's promises that the Holy Spirit would enable His followers to keep God's commandments. Meditate on this, until you have the assurance that Christ equips His disciples to do as He asks. Through the power of the Spirit dwelling in us, we are indeed able to keep His commandments.

Better Promises

But the ministry Jesus has received is as superior to theirs as the covenant of which
he is mediator is superior to the old one, and it is founded on better promises.
HEBREWS 8:6

Jesus the mediator of a new covenant...the sprinkled blood
that speaks a better word than the blood of Abel.
HEBREWS 12:24

The better covenant spoken of here was promised in Jeremiah: "This is the covenant I will make...I will put my law in their minds and write it on their hearts: (Jeremiah 31:33) and "I will make an everlasting covenant with them...to fear me, so that they will never turn away from me" (Jeremiah 32:40).

The Lord also declared, "I will cleanse you from all your impurities. I will put my Spirit in you and move you to follow my decrees and be careful to keep my laws" (Ezekiel 36:25, 27).

Thank You, Lord,
for all such
incredible
promises. And
thank You that
through Your
Spirit You also give
me the means and
power to make
them my own.

The promises contained in these Scripture passages are more than clear: God Himself will do the work. He will plant the desire in the hearts of His children to never depart from Him, and He will cause them to follow His laws. This is the New Covenant of which Jesus is the Mediator.

Through the Holy Spirit, He lives in us to keep us from sin, so that we shall have the desire and the power to do God's will in all things. Soon after the Savior's birth, Zechariah prophesied that Christ would "rescue us from the hand of our enemies...to enable us to serve him without fear in holiness and righteousness before him all our days" (Luke 1:74–75). These are the very words of God and show what He will do for those who desire and seek Him.

Fellowship with God

*We proclaim to you what we have seen and heard,
so that you also may have fellowship with us.
And our fellowship is with the Father
and with his Son, Jesus Christ.*

1 JOHN 1:3

Fellowship with God is the unique blessing of the gospel. Christ died to bring reconciliation between God and us—that the prodigal might return to the Father's house and to a life in the Father's love. By His blood He dedicated for us a new and living way into the Holy Place where we may walk in the light of God. The promise is, "The LORD will be your everlasting light, and your God will be your glory" (Isaiah 60:19).

Fellowship with God must be the preacher's theme. Preachers will fail grievously in their work if they are satisfied to preach only of conversion, forgiveness of sin, and safety after death. Christians should be led into the practice of fellowship with God, for therein lies the secret of holy living.

Fellowship with God is the preacher's only source of power. If fellowship with God is the blessing of the gospel and the burden of the pastor's preaching, then it follows that the preacher must show in his own life the possibility and blessing of such a walk with God. Experiencing it himself, he will be able to tell others about its wonder and joy, and will win them to the same happy fellowship with God. What God can do for me He can do for you.

May fellowship with the Father and the Son be our daily experience—in our quiet times, in our daily work, and in our witness to others so that they, too, may share in the same glorious salvation.

Lord, thank You that You invite me into fellowship with You. Enable me to truly experience such fellowship in all its fullness.

The Fullness of Christ

The Word became flesh and made his dwelling among us.
We have seen his glory, the glory of the One and Only,
who came from the Father, full of grace and truth.
From the fullness of his grace we have all received one blessing after another.

JOHN 1:14, 16

Read these words until you are gripped by the transcendent fullness of Christ. Let the Spirit lead you into worship appropriate to the One in whom all fullness dwells.

I may receive a purse containing very little or nothing at all, or it may contain a substantial amount. Thus it is with Christians. Some receive Christ in terms of the forgiveness of sin and the hope of heaven, yet know little of His fullness and the wealth that is to be found in Him.

Others will sacrifice everything in order to be able to say, "From the fullness of his grace we have…received one blessing after another." Paul was such a one. He said, "I consider everything a loss compared to the surpassing greatness of knowing Christ Jesus my Lord" (Philippians 3:8). Such is the Christian who perceives and desires to be united to the Christ who, in His fullness and love, was utterly devoted to the Father and humankind.

Have you come to know the Christ in whom such fullness dwells? Or do you live as a pauper, largely dependent on the world for your joy? It is God's will that Christ should fill all things, including your heart and its needs! Allow the Holy Spirit to imprint deeply upon your heart the words of our text in all its fullness.

Lord, open my eyes that I may see the fullness and love of Christ, and be gripped thereby until I give all to appropriate it.

The Heavenly Life

For you died, and your life is now hidden with
Christ in God...Christ, who is your life.
COLOSSIANS 3:3–4

It is of the utmost importance for a Christian to know that the new life he or she receives actually is the life of Christ, which He lives in the Father. Our life is hidden with Christ in God and needs to be renewed daily.

It requires time and thought to grasp the truth that the life Christ lives in the Father is the same life He lives in you and me. Christ does not live one life in the Father and another in you. His explicit words are, "Because I live, you also will live. On that day you will realize that I am in my Father, and you are in me, and I am in you" (John 14:19–20). As Christ is in the Father, so you are in Him and He in you.

How poorly we have grasped this! How little trouble we take to experience it. Here is the secret: a necessary daily quiet time with prayerful meditation to become deeply impressed with the truth that the Lord Jesus, whose life is hidden in God, also has His life hidden in us. Only in this way can we truly come to know that our glorious heavenly Christ lives in our hearts to enable us to live as children of the heavenly Father.

If we allow the Spirit of God to daily keep alive in us this heavenly life in Christ, we shall then know what it is to be able to testify to having died in Christ that we might experience His very own heavenly life. Then we shall enjoy a walk with God that participates in his Holiness and love.

Lord, I still have much to learn about my life that is hidden in You. Lead me into the fullness of such an experience.

A Royal Priesthood

But you are a chosen people, a royal priesthood.
1 PETER 2:9

In the Old Testament the concept of the kingdom is foremost; in the New Testament prominence is given to the priesthood.

One of the chief causes of the feeble life in the church is the mistaken idea that our happiness is the main object of God's grace. God's objective is far holier and far higher! He has saved us that we in turn might save others. Every believer is ordained to be the means of imparting to others the life he or she has received.

Those who are saved have the high calling of becoming channels for God's grace. The powerlessness of the church can largely be ascribed to the fact that most Christians see the gift they have received of everlasting life after death as being the main object of their salvation. The church needs to proclaim the gospel that we are saved to *serve*—that we are a royal priesthood.

A royal priesthood! The priestly heart is above all things a sympathetic heart, in which the love of God compels us to win others for Him. Two compelling motives are required: love towards Christ and love toward others—a love that constrains me to sacrifice all, so that others may share the same heavenly life I have been given.

Such a heart knows access to God, and intercedes for those who have yet to come to know Him. *A priestly heart!* Such is the heart of one in whom Jesus, the great High Priest, continues to intercede and in whom Christ's power to save is manifested.

Spirit of God, write upon my heart with indelible letters, "A royal priesthood."

Apart from Me—Nothing

If a man remains in me and I in him,
he will bear much fruit; apart from me you can do nothing.
JOHN 15:5

The nature we inherit from Adam is so corrupt that nothing good dwells in our natural selves; we are under the power of sin to such an extent that we are unable to do anything well-pleasing to God.

What a call to repentance! How often we as Christians have thought that we are able to do that which is good. How often we have thought that we are improving ourselves. We need to remember that Christ said, "Apart from me you can do nothing," and in the future rely only upon Him.

What cause for thanksgiving! Christ has united us to Himself, and thus now lives in us. He is able to work in and through us every day. This is the secret of the spiritual life—the Lord Jesus working in us, enabling us to do His work.

What cause for joy and encouragement! All in a Christian's life that seems too high and unattainable, Christ will nonetheless accomplish. I have but one thing to attend to and that is to remain entirely dependent upon Him. Whenever I remember the words, "Apart from me you can do nothing," I remember, too, "If a man remains in me...he will bear much fruit."

He Himself will see to it that He remains in me and I in Him. This, praise God, is the great work of the Holy Spirit: to make me capable. Thank God for the life of Christ in me!

Thank You, Lord Jesus, for the assurance that You are in me and I in You. I praise You for this. I do not want to struggle any further on my own.

The Thrice-Holy God

The God of peace, sanctify you through and through.
May your whole spirit, soul and body be kept blameless at the coming of our
Lord Jesus Christ. The one who calls you is faithful and he will do it.
1 THESSALONIANS 5:23–24

The God of peace. What inexhaustible meaning is locked up in these words! God gives us the assurance that He Himself will do the work. He will sanctify us completely. Our entire spirit and soul and even our body are to be preserved without blame at the coming of our Lord.

This promise is so great it appears incredible. Paul himself senses this and adds the words, "The one who calls you is faithful and he will do it." That leaves no room for doubt, but calls us to a place of confidence in the faithfulness of God.

The Trinity accomplishes this work. God the Father says, "Be holy, because I am the LORD...I am the LORD, who makes you holy" (Leviticus 20:7). The Son prayed, "For them I sanctify myself, that they too may be truly sanctified" (John 17:19). The Holy Spirit is the Spirit of sanctification, and it is He who facilitates our sanctification.

Lord, You are faithful and will keep Your promises. What cause this gives me for adoration! What encouragement to wait upon You, and to walk with You!

The thrice-holy God accomplishes the great work of sanctification through His continual indwelling and fellowship, breathing His life into us. It is like being exposed to warm sunbeams on a cold winter's day and feeling their warmth penetrating the body. Thus the one who takes time for communion with God becomes permeated with the strength and holiness of the triune God.

What encouragement to wait upon Him, to walk with Him, to know Him, to be assured that He is able to do everything He promised! He will sanctify us wholly and preserve our spirit, soul, and body without blame.

The Spirit of His Son

Because you are sons, God sent the Spirit of his Son into our hearts,
the Spirit who calls out, "Abba, Father."
GALATIANS 4:6

The Spirit that dwells in the child of God is the same Spirit that is in Christ Jesus. He teaches us to know the Father's love, and to respond with childlike love and obedience. As He was in Christ, so He is in us, the Spirit of Sonship expressing itself in a life of prayer.

I can rely on the Spirit of God to manifest the life of Christ in me. The Spirit will bring into fulfillment all that which Christ has said concerning His remaining in me and I in Him. Through the Spirit, Christ's indwelling becomes an experiential reality, forming and manifesting in me the mind and disposition of the Savior.

Furthermore, the Spirit of God equips me for God's service. As the Spirit that sanctifies, He will reveal Christ to me as my sanctification. The Spirit will enable me to overcome the world and its entanglements, and bear witness to the wonder and possibilities of Christ's life in me. He will fill me with love for God's people; with love for those who dislike or ignore me; and with love for those who do not yet know Christ, so that I shall pray for them and be ready to help them. He will give me love for the whole world and fill me with enthusiasm for those activities that bring the gospel to all humankind.

Lord, I come before You, believing that the Holy Spirit will manifest Your life in me.

Take time each day to spend with the Lord, allowing Him to fill your heart with confident expectation concerning what the Spirit of God can do through and in you.

You Were Bought at a Price

Do you not know that your body is a temple of the Holy Spirit,
who is in you, whom you have received from God? You are not your own;
you were bought at a price. Therefore honor God with your body.
1 CORINTHIANS 6:19–20

Your body is God's temple. As such, you are not your own, you do not have the right to please yourself.

The Holy Spirit is the Spirit of God's holiness; He comes to make us holy. And He expects us to obey Him fully. The Spirit asks that I, as one bought at a great price with the blood of Christ, and thus no longer my own, shall seek to please Him and follow His direction. All that I owe to God, and to the Lord Jesus, should be discerned in my conduct toward the Holy Spirit. He must in all things guide me, for as God He has the absolute right to me. He expects me each morning to say, "Speak, for your servant is listening" (1 Samuel 3:10).

Lord, I acknowledge that my body is Your temple. Strengthen me, that I may seek in all things to please and obey You.

He expects me to yield myself to obey the prompting of His voice within me. He expects absolute obedience. Furthermore, He expects me to keep in close touch with Him by taking time each day to renew the bond between Him and me. My whole life must be yielded to Him, so that He may pursue and bring to completion His work in me.

He also expects that in his strength I shall witness for Jesus Christ, and help those around me to come to Jesus. The Spirit expects that my body, which was purchased at great price, shall be a temple of God from which adoration and praise to God the Father and His Son shall continually rise.

Restoration

Restore us, O LORD God Almighty;
make your face shine upon us,
that we may be saved.
PSALM 80:19

Israel was in great need. Their enemies mocked them, saying that God had forsaken them. Thus the psalmist repeats the cry three times: "Restore us...that we may be saved!"

In our present day the enemy rejoices that in spite of our many churches, Christianity seems powerless to overcome the evils of drunkenness, immorality, worldliness, and materialism. God's children ask, *Can nothing be done? Is there no hope of revival? Is God reluctant to lead His people into a fuller, deeper life of victory over sin and all that opposes Christ? Did God not promise that in answer to our prayers He would send His Spirit?*

Revival and restoration are much needed. And both are possible. God longs for us to claim His promises and exercise our right as members of the royal priesthood (see 1 Peter 2:9).

Lord, restore us that we may be saved!

Where must such restoration begin? With ourselves! He waits for us to offer ourselves as instruments to be used by the Holy Spirit. He waits for us to separate ourselves from sin and devote ourselves to the witness of the gospel. Christians need to realize and demonstrate that the aim of their life is to serve God and to rescue those for whom Christ shed His blood. Restoration is, in fact, happening wherever God's people are sacrificing everything to live and work and suffer as Christ did.

It avails little to desire a deeper or more abundant life unless your main objective is to witness for Christ and win others for His service.

A Threefold Cord

Whatever you ask for in prayer,
believe that you have received it, and it will be yours.
MARK 11:24

To know, to desire, and to will—these are the three main activities of the soul. As a Christian begins to realize what fullness there is in Christ and the abundant life He gives, these three words will show him the way to participate in these riches.

To know: We must not be content with our own ideas concerning our growth in grace. We must ensure that we really know what God promises to do in us, and what He requires of us. God's Word teaches us that if we come openly, with all our sin and impotence, and sincerely yield to Christ our Lord, He will do in us far beyond our wildest imagining.

Lord, I am beginning to realize that I can experience such fullness in Christ as I have never imagined. Help me to enter into the purposes You have for me.

To desire: We must be sure to desire with our whole heart that for which we pray, and be willing to pay a price for it. It may be that our desire is half-hearted. God will create the desire, if we pray. It may cost a struggle, and much sacrifice on our part, to turn from the world and self, but the Spirit will come to our aid.

To will: This aspect is the most important. It requires a firm resolve if faith is to have the courage to appropriate what God bestows. Often in the midst of anxiety and struggle we will, almost in despair, grasp that which God offers. Our confidence must be in God alone. When our desire has developed into a firm will, we shall have the courage to believe all that God has promised.

Deeper Life

Some fell on rocky places, where it did not have much soil.
It sprang up quickly, because the soil was shallow.
MATTHEW 13:5

The seed sown upon the rocky place quickly withered because there was no deepness of soil. We have here a striking picture of religion that seems to start well but fails to last. The Christian needs a *deeper* life. Let your whole life be an entering into that love of which Paul prays in Ephesians 3:17–19, "That you, being rooted and established in love, may have power…to grasp how wide and long and high and deep is the love of Christ, and to know the love that surpasses knowledge—that you may be filled to the measure of all the fullness of God."

How can we attain this? Paul answers, "I kneel before the Father. I pray that out of his glorious riches he may strengthen you with power through his Spirit in your inner being, so that Christ may dwell in your hearts through faith" (Ephesians 3:14–17). The apostle here emphasizes three essential components of spiritual growth: humble prayer, reliance upon the powerful working of the Spirit, and—most importantly—fellowship through faith with the indwelling Christ.

Take time, therefore, to kneel before God in prayer each day, and to meditate upon and appropriate the potential riches of which Paul speaks. Commune with the Christ, whose love for you is the same as the love with which the Father loved Him, so that you can get an insight into the greatness of the condescension of that love to you.

Father, grant me insight into the greatness of Your love towards me, that thereby I might be filled to the measure of all the fullness of God.

Winning Others

If a man remains in me and I in him, he will bear much fruit;
apart from me you can do nothing.
This is to my Father's glory, that you bear much fruit.

JOHN 15:5, 8

Fruit is that which a tree or grapevine bears to the advantage of its owner. Likewise, all that Jesus teaches us about His living in us, and we in Him, is not for our benefit, but for His pleasure and for the honor of the Father. We, as branches of the vine, receive and enjoy such astounding grace that we may win souls for Him.

Does unbroken fellowship with God somehow seem to evade you? Perhaps you have failed to see that the purpose of such fellowship and communion is that you may bear fruit by leading others into the same incredible grace. Perhaps you have focused on your own sanctification and growth to such an extent that you have forgotten that the purpose of such spiritual development is to carry on the work that Christ began.

In His earthly ministry Christ declared, "I am the light of the world" (John 8:12); but speaking of the time after He would be taken away, He said, "You are the light of the world" (Matthew 5:14).

Maybe you have on numerous occasions surrendered to the Lord for keeping and purification—but not out of concern for the salvation of others. Let us acknowledge our failure here, and humbly offer ourselves to the Lord for His service.

Christ said, "Apart from me you can do nothing." He knows our weakness, and thus has promised, "If a man remains in me...he will bear much fruit."

Lord, help me to realize that all that I learn of the more abundant life is meant not only for my benefit, but also for the winning of others.

Intercession

If anyone sees his brother commit a sin…
he should pray and God will give him life.
1 JOHN 5:16

On the last evening, when Jesus promised to send the Holy Spirit, He said, "Remain in me, and I will remain in you. If a man remains in me and I in him, he will bear much fruit" (John 15:4–5). This, He taught, would be attained through prayer. If we pray, God will grant us our desires.

Christ made a sevenfold promise: "I will do whatever you ask in my name" (John 14:13); "You may ask me for anything in my name, and I will do it" (v. 14); "If…my words remain in you, ask whatever you wish, and it will be given you" (John 15:7); "The Father will give you whatever you ask in my name (v.16); "Ask and you will receive, and your joy will be complete" (John 16:24); and "In that day you will ask in my name" (v. 26).

The believer has the privilege of praying for others, knowing that Christ and the Father will answer that prayer. Remember that you are a branch of the Vine, not only for your own salvation, but to bear fruit by leading others to conversion. As an intercessor, grace is granted you to pray for others in the firm belief that God will answer your prayer.

Think of the change that would come over a community if every believer took time to pray for those who do not believe. How God would be glorified in our bearing much fruit!

Thank You, Lord,
for the wonderful
promises You have
given concerning
the bearing of
fruit through
intercession.
Make me faithful
in my prayer
life—for myself
and for the world.

Christ Our Life

You died, and your life is now hidden with Christ in God.
Christ…who is your life.
COLOSSIANS 3:3–4

Let us summarize what has been said in the past month about the new life in Christ.

Paul writes to the Colossians, "You died, and your life is now hidden with Christ in God." Only God's Spirit can enable us to understand and appropriate the truth that we were actually crucified and have died with Christ. The new life that we receive in Christ through the Spirit is life out of death. It is in Christ that the power of that life is shown as a crucified life. The Holy Spirit gives me the assurance that I died with Christ, and the power of His death works in me.

Lord, bring me to the place where I truly grasp that I died and my life is hidden with Christ in God. Spirit of God, let me rely upon You to make this true in my life.

Your life is hidden with Christ in God. In this manner Christ also spoke on the last night before His death, "You will know that I am in the Father, and you in me" (John 14:20). My life is hidden with Christ in God, and from there by faith I receive it anew each day through the working of the Holy Spirit.

An inability to grasp this important truth may be the reason for the lack of spiritual growth in so many Christians. They do not know that the life of Christ who died on the cross and now lives in heaven is truly *their* life hidden in God, and is one that must daily be received afresh from God in the sanctuary of prayer. What joy to know that the new life of God's children around me is also hidden with Christ in God! How sincerely we should love and pray for each other.

The Secret of the Cross

Why is it that, although they attend church, read their Bibles, and pray regularly, so many Christians seem unable to overcome sin and enjoy a life full of the love and joy of the Lord?

The answer most frequently lies in the fact that such believers do not know what it is to die to self and the world. They have repented of certain sins, but do not know what it is to turn, not only from sin, but also from their old nature and self-will.

Jesus told His disciples that if they wished to follow Him, they were to consider their life as sinful and under sentence of death. They should surrender themselves, their will and self-effort, and any goodness of their own, and learn instead what it is to live their life in the fullness of God.

Paul, in more than one of his epistles, makes it clear that we are dead to sin, with Christ, and we receive and experience the power of the new life through the working of the Holy Spirit in us every day.

The great work of the Holy Spirit is thus to reveal Christ in our hearts and to live as the Crucified One, who now lives within us. God desires to teach us what it is to die with Christ, to ourselves and to the world, and to be raised with Christ to a new life of love and joy in Him.

The Redemption of the Cross

Christ redeemed us from the curse of the law by becoming a curse for us.
GALATIANS 3:13

Scripture teaches us that there are two basic truths concerning the death of Christ on the cross. The first is the *redemption of the cross*—Christ dying for us as our complete deliverance from the curse of sin. The other, *the fellowship of the cross*—Christ including us in His death, thereby making us partakers in the effectiveness of His own death.

In Galatians 3:13 we find three profound thoughts. The first is that through the law God placed a curse on all sin and on all that is sinful. The second is that Christ took that curse upon Himself—indeed became a curse Himself—thereby destroying its power. The third is that in the cross we now have redemption from sin and all its power.

In paradise, God pronounced a curse on the earth and all that belongs to it, and thereafter continually reminded the people of Israel that "anyone who is hung on a tree is under God's curse" (Deuteronomy 21:23).

Such is the love and grace of God, however, that His Son eventually took that curse upon Himself, so that the repentant sinner can now rejoice in the absolute assurance that it is forever put away for those who believe in Jesus Christ.

Thank You, Father. I praise You for the marvelous redemption of the cross.

The message of the redemption of the cross is the foundation and center of the gospel. For those who receive it, it becomes the source of their deepest joy, enabling them to live in and to make known the fullness of God's love in Christ.

The Fellowship of the Cross

Your attitude should be the same as that of Christ Jesus.
PHILIPPIANS 2:5

Paul names those things that were noticeable in Jesus' attitude: He emptied Himself, He took on the demeanor of a servant, and He humbled Himself, even to the point of dying on a cross. This attitude is to be our motivation. By making it ours we enjoy and participate in the fellowship of His cross.

Paul urged the Philippians to manifest the disposition of Christ in their lives, through the power of the Spirit. As they strove to do this, they would realize their need for a better understanding of their oneness with Christ. They would begin to comprehend something of their own crucifixion with Christ, that they had indeed died to sin and the affections and lusts of the self in Christ's death, and that they were now living to God in the power of Christ's own life.

So would they gradually enter more deeply into the meaning and the power of their high calling. Each in their own measure would display in their lives the imprint of the cross through the denial of self and a growing conformity to Christ in His humility and the surrender of His will to the Father.

The way of the cross is neither easy nor quick. But it will—through a personal experience in the fellowship of the cross—lead to a greater respect for, and a deeper understanding of, the redemption of the cross.

Father, create in me the same attitude as that which was in Jesus Christ, so that I can know what it really means to be dead to sin.

Crucified with Christ

I have been crucified with Christ and I no longer live,
but Christ lives in me.
GALATIANS 2:20

The thought of fellowship with Christ in His bearing the cross has often led to attempts in our own power to imitate Him and portray His disposition. Such is impossible, until we first learn something of what it means to say, "I have been crucified with Christ."

When Adam died spiritually, all his descendants shared his sin and died with him. The power of that sin and death still works in every one of us today. But then Christ came as the *second* Adam, and in His death on the cross every believer likewise has a share. We can therefore say with absolute conviction, "I have been crucified with Christ."

As the representative of His people, He took you and me to the cross with Him, and now gives us *His* life—the life with which He entered heaven and was exalted to the throne. The power of His death and life is active in me. As I hold fast the truth that I have been crucified with Him, and that it is no longer I, but Christ who lives in me, I receive the strength to overcome sin. The life I have received from Him is a life that has been crucified and freed from the power of sin.

Lord, as a believer, I cling to You as the crucified Christ in me.

In this we have a profound and precious truth, concerning which many Christians have little insight. Such knowledge is not easily or speedily gained. It requires a real longing to be dead to all sin and a strong faith worked by the Holy Spirit, that the life He imparts to His children is likewise a crucified life with its victory over sin and access into God's presence.

Crucified to the World

May I never boast except in the cross of our Lord Jesus Christ,
through which the world has been crucified to me, and I to the world.
GALATIANS 6:14

Paul says that his only glory is that in Christ he has been crucified to the world and entirely freed from its power. This is not only a spiritual truth, but also an actual, practical experience in relation to the world and its temptations.

Christ had spoken of the world hating Him, and of His having overcome the world. Paul knows that when the world crucified Christ, he himself had been nailed to the cross with Him. He boasts that he now lives as one crucified to the world, and that the world, as an impotent enemy, was now crucified to him.

Many Christians today agree that they ought not to commit the sins of which the world approves. Yet they choose to remain on friendly terms with the world, and feel at liberty to enjoy its pleasures as long as they refrain from committing open sin. They do not realize that the most dangerous source of sin is the love of the world with its lusts and pleasures.

Be aware that when the world crucified Christ, it crucified you with Him. However, be aware also that when Christ overcame the world on the cross, He made you a conqueror, too.

Let us fervently pray that the Holy Spirit will reveal to us what it means to boast in the cross of our Lord Jesus Christ, through which the world has been crucified to us, and we to the world.

Lord, preserve me from seeking my joy in the attractions and pleasures of the world. Do not allow the world to get a grip on me.

The Sinful Nature Crucified

Those who belong to Christ Jesus have crucified their sinful nature with its passions and desires.
GALATIANS 5:24

Concerning the sinful nature, Paul taught us, "I know that nothing good lives in me, that is, in my sinful nature" (Romans 7:18) and "The sinful mind is hostile to God. It does not submit to God's law" (Romans 8:7). When Adam lost the Spirit of God, his sinful nature took control, a condition that has been passed on to every one of us as his descendants.

Father, I fear I have become so used to my sin that it ceases to bother me much. Please change me!

When the disciples heard Jesus' invitation to follow Him, it was their sincere intention to do so. Later, when they realized what it would entail, they were far from being ready to yield immediate obedience.

Today, too, many of His followers do not appreciate all that is involved in following Jesus, for such a surrender implies the crucifixion of the sinful nature, and the regarding of it as a thing cursed and nailed to the cross.

Sadly, many Christians have yet to see it thus. Perhaps the preaching of Christ crucified has been defective, in that it has failed to point out that we have been crucified with Christ. Perhaps there is a recoiling from the self-denial that it requires, and that the Spirit of God has thereby been unable to exert His power.

Paul taught, "Those who are led by the Spirit of God are sons of God" (Romans 8:14). The Spirit of God, however, can only lead when the sinful nature is kept nailed to the cross. We need, therefore, to live in the Crucified One and, like Paul, to glory only in the cross on which the world and the sinful nature are crucified.

Bearing the Cross

Anyone who does not take his cross and follow me is not worthy of me. Whoever finds his life will lose it, and whoever loses his life for my sake will find it.
MATTHEW 10:38–39

We have considered some of Paul's great words to the Galatians about the cross and our being crucified with Christ. Let us now turn to the Master Himself to hear what He has to teach us. That which Paul taught had its origin and counterpart in the original words spoken by the Lord.

When Christ commissioned His disciples He gave expression to the fact that following Him would necessitate the taking up of a cross. The disciples would have understood these words in terms of that which they had often seen: evildoers, under sentence of death, bearing their crosses to a place of execution. Christ wanted His disciples to understand that, because of the evil and corrupt condition of their fallen natures, it was only in losing their natural life that they could find true life.

The disciples could not at first have understood this. Christ, however, planted within them the seeds of that which would later on be fully revealed. Not only did His disciples need to comprehend that they were, in their natural selves, under the sentence of death, but they also needed to learn that in following the Master to His cross, they would be enabled to lose their lives in order to receive His risen life.

Lord, You ask of Your disciples that we should forsake all and take up our cross to follow You. Help me to fully surrender the self life with its self-pleasing and self-exaltation. May I bear the cross in fellowship with You, thereby sharing in Your victory.

Self-Denial

Then Jesus said to his disciples, "If anyone would come after me,
he must deny himself and take up he cross and follow me."
MATTHEW 16:24

When, for the first time, Christ clearly stated His coming suffering, death, and resurrection, Peter took Him aside and began to rebuke Him. "Never, Lord! This shall never happen to you!" Christ's answer was, "Get behind me, Satan!" (Matthew 16:22–23). Using Peter, Satan sought to turn Jesus away from the cross and its suffering, thus to prevent that which God had appointed as our way of salvation.

In continuing His response, Christ then used a most significant expression: "If anyone would come after me, he must *deny* himself and take up his cross and follow me." When Adam sinned, self-pleasing, self-sufficiency, and self-exaltation became the law of his life. Jesus Christ invites all those who desire to follow Him to deny themselves.

Herein lies the secret of true discipleship: to bear the cross, to acknowledge the death sentence that has been passed on self, and to deny any right that self has to rule over us.

Let us listen to the voice of Jesus when He invites us to deny ourselves. He also asks that, as the disciples of Him who denied Himself for us, we may ever live as those in whom self has been crucified with Christ, and in whom the crucified Christ now lives as Lord and Master.

Lord Jesus, the demand You make of me as my Lord and Master is very clear. Help me to deny myself and take up my cross.

They Cannot Be
My Disciples

If anyone comes to me and does not hate his father and his mother,
his wife and children, his brothers and sisters—yes, even his own life—
he cannot be my disciple.

LUKE 14:26

Christ says that no one can be His disciple unless He relinquishes His own life and His possessions. Why such a demanding condition for discipleship? The reason is that the fallen nature in Adam is so revolting and sinful that we would flee from it if we saw it in its naked ghastliness. The sinful nature is enmity towards God, and the person that seeks God cannot but hate this corrupt nature.

The discarding of our old life will make us willing to take up our cross. We will carry about with us the death sentence of the sinful nature, together with its discarding. We will first have to acknowledge how revolting the old nature is before we will be willing to let it die. Christ has also said that no one can be His disciple unless he is prepared to give away all his possessions.

Christ asks everything of you. Christ satisfies all needs, and then gives back a hundredfold more than what you have sacrificed. It is only once you learn to know and love Christ through faith and receive that from Him after which your immortal soul hankers, that giving up things becomes a privilege—things that once seemed difficult to do without. Then you will know what it means to receive Christ as gain.

Lord, thank You that You supply all that You expect from me. Help me, too, to be aware of the sin in my life in all its ugliness.

Follow Me!

Jesus looked around and said to his disciples,
"How hard it is for the rich to enter the kingdom of God!"
MARK 10:23

The disciples were amazed at the words of Christ to the rich young man. To the question of who then could be saved, Jesus replied that with God all things are possible.

Here it is implied that only by the power of God can one take up the cross and lose one's life, one's self, and all the possessions to which one is naturally so attached. So Christ also had occasion to tell Peter that it was the Father in heaven that had revealed to Peter that Jesus was the Christ.

Thank You, Father, that I need not achieve my redemption and devotion in my own strength. I place my hand anew in Your hand. Guide me each day in Your way.

Many have tried to follow Christ and obey His commands, but have failed. Often people feel that the demands of God are too high, and they then try to be Christians without the whole-hearted devotion and self-denial that are asked.

In our study of what the "fellowship of the cross" really means, let us take the message to heart: It is only by placing our faith in God, and by belief in the power He exerts in our hearts, that we can be disciples who give up everything to follow Christ—becoming followers in the fellowship of the cross.

A Grain of Wheat

I tell you the truth, unless a kernel of wheat falls to the ground and dies,
it remains only a single seed. But if it dies, it produces many seeds.
The man who loves his life will lose it, while the man who hates
his life in the world will keep it for eternal life.

JOHN 12:24–25

In nature a basic fact of life is proved: namely, that death is a condition for life to continue. Every wheat grain speaks of this. Through death runs the road to a fruitful life.

So it was with the Son of God. He first had to walk the road of death through suffering before He could ascend to heaven and bestow life on His people. Beneath the shadow of the cross, He addressed His disciples: *He, who in this life, for My sake, counts his life as nothing, will keep it.*

One would suppose that Christ, having led such a righteous life, would not need to lose it first in order to regain it. Nevertheless, God through His Son took the sins of everyone upon Himself, thereby fulfilling an inescapable law of life: Through death comes new life and fruitfulness.

In this manner you must, as a follower of Christ and as heir of sin and death in Adam, be thankful that you may die to your sinful nature. In a spirit of thanksgiving you must listen for the call to carry your cross and to see your sinful nature crucified in the death it deserves. The thought of the power of eternal life, functioning in you, should make you glad in the knowledge that, by this, you also live in the power of the risen Christ.

Thank You, Lord Jesus, that You were prepared to die for me. Help me to crucify the remnants of my old self.

As You Will

"My Father, if it is possible, may the cup be taken from me.
Yet not as I will, but as you will."
MATTHEW 26:39

The death of Christ on the cross is the greatest and the best that we know of Him. And the greatest and the best that His Spirit can do in us is to keep us in the fellowship of the cross. This truth we must remember: Christ could not enter into the glory of heaven until He had died; He first had to submit to death. Once we realize this great truth, it will help us understand that it is impossible for us to become a part of His life until we are willing to die to sin and the world. Otherwise, we cannot enter into the fellowship of the crucified Christ.

Only Christ can teach us what it means to have fellowship in His suffering and to be one with Him in His death. In Gethsemane, Christ had foreknowledge of what His death on the cross would mean, a death without the light of God's presence. He passionately prayed that the cup would pass Him by. When the answer came and He realized that He would first have to drink the cup, He submitted Himself absolutely with the words "Your will be done."

You have prepared the way for me to die to self. For this, I praise Your name, Lord.

With this panic-stricken cry, you can, as a Christian, join in fellowship with Him. You can also believe that God will give you the strength to forfeit everything because you have been crucified with Christ. "Your will be done": Let these be the most profound and most exalted words of your life, in daily submission to the will of God.

The Love of the Cross

Jesus said, "Father, forgive them,
for they do not know what they are doing."
LUKE 23:34

The words spoken from the cross demonstrate the spirituality that was in Christ. They tell us what the spirit of God's children should be.

Christ prays for His enemies; yes, in their hour of triumph over Him, He prays for them. This is what those who believe in the crucified Christ should also do—follow His command to love our enemies, bless them that curse us, do good to those who hate us, and pray for those who insult and persecute us.

Jesus surely felt the deep anxiety and sorrow of His mother, because He commended her to the care of the disciples. He knew John would regard it as an honor. In like manner, we should comfort others. Those who belong to the Lord, we must assist lovingly.

Christ also took pity on the criminal on the cross beside Him. Be it the love which prays for others, or the love that cares about its friends, or the love which rejoices over a repentant sinner—Christ showed us that the cross is a cross of love, and that the Crucified One is the personification of love that transcends knowledge.

You have the privilege of proving, with all that you are, that the spirit of the crucified Christ lives in you, and that you believe in His love—not just for your own sake, but also for the sake of the world around you.

Lord Jesus, as I meditate on Your suffering and the message of the cross, I thank You that You again defined the message of love so clearly for me.

The Sacrifice of the Cross

"My God, my God, why have you forsaken me?"
MATTHEW 27:46

*Later, knowing that all was now completed,
and so that the Scripture would be fulfilled, Jesus said, "I am thirsty."*
JOHN 19:28

These words from the cross tell something of the total darkness that enveloped Christ. It was this heartrending desolation, separated from His Father in whose company He had always walked, that made Him sweat drops of blood in Gethsemane.

In Gethsemane, He first prayed that the cup would pass Him by, then that His Father's will be done. In His love for God and mankind, He surrendered Himself completely and in the extreme to the cup He was to drink. Thus, *we* must also learn to say, "Abba, Father, Your will be done."

Jesus then said that He was thirsty. His body spoke of the terrible experience of God's furious rage against sin. Jesus referred to the rich man who cried out, "I suffer terribly in the fire." Physicians state that the body suffers excruciating pain and fever during crucifixion; therefore the cry that He was thirsty.

Again, you must act in imitation of Him. As your confidence in Jesus grows, you must grow toward a fuller submission, a burnt offering in the service of God and His love.

Thank You that You did everything that was necessary to redeem me. Thank You, Jesus, for Your sacrifice on the cross. Let me be a living sacrifice for You.

It Is Finished!

When he had received the drink,
Jesus said, "It is finished!"
JOHN 19:30

Jesus' words on the cross reveal to us His spirit. At the very beginning of His ministry, He said that He was coming to do His Father's will (see John 4:34). Later, in the prayer of the high priest, Jesus said that He had accomplished the work that His Father had given Him to do (see John 17:4).

With the words on the cross, "It is finished!" Jesus told us that He had laid down His life. This should also be the spirit of the child of God: in everything to do the will of God and to accomplish God's work. If in the smaller things we have not the necessary dedication, we can spoil His work. Or maybe we recoil from bigger tasks that require some sacrifice.

May you draw strength from the example of Jesus as someone who has completed His task. His finished work has assured us victory over every enemy. In Christ's words from the cross, you will draw strength for your daily existence—in fellowship with His death, and with a firm faith in what He achieved on the cross.

Lord, thank You for the place You made for me in Your kingdom so that I may serve You. I pray for the grace to complete the task You have entrusted to me.

The Death on the Cross

*Jesus called out with a loud voice,
"Father, into your hands I commit my spirit."
When he had said this, he breathed his last.*

LUKE 23:46

Like David, Christ often gave His life into His Father's hands for His daily needs (e.g., Psalm 31:6). But here was a new turn: Jesus gave himself over to death, thereby giving up all control over His life. He declared Himself willing to face the darkness and death of the grave—there where He could neither think nor pray. He trusted His Father to care for Him in His hour of darkness, and to waken Him at the right time.

These words are of great importance in every Christian's life. Yes, you should consider what it means to be willing to lose your life.

Thank You, Father, that the same power with which You raised Jesus from the dead also works in me. I wait in anticipation to see how my new life will develop.

We died in Adam and the "life" we received from him, is death. By nature nothing good lives in us. We must therefore die of a sinful nature. Many try to live in God before the old being has died. But a grain of wheat cannot germinate before it has died.

The answer for us lies in the manner of Christ's dying. "Into your hands I commend my spirit," Christ said. We must, like Jesus, trust God to uplift us to a new life with the same power with which He raised Christ.

That is the test of faith: to live every moment in dependence on that new life given us by the Holy Spirit.

Dying to Sin

We died to sin; how can we live in it any longer?
ROMANS 6:2

In the first part of his letter to the Romans (1:16–5:11), Paul expands on the absolution by faith. In the second part, he writes about the related doctrine of the new life in faith through Christ. He offers Adam as a prototype: All died in Adam and therefore death reigns in us. Yet all died in Christ because of sin, and in this way we have been set free to be partakers of the new life in Christ.

Quite rightly then, Paul asks, how can those who have died to sin still live in it? A profound spiritual truth lies in this, namely that in Christ we die to sin. Through this we are also set free from the grasp of sin.

In his explanation of the truth, Paul reminds the Romans that they were baptized by the death of Christ. We are united with Him by the similarity of our death to His. Our old self has been crucified with Him; it has been declared invalid and made powerless.

It is worth the trouble to take time to meditate on these words until you grasp their full meaning: *I am dead to sin through Christ Jesus.* As you become more familiar with your unity with the crucified Christ, you will feel the power of His life in you that releases you from the power of sin.

Lord Jesus, thank you that I may identify with your death on the cross, through the working of your Holy Spirit.

It is only by the working of the Holy Spirit that you can accept the truth within yourself.

The Absolution from God

Abraham believed God, and it was credited to him as righteousness.
He is our father in the sight of God, in whom he believed—
the God who gives life to the dead.
ROMANS 4:3, 17

The first part of Romans deals with absolution through faith in Christ. Paul first refers to the sins of the heathens (see 1:18–32), then to the sins of the Jews (see 2:1–29), and then says that both Jews and non-Jews were guilty before God, because all have sinned. Further, he explains the redemption there is in Christ Jesus (see 3:21–31).

In chapter 4 of the letter to the Romans, Paul refers to Abraham, who understood that God had absolved and declared him righteous through grace, and not through anything that Abraham had done. Paul then goes a step further, declaring that God raises the dead to life.

Lord Jesus, thank You for all that You have made possible for me by Your work on the cross. I praise You for Your wonderful provision for my deepest needs.

These principles indicate the basic requirements that are dealt with by redemption in Jesus Christ. First, there is the need to be absolved by faith; second, there is the need for an enlivening of the spirit, a rebirth through faith.

In the following section (see Romans 5:12–8:39) Paul writes of the wonderful unity in Christ through the faith whereby we died with Him and whereby we are declared free—not only from punishment, but also from the hold of sin on us. By the power of the Holy Spirit we can lead a life of righteousness, obedience, and sanctification.

Died with Christ

Now if we died with Christ,
we believe that we will also live with him.
ROMANS 6:8

The reason why God's children so seldom live in the power of the resurrection is that they have so little insight into dying with Christ. This becomes clear with Paul's words: "If we have died with Christ, we believe that we will also live with him.... The death he died, he died to sin once for all." (Romans 6:8, 10).

Therefore, says Paul, we must remember that we are dead to sin and alive for God in Christ Jesus. These words give us God's assurance of who and what we are in Christ. It is a truth that we cannot master with our minds or call our own, but which the Holy Spirit must reveal to us. Through His power, we must experience the death of the cross as the power for our daily lives.

Then together with Paul, we can also declare that we will not place any part of our bodies in the service of sin or as an instrument in the pursuit of godlessness (see Romans 6:13). Every part of our bodies will be given to the service of God, for a holy life (see Romans 6:19).

The whole of Romans 6 is a wonderful extension of the words in verse 2: "We died to sin; how can we live in it any longer?" All depends on our acceptance of God's assurance: If we have died with Christ, we go on living only with God.

Thank You, Lord Jesus, for the power that is mine in Your death and resurrection. Help me each day, to acknowledge that power and to live by it.

Dead to the Law

You also died to the law through the body of Christ.
Now…we serve in the new way of the Spirit,
and not in the old way of the written code.
ROMANS 7:4, 6

The believer is not only dead to sin, but also to the law. It is a profound truth of faith that releases us from a life of striving and of failure and of "you must." It opens up a new way of life in the power of the Holy Spirit.

The remainder of Romans 7 gives a description of a Christian who tries to uphold the law. Throughout, the "I" is at the forefront, without any reference to the support of the Holy Spirit. But after his desperate cry for support at the end of the chapter, Paul comes to realize that he is no longer under the law, but under the guidance of the Holy Spirit (see Romans 8:1–2).

Lord, I find myself
time after time
trying to add to
what You have
done on the cross.
Forgive me
my efforts.

In Romans 7 we have an image of an ordinary Christian doing his best to fulfill the requirements of the law and to live by them, yet never succeeding because of shortcomings and failures. In Romans 8 someone is described who knows that he lives in Christ Jesus and is dead to sin and alive for God. By the Spirit of God, he is free of the hold which sin and death have on him.

May you each day discover the great truth of Romans 7: Nothing good lives in the sinful nature of man; there is redemption only through submission to the power of the Holy Spirit who releases us from our sinful nature. The demands of the law are thereby fulfilled in the power of Christ.

The Sinful Nature Nailed to the Cross

For what the law was powerless to do in that it was weakened by the sinful nature, God did by sending his own Son in the likeness of sinful man to be a sin offering. And so he condemned sin in sinful man.

ROMANS 8:3

In this same chapter, Paul writes that the things with which sinful man occupies himself are enmity towards God (see Romans 8:7). Here Paul touches on the extent of the sinful nature of man. In chapter 7 he said that nothing good lives in the sinful nature. In chapter 8 he goes a step further and states that the inborn nature of man hates God and His law. Therefore, God had sin nailed to the cross, and the curse that was on sin was therefore transferred to the body of Christ.

As the believer comes to accept this truth, he or she will no longer strive to overcome the sinful nature in their own power. No, the Holy Spirit does this for us. Only then can we fulfill the demands of the law—when we are no longer ruled by the sinful nature, but by the Spirit of God (see Romans 8:4). We are only able to fulfill the demands of the law by remaining in the Spirit.

May you, as one of God's children, therefore learn the truth: In our sinful nature in Adam, nothing good lives. No discipline or struggle or prayer can change that. On the cross, the Son of God condemned sin. That is the only reason why there is no condemnation for those who remain in the Spirit and accept the truth for themselves.

Thank You, Lord, that You free me of my own feeble efforts to gain Your redemption. Thank You that You also nailed my sinful nature to the cross.

Jesus Christ the Crucified

I resolved to know nothing while I was with you
except Jesus Christ and him crucified. My message and my preaching were…
a demonstration of the Spirit's power.

1 CORINTHIANS 2:2, 4

Paul's whole ministry and bearing were in agreement with Christ: crucified in weakness, yet alive by the power of God (see 2 Corinthians 13:4–5). Paul strove in all things to be the same as Christ.

Shortly before, Paul had written that the cross is nonsense to those that are lost, but for those that are saved it is the power of God (see 1 Corinthians 1:18).

Lord, at the Passiontide, I pray especially for our ministers, that You will provide powerful preaching.

Paul sought after the same sort of weakness as that in which Christ was crucified. In everything he emulated the spirit of the crucified Christ. He tried above all not to convince with words of human wisdom, because that would diminish the power of the cross (see 1 Corinthians 1:17). His message was not proclaimed by learnedness or fluency of speech, but by the powerful working of the Spirit (see 2 Corinthians 2:4).

Is that not perhaps why the power of God is so seldom felt in the ministry these days? Christ may well be the subject, but we can also place too much store in human learnedness and fluency. Then too little is seen of the image of Christ who gives godly supernatural power to the ministry. Pray that God will give to the life of every preacher and every believer the stamp of Jesus Christ, the crucified.

Moderation in All Things

Everyone who competes in the games goes into strict training.
I beat my body and make it my slave.
1 CORINTHIANS 9:25, 27

Paul reminds us of the well-known principle that anyone competing in a race for a prize must deny themselves certain things; that means *anything*—no matter how enticing—that could be a hindrance in the race.

If the principle holds good for an earthly competition, how much more should short shrift be given to those things that prevent us from receiving the everlasting crown?

Paul says that he exercises his body tirelessly and brings it under control. He will not allow anything to hinder him—no self-satisfying eating or drinking, no comfort or ease must prevent him from carrying the spirit of the cross in his daily life, or from keeping everything faultless for his Master.

The cross was the theme of Paul's ministry and the compass in his life in all matters, however insignificant.

You must pray that this attitude will be that of every Christian and preacher, by the power of the Holy Spirit. If the death of Christ works powerfully in the preacher, the people will know the life of Christ. You must pray, therefore, that the fellowship with the cross be restored to a position of honor. Jesus humbled himself and became obedient to this death. Since you became one with Him in His death, you will surely also be one with Him in His resurrection.

Lord, there are still so many distractions that I cannot dedicate my life fully to You. And I think up such convenient excuses. Forgive me, and help me to surrender my life totally to You.

The Death of Jesus

We always carry around in our body the death of Jesus,
so that the life of Jesus may also be revealed in our body.
So then, death is at work in us, but life is at work in you.

2 CORINTHIANS 4:10, 12

Here Paul speaks directly about the close relationship between Christ who lives in him, and the tangible, earthly life—which includes suffering.

Paul declares that he always carries the death of Christ about with him, and therefore the life of Jesus becomes visible in his body. It is because the death of Christ works in and through him that the life of Christ works in the congregation of the Corinthians (see 2 Corinthians 4:12).

Lord Jesus, help me in this day, too, to carry your crucifixion with me in my body.

We often speak about how we should remain in Christ, but we forget that this means we must remain in a *crucified* Christ. It would seem that many Christians are under the impression that a single identification with Christ's crucifixion is sufficient—that no more is required and that it is over. But it does require a continued daily fellowship and identifying with the crucified Christ, including His humiliation and obedience to the point of death on the cross.

If we wish to live for the benefit of those around us, and sacrifice ease and pleasure in order to win people for the Lord, then the life of Christ may also work in these others. It is through our fellowship in the suffering of Christ that the crucified Lord can fulfill His work.

When you therefore pray that Christ Jesus must live in you, it means the crucified Lord in you.

The Cross and the Spirit of God

How much more, then, will the blood of Christ...cleanse our consciences
from acts that lead to death, so that we may serve the living God!
HEBREWS 9:14

The cross is the pinnacle of Christ's glory. The glory that He eventually received from the Father was because of His willingness to humble Himself on the cross. The most important work that the Holy Spirit did in the Son of God was to enable Him to give Himself as a sacrifice, a sacrifice that was a pleasing aroma before God.

The Holy Spirit can do no greater work in us than to lead us to fellowship with the crucified Christ. Perhaps you pray too seldom that the Holy Spirit should glorify Christ in you, as a partaker also of His suffering.

The Spirit of God and the cross are indissolubly bound together. The Spirit of God led Christ to the cross; this cross brought Christ to the throne of God, to receive the fullness of the Spirit to give, in turn, to His children. The Spirit taught Peter to preach the crucified Christ, and three thousand people received the Holy Spirit.

Is not the lack of insight and knowledge of the crucified Christ a reason for a lukewarm, lifeless church—insight into death to self and the world in order to achieve life for those who are dying?

Holy Spirit, glorify
the crucified
Christ in me. I
want to receive
that fullness that
You intend for me.

Ask God earnestly to teach you that you have been crucified with Christ, that you carry His death in you. Thus you will be prepared for filling by the Spirit, which the Father desires to give you.

The Veil, the Body of Christ

Therefore, brothers, we have confidence to enter the Most Holy Place,
by the blood of Jesus, by a new and living way opened
for us through the curtain, that is, his body.
HEBREWS 10:19–20

In the temple the veil hung like a curtain between the Holy and the Most Holy Places. At the altar in the entrance, the blood for the forgiveness of sins was sprinkled. The sprinkling of blood gave the priests permission to enter the Holy Place to burn incense there as part of the offering. But into the Most Holy Place only the high priest could go, and only once a year.

The veil can be seen as a symbol of the sinful nature. In spite of the forgiveness of sins by the sprinkling of blood, entry all over and fellowship with God were forbidden. But when Christ died, the veil was torn. Christ showed the new, living way to God through the torn veil—His body.

Thank You, Jesus, that through the cross You gave me unconditional access to the throne of God.

The new way, through which all believers now have access to the Most Holy, always goes through the torn veil, the body of Christ. Every step on the new and living road of access to God includes, therefore, fellowship with the cross of Christ.

The torn body of the sinful nature does not only refer to Christ and His death on the cross, but also to our growth in the image of Christ. Let Christians therefore see the sinful nature as cursed and nailed to the cross. There is no other way to God than through the torn body of Christ.

Eyes Fixed on Jesus

Let us run with perseverance the race marked out for us.
Let us fix our eyes on Jesus, the author and perfecter of our faith,
who for the joy set before him endured the cross, scorning its shame.
HEBREWS 12:1–2

When we run a race, our attention is fixed on the goal and a possible reward. That is the metaphor Paul uses in this verse. Here Jesus is the focal point in the race—Jesus who was willing to endure the cross for the sake of the large reward afterward. This should be our inspiration. In like manner we should also be willing to endure the earthly cross for the sake of the anticipated joy and reward.

The lack of power of the church today can be ascribed to the fact that a willingness to carry the cross is so seldom preached. Many Christians think that as long as they do not actually commit sins, they are free to be a part of as many superficial, worldly pleasures as possible. There is too little perception that the sinful nature, which loves these worldly things, is enmity towards God. That is why many Christians pray for years on end to be remolded in the image of Christ and it just does not happen.

Only in the fellowship of the cross of Christ do we become like Him. As believers get to understand the truth and run the race with the crucified Jesus in view, they will receive power to win for Him people for whom He died on the cross.

Lord, I try to keep my eyes on You, but I find it so difficult to die to the superficial pleasures of the world. Make me more like You.

Outside the Encampment

The high priest carries the blood of animals into the Most Holy Place
as a sin offering, but the bodies are burned outside the camp.
And so Jesus also suffered outside the city gate.
Let us, then, go to him outside the camp, bearing the disgrace he bore.
HEBREWS 13:11–13

The blood of the sin offering in the Old Testament was brought into the temple, while the carcass of the sacrificed animal was burned outside the encampment. So it happened with Christ: His blood was offered, but His body was discarded like something cursed, outside the city walls.

Now we may freely enter the Most Holy Place, which is the presence of God, through the blood of Christ. The better my insight into this truth, the greater my joy in the privilege. And the better my insight into the shame of the cross, where He also had to suffer outside the city wall, the easier for me to follow Him in His suffering.

Christians rejoice at the privilege of being able to go into the Most Holy Place, but they do not show the same enthusiasm to be a part of the abuse and rejection of Christ. They do not separate themselves from worldly interests with the same joy they have for going into the Holy Place.

To be a follower of Christ means to be a witness for Him in the midst of the world. It also means identification with the cross and a willingness to sacrifice the self so that the Father may be glorified and people can be saved.

My Redeemer, teach me to follow You. With Your spirit and love, allow me to search for those who are still lost.

Live for Obedience

*He himself bore our sins in his body on the tree
so that we might die to sins and live for righteousness.*
1 PETER 2:24

Here we find the same scriptural truths as those of which Paul repeatedly writes. First, there is the idea of the reconciliation of the cross, of Christ who bore our sins in His body on the cross. Second, there is the idea of fellowship in the crucifixion death of Christ: We must see ourselves as dead to sin and in the future live in obedience to the will of God.

To make this a reality in our lives, we need the guidance of the Holy Spirit. Only then will we know that sin no longer has power over us, and only then can we commit ourselves as obedient children to the will of God, to be used by Him.

It cost Christ so much to carry the cross. The passionate words on that last day, "Father, save me from the hour!" are witness to this. Only the Holy Spirit can teach us how to identify with Christ on the cross. Through Him, by faith, we learn what it means to die with Christ on the cross, what it means that He lives in us, and how we can live in continuous fellowship with Him, the crucified. It implies self-sacrifice and serious prayer. It also asks wholehearted commitment to, and unbroken fellowship with, our God.

*Lord, let your
Spirit imprint
these words deep
into my heart,
that sin no longer
has a hold on me
because of Jesus'
sacrifice.*

Let us therefore pray that God will teach us these things through the Holy Spirit.

Followers of the Cross

This is how we know what love is:
Jesus Christ laid down his life for us.
And we ought to lay down our lives for our brothers.
1 JOHN 3:16

Elsewhere, Jesus says that no one has greater love than to lay down his life for his friends (see John 15:13). So we, too, should be willing to lay down our lives for our brothers. Our interactions with others show whether or not we radiate the image of Christ.

The cross of Christ is the measure by which we can know how much Christ loves us. And by the same cross we can measure our love for others. Our fellowship with the cross is shown by the manner in which we love our neighbor. We can, however, only love our neighbor once the love of Christ on the cross possesses and inspires us.

Lord, You gave
your life for me.
Make me willing
to give my life for
others in practical
ways. Keep me
close to You and
the cross.

The ideal expressed here by John is something of which natural man is not capable. Only the faith of Christ Himself living in us can enable us to accept the challenge in the verse, in the knowledge that Christ will bring about the success in us. It calls for a death with Christ on the cross, the death of our sinful nature.

Thus a daily unbroken fellowship is necessary with Christ. The way in which you have love for your fellow beings will convince the world that you are Christ's disciple and will eventually bring them to believe that God loves them just as He loves Christ.

Those Who Follow the Lamb

They follow the Lamb wherever he goes.
REVELATION 14:4

Of one thing we can be certain: that the Lamb on earth was the exact likeness of the glorified Lamb in heaven. So followers of Christ also reflect something of the heavenly glory on earth.

And what does it entail to follow in the footsteps of the Lamb? He humbled Himself—like a lamb being led to the place of slaughter, He did not open His mouth (see Isaiah 53:7). His gentleness, His tenderness, and His humility serve as a model for His followers.

Paul warns us that the same attitude that was in Christ must be in us. He was God but became man and slave; He humbled Himself and became obedient even to death on the cross. The Lamb opened the only way that leads to the throne of God. The way—the way of humility, thoughtfulness, and obedience—leads through the torn veil into the Most Holy Place, and into the presence of God.

Therefore God exalted Christ to the highest place and gave Him the name that is above every name (see Philippians 2:9). Sadly, it is because Christians do not bear the same mark of thoughtfulness and humility that the world does not believe in a Christ-filled life.

Thank You, Lord, that You showed me the way to follow the Lamb, even into the glory of the throne of God in heaven.

Let Paul's words be the model by which you organize your life: "I am crucified with Christ, and I no longer live but Christ lives in me" (Galatians 2:20).

To Him the Honor

To him who loves us and has freed us from our sins by his blood,
and has made us to be a kingdom and priests to serve his God and Father—
to him be glory and power for ever and ever! Amen.
REVELATION 1:5–6

Perhaps you feel that it is not so easy to carry out the message and commands that are confined in the cross. But Christ says that His yoke is easy and His burden is light. Love makes everything easy. Do not think of your love for Him; rather think of His great love for you, which He gives through the Holy Spirit. Think of it by day and by night; mull it over, until you have the assurance: *His love for me is indescribably great.* It is through the love of Christ on the cross that people are drawn closer.

Here in His love you have the answer to that which enables you to find fulfillment in fellowship with the crucified Jesus. The answer lies in the continual guidance and inspiration of the Holy Spirit in your heart. Think of the everlasting love that longs to take possession of you and to fill you with unspeakable joy.

Yes, Lord, to You who love me, who washed me of my sins in Your blood and made me king and priest, to You belong the glory and the power for all eternity.

His blood redeems us from our sins. Is that not enough proof that He will never reject you? That you are precious in His sight? That the power of His blood has made you acceptable to God?

Priest for God the Father, He guards you in His power and you will be strengthened by His Spirit to overcome sin and to appear as a priest for others. To Him, therefore, belong the glory and the power for all eternity!

The Secret of a
Life of Faith

We have followed Jesus on the way of the cross and pondered
the secret of the cross. You have noticed that it has often
been emphasized how necessary it is to, by faith, claim the
offer of Jesus on the cross as your own. Now that we are
approaching Pentecost, we are specifically going to speak
about the secret of living a life of faith.

Jesus said to the father of a boy possessed by a demon,
"Everything is possible for him who believes" (Mark 9:23).
Maybe the father of the boy felt that the responsibility for
the boy's recovery rested with him—that is, if he believed, his
son would be healed. But when he looked into Jesus' eyes, he
was assured of a love that was willing to heal, and also willing
to strengthen his faith. Christ listened to the man's plea and
the child was restored to health.

There is great comfort in this for all those who feel that their
faith falls short. The same Redeemer who waits for our faith
supplies that faith Himself. He hears our cry, a cry that has
its trust in Christ, "Help me in my unbelief!" Even if our
faith is as small as a mustard seed, God will make it stronger.
Jesus Christ completes the work that He has begun.

The Image of God

Then God said, "Let us make man in our image, in our likeness."
GENESIS 1:26

Here for the first time we encounter the thought that it was God's intention to make man a godlike being—someone in God's image. Man would live in complete dependency on God and receive from Him what is holy and blessed. The glory, holiness, and love of God would live in man and radiate from him.

But when sin spoiled the image of God in man, God gave the promise of a descendant of a woman in whom the divine purpose would be fulfilled. "The Son is the radiance of God's glory and the exact representation of his being" (Hebrews 1:3). He was to become a Son of man, in whom God's plan would be carried out.

This idea of the Creation is carried over into the New Testament where the children of God are spoken of as being predestined to alter to a likeness of His Son. The expectancy is worded in 2 Corinthians 3:18 as follows: "And we, who with unveiled faces all reflect the Lord's glory, are being transformed into his likeness with ever-increasing glory, which comes from the Lord, who is the Spirit." We are being changed more and more into a likeness of Christ. Just a few verses earlier Paul spoke of the greater glory of the ministry of the Holy Spirit.

Lord, renew me today through the work of Your Spirit, so that I can reflect Your glory and win people for Your Kingdom.

The promise contained in the text must be remembered. It is for all those who give Jesus Christ the position of glorified Lord. You must remember that you are God's representative on earth, and that the Spirit of God is capable of renewing you in His image.

Faith and Obedience

The LORD appeared to him and said, "I am God Almighty;
walk before me and be blameless. I will confirm my covenant
between me and you, and will greatly increase your numbers."

GENESIS 17:1–2

In Abraham we have an example of how God works through faith. This example implies step-by-step training in faith. Originally God gave the promise to all nations on earth, that they would be blessed through Abraham (see Genesis 12:3). As Abraham entered the Promised Land, God gave him a further promise that this would be the land his descendants would inherit (see Genesis 12:7).

Following the battles against the kings, God said to Abraham, "Look up at the heavens and count the stars—if indeed you can count them. So shall your offspring be" (Genesis 15:5). When Abraham's wife, Sarah, was disbelieving on the plains of Mamre, God asked Abraham, "Is anything too hard for the LORD?" (Genesis 18:14.) Thus God led Abraham step by step until his faith was strong enough for him to offer Isaac. After forty years, Abraham was willing to do that which was seemingly contrary to all God's promises.

If you, as a child of God, wish to follow in Abraham's footsteps, you must be willing to rely solely on the promises of God who desires to work His perfect will in you. It is not always an easy road. It is a road that continually asks the will of God. It is a road that hears God's voice saying, "Walk before me, and be blameless."

Lord, thank you
for the gift of
faith and how you
mold it day by
day. Make me to
be obedient
to you.

After God had appeared to him the first time, Abraham fell to his knees. Only then did God speak to him. That then was the origin of the working of the power of God.

The Love of God

*Love the LORD your God with all your heart
and with all your soul and with all your strength.*

DEUTERONOMY 6:5

God taught Abraham what it meant to believe in God with all his heart. Moses taught Israel that the first and greatest commandment is to love God with all their heart and soul. God is the loving Creator, and Man has been created in His image to be the object of His love.

The nation of Israel was not capable of living out this commandment. But at the end of his life Moses could declare, "The LORD your God will circumcise your hearts and the hearts of your descendants, so that you may love him with all your heart and with all your soul, and live" (Deuteronomy 30:6). This was the first indication of a New Covenant that was to come, a covenant of which Jeremiah later also spoke—a law that would be written on the hearts of people by the Holy Spirit so that mankind would walk God's road.

Heavenly Father, I pray that every day Your Spirit will make my love increase in quality and quantity.

Most Christians easily shrug this off as being impossible to do. But the message of the Bible is that all that is worthy of God is an undivided heart that God *Himself will give and work in us.* That is the gift of grace that God will bestow on those who ask for, expect, and eagerly await the fulfillment of His promise.

Think seriously of the promise in Romans 5:5: "And hope does not disappoint us, because God has poured out his love into our hearts by the Holy Spirit, whom he has given us." To love God with your whole heart is surely grace and a glorious reality. Be still before God and wait on Him until He makes His promise a reality in you. This is what a life of faith means.

Rejoice in His Honor

Blessed are those who have learned to acclaim you, who walk in the light of your presence, O LORD. They rejoice in your name all day long.
PSALM 89:15-16

"Rejoice in your name" speaks of a nation that walks in the light of God's presence and sings praises to His name. In the Old Testament it was something done at times by the leading churchmen, but it only became possible for every believer in the New Testament—and then not only on special occasions.

In every healthy family is a father who finds joy in contact with his children, and children who in turn find delight in being in the father's company. Ethan expressed this in Psalm 89:15: "Blessed are those who have learned to acclaim you, who walk in the light of your presence O Lord." Our heavenly Father promises the same to His children. This has been made possible by Christ, who through the Holy Spirit fills our hearts with the love of God. There are many children of God who do not think this is possible. And yet Jesus promised us joy, a joy no one can take away from us (see John 16:22).

Throughout the day let us remember the longing of the Father for His children's trust and love and the children's need of the Father's presence so that they can live in His light. The result will be children who rejoice in His name and praise His deeds as savior.

Can you imagine the witness that goes out into the world when you live each day with so much joy? The happiness of Jesus cannot be taken from you. It is a joy that lasts.

Lord, I do not know if my faith life radiates so much permanent joy that it glorifies Your name. Forgive me for this. I wait on You.

The Thoughts of God

*"As the heavens are higher than the earth,
so are my ways higher than your ways
and my thoughts than your thoughts."*

ISAIAH 55:9

God's promise that we are created in His image, and that the Holy Spirit will mold us closer to this image as we learn to know Christ more intimately, is indeed a thought as high as heaven is above the earth. His invitation to love our God and our neighbors with all our heart, and His promise to change our heart for this purpose, are also thoughts as lofty as the heavens. God's call to walk in His light on earth and to seek His presence unceasingly, is a gift of love from the heart of God.

Holy Spirit, fill my heart with the thoughts of God in all their heavenly glory and power.

Deep respect and humility are necessary to make these ideas a part of your life. Every day you need close fellowship with God in order to make His thoughts your thoughts. There must be an unshakeable belief that God can bring about these things in your life. His promise to you and His disciples is that the Spirit will fill you and make these promises a part of you—promises that are as high above us as the heavens are above the earth. Paul quotes the words of Isaiah as he says, "No eye has seen, no ear has heard, no mind has conceived what God has prepared for those who love him" (1 Corinthians 2:9).

Do not take these promises of God lightly. Do not limit Him according to your own abilities and thoughts. The more you become quiet in His Word, the better you will get to know God's great plans for you.

A New Covenant in Jeremiah

"The time is coming," declares the LORD, "when I will make a new covenant with the house of Israel and with the house of Judah. I will put my law in their minds and write it on their hearts."

JEREMIAH 31:31, 33

Israel could not keep God's covenant on Sinai, for their nature was too carnal and too sinful. In that law there was not yet sufficient room for grace; it only served to point out the sins of the people.

There is mention here of a New Covenant between Israel and God, a covenant written on the heart and impressed on the mind; not written in ink but by the Spirit of the living God. In this covenant the child of God can rejoice and cry out like David, "I desire to do your will, O my God; your law is within my heart" (Psalm 40:8).

In contrast to the Old Covenant, which lacked the power to enable Israel to be obedient to God's law, the New Covenant held the promise of ongoing obedience and a claiming of His promises—actual signs of a believer taking God at His Word.

The difference between the Old and the New Testaments must be kept clearly in mind. In the Old Testament, the principle of grace was already included, but not enough for Israel to remain obedient. In the New Testament there is the definite promise that our hearts will be renewed by the power of the Holy Spirit, enabling us to appear before God without blemish.

Heavenly Father, thank You for the work of Your Spirit in my life and the principle of obedience that I have received. Write Your will on my heart and impress it on my mind.

The New Covenant in Ezekiel

I will sprinkle clean water on you, and you will be clean; I will cleanse you from all your impurities and from all your idols. I will give you a new heart and put a new spirit in you; I will remove from you your heart of stone and give you a heart of flesh. And I will put my Spirit in you and move you to follow my decrees and be careful to keep my laws.

EZEKIEL 36:25–27

In contrast to the Old Covenant, the God-given power that enables the people to stay within His law is the distinctive feature of the New Covenant.

But why does the truth of the New Covenant so seldom become a reality in the life of a believer? The answer is quite simple: It is not preached or believed, and the fulfillment of it is not felt in the believer's life.

Paul is an example of the fulfilling of the New Covenant in a believer's life. The same anxious person who cries out that the power of sin holds him captive, shortly thereafter thanks God that he has, in Jesus Christ, through the Spirit that gives him life, been set free (see Romans 8:1–4).

Why is it that so few people can testify to the truth of this? God links His promises to our faith—however difficult the truth may be for the human mind to fathom. His promises become operative when we believe. Maybe you will put it to the test even today.

Read through the text for today a few times, until you believe and make it your own. Trust the work of the Spirit. "What you believe, will happen" (Matthew 9:29).

Lord, I understand more and more about the life of faith. I can only pray: Help me in my unbelief.

The New Covenant and Prayer

*Call to me and I will answer you and tell you great
and unsearchable things you do not know.*

JEREMIAH 33:3

The fulfillment of the promises of the New Covenant is dependent on prayer. But in our unbelief there is little expectation that God will, or even wishes to, keep His promises, even when we call to him in sincere faith and in expectation. There are people who no longer believe that the promises of God are genuine. We just do not have the faith in God's mighty power that He can do what He has promised. Be honest: Do you believe that the promises of God (all of them!) also specifically apply to you?

The path of faith is through prayer. "Call to me, and I will answer you," says God. It is in practicing persistent prayer that your faith is strengthened; it is a total commitment linked to prayer and faith in God's almighty work. As the faith of individuals is being built up, they can help one another to strengthen the church of God, in the wider expectation that His message of salvation will reach those who are lost.

The state of the church and of its preachers and members calls for continual prayer. One should also pray that believers would realize the necessity of the work of the Holy Spirit, and ask for steadfast faith in the intense expectation of mighty works of God.

Lord, thank You for Your trustworthy Word and all that You have to say to me in it, through Your Spirit. Grant me the faith to believe every promise You have made.

The New Covenant in Hebrews

For I will forgive their wickedness,
and will remember their sins no more.
HEBREWS 8:12

Christ is called "the Mediator of a better covenant" which was grounded on more excellent promises than before (Hebrews 8:6). He fulfilled both sides of the covenant. He came, first of all, for the reconciliation of man with God so that he could be redeemed; and He also broke the power of sin so that we could have free access to God. With this was included an even greater blessing: a new heart, freed from the power of sin, a heart that rejoiced in the law of God and obeyed it.

Lord, I claim the abundance of Your promises for myself. Do this through the powerful working of Your Spirit within me.

These two parts of the covenant may never be separated. And yet there are many Christians who receive forgiveness, but never reach for the abundance of the whole promise. That is, namely, a new heart together with the joy in the law of God and the power of the Holy Spirit in order to obey it—in short, access to the fuller, richer life of the New Covenant. All this, through Jesus Christ, the Mediator of a better covenant written on the heart by the power of His Spirit.

This requires a heartfelt desire for a life committed completely to Jesus Christ. It means we must move prejudices aside and must believe in the power of God. It means submission to Jesus Christ as the Mediator of a better covenant, and a willingness to crucify the self and its sinfulness. It means being prepared to follow Him at any cost.

The Test of Our Faith

*Naaman's servants went to him and said, "My father, if the prophet had told
you to do some great thing, would you not have done it?
How much more, then, when he tells you, 'Wash and be cleansed'!"*
2 KINGS 5:13

In Naaman we have a vivid Old Testament example of the place of
faith in God's dealings with people.

Naaman would do anything to be healed. He would even
humble himself before an unknown prophet. In this passionate desire
to receive blessing lies the root of a strong faith. Too often it is just this
that is lacking in our religion.

For the strengthening of our faith we must
renounce all our preconceived ideas and bow
before the Word of God. That was more than
Naaman originally was prepared to do, and he
turned away in a rage. Fortunately, a wise and loyal
slave gave him some good advice. Faith is often
hobbled by our reluctance to believe that God can
bring about great changes if He is simply taken at
His Word.

A further hallmark of this type of simple faith
is the unconditional obedience to the Word of
God. "Wash and you will be cleansed," was the
simple instruction. Naaman did this seven times
and his skin healed and became like that of a little
boy (2 Kings 5:14).

You have to believe that wholehearted surrender to the promise of God can bring about the
cleansing you so much need.

*Lord, thank You
for the blood of
the Lamb through
which I have been
washed clean.
Help me to live a
purified life and
be able to say to
them, who stand
outside, "Wash
and you will be
cleansed."*

Faith in Christ

Believe in God; believe also in me.
JOHN 14:1, KJV

In Jesus' farewell words to his disciples before His crucifixion, He told them that they must believe in Him with the same faith that they had in God: "If you know me, you will also know my Father." On earth, Jesus could not yet reveal Himself completely to His disciples, but in heaven the abundance of God would be His, and He would do even greater things through His disciples. Faith must concentrate on the person of Jesus Christ in His union with the Father. Everything that God can do, Jesus can also do.

The divinity of Christ is the cornerstone of our faith. Christ the person is also God. The same power that worked in Christ and raised Him from the dead works in us and provides for all our needs. As a child of God, you must worship Jesus in his divine might in the knowledge that He is one with the Father. Trust in Him to provide for all your needs. Be assured of His presence as Redeemer who can equip and strengthen you. Remember that Christ works in and through you, and provides all that God desires for you and all that you need.

Lord Jesus, I know a lot about You, but am uncertain whether I really know You. Reveal Yourself anew to me in all Your glorious majesty.

When you think of Jesus who is one with the Father, your first thought is not of Him hanging helplessly on a cross, but rather as your Redeemer who saved you and sanctifies and strengthens you with His power.

The farewell words of Christ to His disciples were that they must be of good courage because He had overcome the world. Our greatest need is a direct, definite, and unceasing faith in the mighty power of Christ working in us.

The Life of Christ in Us

Because I live, you also will live.
JOHN 14:19

John, the bosom friend of Jesus, says more about a life in Christ than the other three evangelists. It could be that he was closer to Jesus than the others. The other evangelists speak of remorse and forgiveness, but John takes it further when he speaks of a new heart in the child of God in which the law had been put as a living power. It is John who writes of the disciples becoming one with Him, just as He is with the Father. The other three gospels tell of the shepherd searching for His lost ones; John speaks of the shepherd laying down His life for the sheep. His life *became* their life: "I have come that they may have life, and have it to the full" (John 10:10).

Jesus did not promise His disciples the life He had here on earth, but the resurrected life, the life of victory over death, life at the right hand of God. He would remain in them, and the promise is for all those who accept it by faith.

Too often there are those who are satisfied with the first, basic steps of the Christian life but never seek the richer life in Christ. Maybe they do not believe it or are not prepared to make the necessary sacrifices.

Let it be the desire of your heart to be content with nothing less than Christ living in you and you living in Christ. All things are possible through God for those who believe. The life of abundance is especially meant for those who make time to listen to God's promises, take them seri-ously, and believe in the power of God to do what He has promised.

Jesus, risen and living Lord, thank You for the unspeakable privilege that You live in me by faith and give me life abundantly.

The Obedience of Love

If you obey my commands, you will remain in my love.
JOHN 15:10

So often people wonder how they can remain in Christ uninterrupted and thus live for Him alone? One often hears such prayers.

Jesus gives the answer: Obey My commands. Loving obedience is the answer to the joy of His continuous presence.

Over and over, in John 14–15, the Lord sets the condition: He who knows my commands and obeys them, him my Father will love. And then He specifically says, "You are my friends if you do what I command" (John 15:14). In our relationship with Christ, love is everything: the love of Christ for us, and our love for Him as it finds expression in our love for our neighbor.

Thank You, Lord, for the promise of the Holy Spirit to be the power of Jesus' life, working and living in me. I plead for that obedience that You promised.

Too few believers believe this truth. They cannot believe that a heart submitted to Christ is capable of loving Him and living within His commands and love. They do not believe the promise of the New Covenant as spelled out by Ezekiel: "I will put my Spirit in you and move you to follow my decrees and be careful to keep my laws" (Ezekiel 36:27).

These promises of the Holy Spirit were the guarantee that the disciples would love Him and guard His words. To live "in Christ" and "through the Holy Spirit" was the secret of the effectiveness of the disciples' prayers to bring down God's blessing on all their work.

The Promise of the Spirit

If I go, I will send him [the Counselor] to you. He will bring glory to me by taking from what is mine and making it known to you.
JOHN 16:7, 14

After His ascension to heaven, the crucified Christ was glorified on His throne at the right hand of God. And from that glory He sent the Holy Spirit to His disciples, fulfilling His promise to them. It is the Spirit that searches for the deep secrets of God, who is an indissoluble part of God, who was with Christ during His life on earth and at His death on the cross.

The same Spirit would now support the disciples and make them aware of the presence of the glorified Christ. The Spirit of God would be their power in a life of obedience, and their instructor in all for which they had prayed. It would be by the power of the Holy Spirit that the disciples would defeat God's enemies and proclaim the gospel to the world.

The Spirit is God. He wants to appropriate your entire life. He is not just a casual helper. No, your whole heart and life must be under the control of the Spirit—from hour to hour and from day to day. The Spirit, who surveys all the secrets of God, lays hold of your innermost being, where He reveals Christ as your master. Believe Jesus' promise that the Spirit of God desires to glorify Christ in you. Your life can, through loving obedience and the indwelling of the risen Christ, be a very strong witness in the world, in the power of the Holy Spirit.

Spirit of God, You who examine the secrets of God and make them known to us, forgive my feeble faith. Empower me that Christ might be glorified in me.

In Christ

*On that day you will realize that I am in my Father,
and you are in me, and I am in you.*
JOHN 14:20

God the Father and Jesus Christ were one, and although Christ was on the earth, He was also in the Father. What He did, the Father achieved through Him.

The unity of the Father and the Son is also the image of Christ in us and us in Christ. As God worked through the Son, so Christ in turn works in us if we believe that we are in Him and expose ourselves to His power in us.

As the Son waited on the Father and the Father then worked through Him, the disciples had to make their desires known through prayer, and He would work through them. Their life in Him was an image of Christ's life in God. As the Father worked through the Son because the Son lived in the Father, Christ would work in them if they remained in Him.

For this, they had to wait for the coming of the Holy Spirit who would equip them with supernatural power. They also had to stay in daily fellowship with Him in prayer so that He could accomplish the greater work through them that He had promised. Herein also lies the power of the church and its members.

Ask God each day for submission to the Holy Spirit—God the Trinity in you and you in Him.

Gracious Lord, humbly and sincerely I plead with You, that You will show me how to submit myself completely to Your Spirit while I wait on His doctrine and knowledge, so that Jesus may be glorified in me every moment.

Remain in Christ

Remain in me, and I will remain in you.
JOHN 15:4

In the parable of the vine and the branches, Jesus drew attention to the importance of close, daily contact with Himself.

He first refers to the relationship between Him and His Father. "Remain in me," He says. "No branch can bear fruit by itself; it must remain in the vine. Neither can you bear fruit unless you remain in me" (John 15:4).

You have no doubt often read this fascinating chapter and pondered over the imagery of the vine. And yet you have probably never nearly experienced that close unity and strength which Jesus has in mind.

Jesus casts more light on it with two clear examples: one from heaven (as I am in My Father) and one from nature (as the branch is in the vine).

I think the most important thing is for you to wait on the Spirit of the Lord until the two great truths of this passage become a reality in you. Jesus did, after all, explain that He would work with power through His disciples to enable us to really understand these two points.

God says this to the weakest and the strongest of His children: *Remain in me, and you will bear much fruit. It is the condition for a life of power and blessing.*

Do you believe that the Lord meant this for You as well? Be still before Him.

Lord, thank You that You are in me and that I can be anchored in You. I do believe that this passage of Scripture was also meant for me. I desire to remain in You and Your love.

The Power of Prayer

If you remain in me and my words remain in you,
ask whatever you wish, and it will be given you.

JOHN 15:7

Before the Lord ascended to heaven, He taught His disciples two important lessons about their relationship with Him and the tasks that awaited them. One was that in heaven He would have more power than on earth and that He would use the power to save people through them.

The other lesson was that without Him, they would not be able to do anything and would, for all intents and purposes, be powerless. They could depend on Him to work in and through them, in that way fulfilling His perfect will. His first and most important instruction was to bring everything to Him in prayer.

Lord, I think I do not have the slightest idea yet of the power of prayer. Convince me more and more each day.

With these truths He sent them out into the world. They could begin work with confidence. The glorified Jesus desired to do even greater things in and through them than He Himself had done on earth. The condition for the disciples was that they retain a spirit of dependent prayer and supplication.

Too often powerless lives bear witness to our inability to remain in Christ and to take hold of His wonderful promises and believe in them. It is so important for the members of the body of Christ to have a meaningful fellowship with Him and to live in utter dependence on Him, constantly pleading with Him in prayer, that the work to be done should be to His glory.

Today the Lord asks you, as He asked Martha in another context, "Do you believe this?" She answered, "Yes, Lord, I believe that you are the Christ" (John 11:26–27). And you? Do you believe?

The Secret of Love

*May they be brought to complete unity to let the world know that
you sent me and have loved them even as you have loved me.*
JOHN 17:23

In the last discussion with His disciples around the communion table,
Jesus again stressed the thought of the disciples being in Him and
remaining in Him. Here in His prayer as the High Priest in John 17,
Jesus gave more prominence to the thought of His *being in them,* just
as the Father was in Him.

The world could only be convinced that God loved the disciples
as He loved His Son if believers allowed Christ into their lives and
proved it by loving their fellow beings as Christ loved them.

One of the most wonderful promises was given to the beloved
followers of the Lord: "He who loves me will be loved by my Father,
and I too will love him and show myself to him"
(John 14:21). This is actually what the life of faith
is all about: to live the life of love in the power of
the Spirit. You should not be satisfied with anything less.

The weakness of the church can be ascribed
to the fact that the world does not see the unity of
Christ in us and us in Him. That is what is necessary, together with an outpouring of love towards
all people.

God longs to bestow this on you through the
Holy Spirit. Through the love of believers toward
each other and to others, the world is convinced of
the fulfillment of God's Word and His promises. *I
in You and You in me*—that is the secret of love.

*Thank You, Lord,
that You are in
me. Grant me
overflowing love
so that my witness
will not
deteriorate into
disfavor.*

Christ Who Absolves Us

And [they] are justified freely by his grace through
the redemption that came by Christ Jesus.

ROMANS 3:24

The first three Gospels emphasize the redemption as the freedom from sin. Paul speaks of it as the absolution that we receive. John takes it a step further and mentions the fullness of a life of Christ in us. It is a rebirth and, therefore, a renewal. Paul combines these two truths of faith into a harmonious unit.

In Romans, for instance, Paul first speaks of absolution (see Romans 3:21–5:11). After that he speaks of a life unified with Christ (see 5:12–8:39). He uses Abraham as the example in which all the aspects of faith are combined. God saw Abraham's faith as a reason for absolution. Then God led him to faith in the God who gives life and brings into being things which do not exist through His Word (see Romans 4:17).

Lord, thank You that You walk the road with me. Help me not to remain bogged down in the basic things.

Absolution is the first step. This we obtain through faith in Christ, but that is only the beginning. Gradually the believer realizes that he or she has also been born again, that there is a new life, that Christ lives in him or her, and that all have the calling to remain in Christ and to live and work in Him.

Most Christians see their faith only as absolution. With this they motivate themselves to a life of thankfulness and obedience. Yet they fail because they do not know the secret of a life of submission to Christ. The secret is belief in a God that renews their life daily in Christ, the One in whom there is abundance.

Christ Our Life

For if, by the trespass of the one man,
death reigned through that one man,
how much more will those who receive God's abundant
provision of grace and of the gift of righteousness
reign in life through the one man, Jesus Christ.
ROMANS 5:17

In the same way, count yourselves dead to sin
but alive to God in Christ Jesus.
ROMANS 6:11

Paul explains in his letter to the Romans that all who are baptized in Christ Jesus are also baptized in His death (see Romans 6:3). We were buried with Him, and rose again with Him. The old self was crucified with Him and rose with Him from the dead. Now all believers must see themselves as dead to sin and alive to God.

As the new life is unity with the resurrected Christ, so our death to sin is unity with Christ on the cross. It is when, through the power of the Holy Spirit, we see ourselves hanging on the cross and then rising again, that sin no longer has power over us. It is then that we are no longer slaves to sin (see Romans 6:6). It is then that we are dead to sin. All is made possible through the working of the Holy Spirit.

May you, as a child of God, have insight into these spiritual truths—what the full power of Christ in you means once you realize you are dead to sin: Christ in you for a life of fruitfulness and service.

Lord Jesus, You are my life. Thank You that I could die and rise again with You. Make this truth a greater reality in my life each day.

Crucified with Christ

*I have been crucified with Christ and I
no longer live, but Christ lives in me.*
GALATIANS 2:20

Mankind died with the fall of Adam beyond the perfect will of God. In Christ, however, we have another kind of death. We die to sin and come alive again within the will of God. It was for this that Christ died on the cross and we identify ourselves with His death.

The text tells us how very real the doctrine of faith was to Paul. The crucified Christ lived in him and helped him understand the deepest significance of the cross. Like Christ, Paul considered himself lowly and became a slave, obedient to death.

Lord, thank you that I could die with you. Please let the remains of my old self die altogether. Thank you that I may know that I rose again with you.

The death of Christ on the cross testifies to His holiness and His triumph over sin. By faith, the believer shares in the power and blessing of the crucified Christ. The measure in which the believer claims the truth for himself is how much he dies to the world—the superficial pleasures of the world, its desires, and its selfishness. He learns that the deepest meanings of the cross open the way for fellowship with Christ and association with His suffering. He learns that the crucified Christ is the power and wisdom of God.

May you experience this wonderful power every day, of the faith God gave you, to enable you to grasp the truth and live according to it: dead to sin and alive to God and Christ.

A Life of Faith

The life I live in the body, I live by faith in the Son of God,
who loved me and gave himself for me.
GALATIANS 2:20

Many devoted believers would like to ask Paul what he meant when he said that he no longer lives, but that Christ lives in him. Has he any further role to play, or has he merely become some sort of robot? This, and similar questions, he would answer with the words of our verse.

Paul explains that his earthly life is a continuous, moment-by-moment faith of trust in the love of Christ that has been bestowed on him. Faith is the power that took possession of him and permeated his entire being and all his actions.

This is the secret of the life of Christian faith. The Christian life is more than a belief in certain promises of God or promised blessings. It is also a picture of how completely Christ gives Himself to us every moment. On our part there must be the continual trust of faith that the Holy Spirit maintains life in us, moment by moment. It is as vital as the air that we breathe. Jesus can, by the work of the Holy Spirit and His omnipresence, be an indwelling guest. We can associate with Him every moment. He maintains our life as if each of us were the only one in whom He lives. As the Father lives in Him, so He dwells in us. Faith is nourished by the omnipresence of Christ in the Holy Spirit. May God reveal to you the indissoluble unity between Christ and yourself.

Thank You for the assurances of Your Word. Strengthen my faith, Lord, so that it can be revealed each day in a life that pleases You and calls the world to repentance.

Total Submission

What is more, I consider everything a loss compared with the surpassing greatness of knowing Christ Jesus my Lord.

PHILIPPIANS 3:8

What made the disciples suitable to receive the Holy Spirit? Why were they so privileged to spend those last days with Him and to receive His instruction?

The answer is simple. When Jesus called them, they left everything behind and followed Him. They renounced their lives, counted them as unimportant, and were willing to do His bidding. They followed Him right to Golgotha, and held fast to Him alone. Therefore, they were ready to be witnesses to His resurrection and to receive the Holy Spirit.

Just as Jesus Christ had to sacrifice all to be an offering to God, so Abraham, Jacob, and Joseph had to give up everything in order to become a sacrifice to God. Therefore, the disciples also had to give up everything to follow God's call, separated to God alone. Only then could God fulfill His purpose in them.

The same applied to Paul. He held everything as worthless in order to know Christ. Christ asks an undivided heart, all our strength, and our whole life if we want to share the victory with Him.

Christ requires meaningful fellowship and constant association with Him every day; He asks for people who do not belong to themselves, people who hold everything as worthless in order to know Christ. In this way we receive the abundant blessing of the Holy Spirit.

Lord Jesus, I believe in my heart that this life is also meant for me. I do not want to be satisfied with anything else. Thank You that I can be more than a conqueror in You.

Devoted to Him Alone

May God himself, the God of peace, sanctify you through and through. May your whole spirit, soul and body be kept blameless at the coming of our Lord Jesus Christ. The one who calls you is faithful and he will do it.

1 THESSALONIANS 5:23–24

What a promise! One would expect to see all God's children clinging to it, claiming its fulfillment! However, it seems as though many believers do not see the riches of the promises in this text as being for themselves. Just listen to what is written here.

God who gives peace. The peace spoken of here is the peace brought by the sacrifice on the cross, the peace that passes all understanding, a peace that only God can give. God, who gives peace, promises to make you devoted to Him in Christ and in the Holy Spirit.

As if he knows that the riches of promises in the verse will be too much for us, Paul repeats and strengthens it in the second part of the verse: spirit, soul, and body: *spirit,* the inner core of one's being, created to live in fellowship with God; *soul,* the center of life; and *body,* the means by which sin and death got a foot in the door, but which was made alive in Christ.

I have but one prayer in Your presence: Make me wholly devoted to You.

And then he adds that God is faithful to keep the promise. All He asks is that you stay close to Him each day. As the sun warms your body, so the warmth of His nearness will awaken your devotion. May you experience this.

The Majesty of the Almighty

I pray also that the eyes of your heart may be enlightened in order that you may know the hope to which he has called you, the riches of his glorious inheritance in the saints, and his incomparably great power for us who believe. That power is like the working of his mighty strength, which he exerted in Christ when he raised him from the dead and seated him at his right hand in the heavenly realms.

EPHESIANS 1:18–20

There are biblical passages for which one needs faith. They are those that mortal man cannot just accept.

Paul was writing to believers who were being led by the Holy Spirit, yet he still felt the need for continual prayer for them to know the full power of the Spirit living within them. It is the same power that raised Christ from the dead.

Thank You, Lord, for Your power at work in me. I do not understand or experience enough of it. I am silent before You in order to experience something of this in my life.

Christ died on the cross under the weight of the sin of the world and the curse that rested on it. Weighed down by this, He went to the grave. By the power of God, Christ was raised up from that grave and glorified. Even today this is a marvelous revelation of power! And now the same power can work through those who believe and trust in God. It is by the power of the Almighty that the risen and exalted Christ can be revealed in our hearts, as our life and our strength.

Believe it, and pray for it every day—for yourself and for other believers. Preachers must pray for their congregations to receive it. The same power that raised Christ from the dead is operative in you. What a difference this could make to your life and to your outlook! Pray without ceasing that the Spirit will reveal the power of the Almighty in your life.

Christ Who Dwells in Us

I pray...that Christ may dwell in your hearts through faith.
EPHESIANS 3:16–17

One of the chief differences between Israel and the surrounding nations was that the God of Israel lived amongst them—in the tabernacle and, later, in the temple. In the New Testament the good news is that Christ lives within the believer. Paul explains it as follows.

"I kneel before the Father" (Ephesians 3:14). The blessing must come from the Father in answer to our prayers—blessing either for the one who prays, or for those for whom He intercedes.

"I pray that out of his glorious riches he may strengthen you with power...in your inner being" (v. 16). These riches must be something very special. The inner strength Paul speaks of includes separation from the sins of the world, and submission to Christ as Lord and Master to live a life of obedience to Christ. Then His promises can be fulfilled in us, and the Father and the Son will live in us.

"So that Christ may dwell in your hearts through faith" (v. 17). The godly nature of Christ desires to dwell in us. Through faith we receive the gift.

Lord, I hold fast to the assurance of Your Word, that You will fulfill Your promises in my life.

"To know this love which surpasses knowledge— that you may be filled to the measure of all the fullness of God" (v. 19). This is a promise, naturally, for as far as it is humanly possible to understand the bounty of God.

Meditate with strong desire and childlike faith on what the Father, the Son, and the Holy Spirit have undertaken to work in you. God is able to do far more than we could pray or ask for.

The Christian Equipment

May the God of peace...equip you with everything good for doing his will,
and may he work in us what is pleasing to him, through Jesus Christ.
HEBREWS 13:20–21

This text makes a strong appeal to your faith to claim it as a truth for yourself and your own life. The promise takes you further than anything you have ever dreamed about. Do not just read it. Believe it.

In Hebrews we have a very moving account of the eternal redemption which Christ, as the High Priest and Mediator of the New Covenant, brought about by His crucifixion. The letter is ended with deeply spiritual instructions and with the prayer of blessing.

The blessing begins by saying that the God of peace will equip us with "everything" good. Everything! Has anything been omitted? Is there more that you desire? Is there any more equipment that you require in order to live to the full for the Lord? The promise says that you already have everything. Therefore, begin to live.

Lord, thank You for the extent of Your promise and for everything You provide for me to live as You want me to live.

The main idea here is that the meaning of Christ's death and resurrection lies in the fact that God Almighty has free access to work His will in us; that He, through Jesus Christ, brings to pass that which is acceptable to Him.

Christ's deed of reconciliation was so complete that we have the assurance that God Himself completes the work He has begun in someone who trusts in Him.

May you always remember that which is almost too overwhelming for the human mind to grasp: God Himself completes the work in those who wait on Him and have faith in Him.

The God of All Grace

And the God of all grace, who called you to his eternal glory in Christ,
after you have suffered a little while, will himself restore you
and make you strong, firm and steadfast.
1 PETER 5:10

Just as the writer of Hebrews, in yesterday's text, worded God's promise of blessing in glowing terms, Peter does in today's passage.

God must be the subject of our hope and trust. As God is the heart of the universe, the source of power, and He directs and manages it, so He must be the heart of the life of the believer.

Each new day God must fill the thoughts of the believer: *God, and God alone, can equip me for the day.* Each day you must confess your own helplessness and submit to God in childlike faith. It is absolutely necessary to meet with God every morning and to give Him time to reveal Himself to you, to allow Him to guide you through the day. That was the theme with which we began the year in January.

You have no idea of what awaits you in the day. It could be that there is some suffering—even if it has to do with your own sinfulness. But the Lord wants to supply all your needs even there. May this be the spirit in which you awake: having faith that God Himself will uplift you, and make you courageous, strong, and steadfast.

May the words of the text be your prayer each day, to carry you to that ultimate goal that the Father has in mind.

Heavenly Father, open my eyes and the eyes of Your children, that we might understand how You are working in our lives to mold us in the likeness of Your Son.

Remain in Him and Do Not Sin

But you know that he appeared so that he might take away our sins.
And in him is no sin. No one who lives in him keeps on sinning.
1 JOHN 3:5–6

At the first communion meal, John sat next to Jesus. Everything that Jesus said that last evening, John absorbed and saved deep in his heart and life. He remembered the discussions about love, obedience, and how to remain in Christ and His Father.

That is why he cannot but write of how necessary it is to remain in Christ and what the result would be. John tells us how we can prevent ourselves from sinning. Anyone who remains in Jesus does not sin, he says. Although it is in our nature to sin, we will be freed from the power of sin, and lead a life that pleases God—if we remain in Him. John says further that we will receive all that we ask for, if we obey His commands (1 John 3:22).

Lord, You know how I yearn to be free of the grip of sin. Thank You that You will not remove the power of Your Spirit from me.

Let the one who longs to be freed from the power of sin cling to these words: There is no sin in Him, and anyone who remains in Him does not keep on sinning. If I desire to remain in Him in whom there is no sin, Christ will live in me and equip me for a life that is pleasing to Him.

You are called to a life of faith—unbroken faith in the power of God. If you take time each day to submit yourself to the God of peace, the miracle will happen. God works in the hearts of those who wait on Him. Remain in Him and do not sin.

Overcome the World

Who is it that overcomes the world?
Only he who believes that Jesus is the Son of God.
1 JOHN 5:5

Christ often expressed himself about the kingdom of God on the one hand, and the world on the other. The two are irreconcilable. John also said that we must not love the world and the things of the world. If you love the world, the love of the Father is not in you, he warned.

John also taught that worldly things—all that sinful man covets, his preoccupation with possessions—does not come from the Father, but is of the world (see 1 John 2:16). That was how Eve came to fall: She saw that the fruit was good to eat, good to look at, and desirable (see 1 John 5:5). Through the eyes, through selfishness and pride, the world got the upper hand over her.

The world exercises great influence on the Christian who does not realize that in Christ he has been crucified to the world. In the excess of eating and drinking, in a worldly showiness, in everything with a worldly connotation, the world manages to get a grip on the believer. Most Christians are either unaware that they are falling under the spell of such worldliness, or they feel powerless to triumph over it and to shake it off.

Christ said that He has already overcome the world. So His encouraging command is, "Take heart!" (John 16:33). If the child of God remains in Christ, he will triumph.

Hour by hour, day by day you must remain in Christ. Make sure you retain the spirit of victory in your heart.

Lord, I believe in the victory of faith over the world. Each day I place my trust in the mighty power of God and in the presence of Jesus, in whom I remain.

The Secret of Power from On High

This is the month in which we celebrate the ascension of our Lord Jesus into heaven. And following the example of the first disciples, we gather together to pray for power from on high. No, we do not pray for another outpouring of the Holy Spirit. He has already come in all His glory and power! And when you accept Jesus into your heart, you also accept the Holy Spirit because God cannot be divided.

The question today, however, is how to live with the full power and indwelling of the Holy Spirit. This power is still the guarantee of what God can do. If the children of God were to unite each day to wait on His promises, there would be no limit to what God could do for them and through them.

The greatest desire of the Holy Spirit and of the Father is for Christ to be glorified in you. May this also be your greatest desire.

The Dispensation of the Spirit

If you then, though you are evil, know how to give good gifts to your children, how much more will your Father in heaven give the Holy Spirit to those who ask him!

LUKE 11:13

The writer of a booklet on prayer tells how he discovered the secret of a more fruitful prayer life. While he was thinking about prayer, it suddenly struck him that we are now living in the time of the dispensation of the Holy Spirit, and that anything we wish to do in God's service will be of little value unless the Holy Spirit inspires it. This brought me to the well-known, precious, and inexhaustible text, "How much more will your Father in heaven give the Holy Spirit to those who ask him!"

It dawned on me anew that the most important spiritual exercise of each day is to pray that God will send the Holy Spirit to us for our daily crises and needs. Without the Spirit, we can neither please God nor support others. Our prayers must have their origin in God, the highest source of power, if they are to raise our lives to fulfill God's purpose. If the Holy Spirit prays through us, as human channels, our prayers will rise again to God, who is their source, and will be answered by the divine working in ourselves and in others. The writer of the booklet adds that he is convinced that the Christian life depends chiefly on the quality of our prayers and not on the quantity.

Father, grant me in the month of Pentecost the working of Your Holy Spirit, so that I can learn to pray.

When you pray, therefore, ask your heavenly Father to again give you the Holy Spirit today. He longs to do it.

The Fruit of the Spirit

*But the fruit of the Spirit is love, joy, peace, patience, kindness,
goodness, faithfulness, gentleness, and self-control.*
GALATIANS 5:22–23

Christians often think that they have only to ask God to teach them
to pray, and He will immediately do it. This is not always the case.
What the Spirit does is to strengthen our spiritual life so that we are
better able to pray. When we ask God to teach us, it is important to
open ourselves to receive His influence so that our hearts are touched
and we submit ourselves to the work of the Holy Spirit.

This submission also includes naming before Him the fruit of
the Spirit, with an earnest prayer to be filled with the fruit. The advantage of the naming and memorizing of the fruit of the Spirit is that we
thereby express the deep desire to be filled with the fruit of the Spirit.

*Thank You, Lord,
for Your Spirit
that You sent me
and for His work
in my life. I pray
that ever more of
His fruit will be
visible in my life.*

Think, for instance, of the first three aspects
of the fruit: love, joy, and peace—the three main
characteristics of a strong faith. *Love* for God and
for Christ, love for all mankind. *Joy*—proof of the
perfect fulfilling of every need, of courage and
faith for what must still be accomplished. *Peace*—
the blessed state of undisturbed rest and security
during which we are completely filled with the
peace of God.

In the last talk with His disciples, Christ used
these three words, preceded each time with *my*:
"remain in *my* love" (John 15:9); "so that *my* joy
may be in you" (15:11); "*my* peace I give you"
(14:27).

Let us bring the fruit before the Spirit as the
deepest desire of our heart.

Guided by the Spirit of God

Because those who are led by the Spirit of God are sons of God.
ROMANS 8:14

Today we consider another four aspects of the fruit of the Spirit: patience, kindness, goodness, humility and self-control. These are also qualities of our Father in heaven, which will increase in us through prayer and the working of the Holy Spirit.

Patience. In the time of Moses, God's patience with his people was praised. The whole Bible is witness to the wonderful patience with which God dealt with sinful mankind, as the words of 2 Peter 3:9 remind us: "The Lord is not slow in keeping his promise, as some understand slowness. He is patient with you, not wanting anyone to perish, but everyone to come to repentance."

Kindness. We read a great deal about the kindness of God in the psalms. God works in our hearts the same kindness, friendliness, and grace toward all the sin and the misery around us.

Goodness. All goodness is of God, and He gives His children the same quality according to what we ask for and desire. This goodness is manifested in sympathy and love toward all those who suffer.

Humility. Jesus said, "Take my yoke upon you and learn from me, for I am gentle and humble in heart, and you will find rest for your souls" (Matthew 11:29).

The Holy Spirit will bring these attributes of God to ripeness in our hearts so that we may be more and more like God in all our ways and conversations.

Holy Spirit, I desire to receive the fruit of patience, kindness, goodness, and humility, so that I may become more like Christ.

The Spirit Awakens Faith

With that same spirit of faith we also believe and therefore speak.
2 CORINTHIANS 4:13

Why is it so important to remember the text in Galatians 5:22–23 concerning the fruit of the Spirit? It will awaken the desire in your heart to strengthen the fruit of the Spirit within you. Your expectation of the blessing of God will be greater. Therefore, we will look at two more fruits of the Spirit.

Faith. When the disciples asked the Lord why they were unable to drive out a certain demon, His answer was that they had too little faith (see Matthew 17:20–21). Faith is a fruit of the Spirit and leads to trusting solely in God. Faith believes in God's Word, trusts in Him, and waits in trust that His power will bring about that which He has promised.

Lord, let the fruit of the Spirit, with all its wonderful variety, ripen in my life.

Self-control. This fruit referred primarily to eating and drinking and leads us to restraint, carefulness, and unselfishness in our conversations, our desires, and our interactions with others. We should live with self-control, sincerity, and godly fruitfulness, as Paul wrote to Titus (2:12). We should exercise self-control in our dealings with the world and its temptations, being honest in carrying out God's will and devoting ourselves to fervent fellowship with God Himself.

Faith and self-control are both fruit of the Spirit. When we ask the Spirit of God to teach us to pray, we open our hearts to Him so that He may give us the gift of the fruit of the Spirit, including faith and self-control. These will influence our daily lives in our interaction with God and our fellow beings.

Praise God in the Spirit

*For it is we who are the circumcision, we who worship by the Spirit of God,
who glory in Christ Jesus, and who put no confidence in the flesh.*
PHILIPPIANS 3:3

When we approach God, we first ask Him for the guidance of the
Holy Spirit. Next we thank Him for all His blessings. We acknowledge our absolute dependence on Him and our own inability, and
express our reliance on His love and care. We wait on Him until we
have the assurance that He sees and hears us.

Then we direct our prayer to Jesus Christ and ask for grace to
always remain in Him, for without Him we can do nothing. We look
to Him as our Lord, our protector, our life, and commit ourselves to
His care for the day. We express our faith in His measureless love and
in the reality of His presence in us.

Last of all, we address our prayer to the Holy
Spirit. We have already prayed for His guidance.
Now we ask Him to strengthen us in the faith that
what we have asked of the Father and the Son will
be done in us. The Holy Spirit is the giver of the
power and the gifts of the Father and the Lord
Jesus. All the grace we need must be the result of
the working of the Spirit in us.

We do not, by nature, have the ability to do
what is right. We depend on the Lord Jesus to
work in us through the Holy Spirit. Think about
this. It will help to strengthen your faith if you
repeat Galatians 5:22–23 to yourself and ask God
to bestow on your life the gift of the fruit of which
the passage speaks.

*Triune God, I thank
You that I may
come before You
with all the needs
of my heart and
life. I consecrate
myself anew to
You and rely on
the work of the
Spirit in my life.*

Intercession

Pray for each other.
JAMES 5:16

Intercession is an indispensable part of prayer. It strengthens our love and faith in what God can do and is a way of bringing blessing and rescue to others. Prayer must not be just for ourselves, but chiefly for others.

Begin by putting forward those who are close to you, those with whom you live. Pray that you will be a help and not a hindrance to them. Pray for wisdom, for consideration toward them, for goodness and love, and for your self-sacrifice for their good.

Pray for your friends and for all with whom you come into contact. Pray that you will care prayerfully about their spiritual welfare. Pray for all Christians, for spiritual leaders and others in positions of authority.

Lord, I pray that through the work of Your Spirit, You will make a loyal intercessor of me.

Pray for those who do not yet know Jesus Christ as their Redeemer. Make a list of the names that God has laid on your heart and pray for their conversion. You belong to Christ; He needs you to bring the people around you to Him in prayer. The Holy Spirit will strengthen you to actively care about others. Pray, too, for the poor and the neglected.

Pray for the unconverted and for mission work. Use a mission calendar with daily prayer subjects, and bring before the Lord the missionaries, evangelists, teachers, and believers who work among them.

If this takes up too much time in the morning, make time for it during the day. Remember that you have been saved in order to serve, and you are on earth for the sole purpose of making God's love known to others.

Time

Could you men not keep watch with me for one hour?
MATTHEW 26:40

Is it possible that Christians can say that they cannot spend a quarter-hour or half-hour alone with God? We do not find it difficult to make time if a friend comes visiting, or if we must attend an important meeting, or do anything for our own pleasure or profit.

And for God, the great God, who has a rightful claim to our lives and who longs for us to spend time with Him so that He can transfer His power and grace to us, we do not have time. Even His disciples, who could regard it as a special privilege to be able to be with Him in prayer, did not in Jesus' final hours make time to wait on God and receive from Him the necessary strength for their work.

You may never say that you do not have time for God. Allow the Holy Spirit to teach you that the most important and most profitable time is that which you spend alone with God. Pray to Jesus Christ, who found it necessary to pray when He was on earth; pray to the Holy Spirit, who will impress the truth on your heart. It is as necessary as the food you eat and the air you breathe. God has priority over your time, no matter what else must be neglected. Only then will you be able to submit yourself fully to the will of God. If, from day to day, you persevere with dedication, time will no longer be a question.

Lord, enlighten me by Your Spirit, that I may get my priorities in order. Thank You that You eagerly await my fellowship with You.

The Word of God

The word of God is living and active.
HEBREWS 4:12

I find it useful to refer to God's Word in my prayers. Should the Holy Spirit impress a certain verse on my heart, I take it to the throne of grace and plead for the promise locked in it. This habit strengthens my faith, reminds me of the promises of God, and brings me into harmony with the will of God. I learn to pray within God's will and understand that I can only expect an answer if my prayers are in accordance with that will (see 1 John 5:14).

Prayer is like fire. The fire will only burn well if it is kept going with a viable fuel. God's Word is a powerful fuel that must be carefully and prayerfully studied, taken to heart, and lived by. The inspiration and working of the Holy Spirit alone can do this.

Thank You, Lord, for Your Word. Teach me to pray in total surrender to Your Word, and to rely on Your promises so that the fruit of Your Spirit may reach full maturity in my life.

In this way we have a deeper insight into the value and power of God's Word as the seed of everlasting life—a small seed in which life-giving strength is sheltered. Each Word or promise of God is a seed sheltering divine life in it. If I absorb it into my heart by faith and love, and meditate on it, it will produce fruit. Think about this: Even if your heart should feel cold and dead, the Word of God will bring about the kind of outlook He has promised in His Word.

The Holy Spirit uses both the Word and prayer. Prayer is the expression of our human anxieties and needs. The Holy Spirit informs you through the Word of God what He wants to do for you. It is the means by which the Holy Spirit activates your heart.

In the Name of Christ

And whatever you do, whether in word or deed, do it all in the name of the Lord Jesus, giving thanks to God the Father through him.
COLOSSIANS 3:17

It is good to end your prayer with a request that the Spirit will help you to remember, so that your prayer of the morning does not get lost in the activities of the day.

Our text for the day is a demand, although it seems difficult to carry out. God, however, would not have required this of us if it were impossible. The Word of God has the wonderful power to preserve the spirit of thanksgiving in our lives. In the morning, thank Him in the name of Jesus Christ for a good night's rest; and at night, give thanks for the gifts of grace throughout the day. The daily tasks will be lighter when we think of what God is doing for us. Each ordinary task will fill us with gratitude for the strength that He gives us to perform it.

Initially, it may be difficult to remember God in everything, and to do all in His name, yet the mere attempt to do this will strengthen us. As a mother is aware of her love for her child throughout the day, so the love of Christ will help us to live in His presence every moment. To this you must commit yourself: to live for God throughout the day.

Whatever you ask in the name of Jesus Christ, you will receive. Therefore, take the text of the day to heart and strive to live by it.

Thank You, Lord, that I do not need to bring my prayers to You in my own strength or merit, but that You receive me in the name of Jesus Christ. Thank You that I may live in Your presence.

The Spirit Who Glorifies Christ

He will bring glory to me by taking from what is mine and making it known to you.
JOHN 16:14

To understand the work of the Holy Spirit, you have to try to grasp the relationship between the Spirit and Jesus Christ. Before His ascension, Jesus promised that the Spirit would come as Mediator. The Spirit would reveal Himself in their hearts in His full heavenly glory.

The disciples gladly accepted the idea. They would then not miss their Master so much; they would always have Him with them. This led them to pray earnestly for the Holy Spirit as they longed to have Jesus with them always.

That is the meaning of the words "he will bring glory to me." Where there is an earnest desire for the glory of Jesus in the heart of a believer, the Holy Spirit will make His presence a reality all day long.

You must not make a big issue of struggling to know God's presence. Just try to live quietly in fellowship with Christ at all times, to love Him, obey His commands and to do all that you must do in the name of Jesus. Then you will be able to rely with assurance on the quiet but powerful working of the Spirit of God within you.

Now you will realize the value of memorizing and meditating on Galatians 5:22–23. If your thoughts revolve around the Lord Jesus—His love, His joy, His peace—the Holy Spirit will bring these qualities to maturity in you.

Lord, I praise You for the wonderful plan of redemption that You brought about for us. Thank You that I can rely on the Spirit to work in me.

Pray Through the Spirit

Pray in the Holy Spirit. Keep yourselves in God's love.
JUDE 20–21

Paul begins the closing part of his letter to the Ephesians, "Be strong in the Lord and in his mighty power" (Ephesians 6:10). He speaks of the armor of God, and ends by saying that the armor must be put on with prayer and supplication, while one prays through the Spirit.

The Holy Spirit does not come to us just at times when we think we need Him or at times when we think we need His help. The Spirit comes to us as our lifelong companion. He wants to view us as His possession, completely and at all times.

Many Christians do not understand this truth. They desire that the Spirit of God help and teach them, but they do not grasp that He wants to live within them continually and have full possession of their lives.

Once we understand this, we will realize that it is possible to live while we continually pray through the Spirit. By faith, we will have the certainty that the Spirit will lead us to a prayerful attitude and make us aware of the presence of God, so that our prayer will be an exercise in our fellowship with God and His great love. As long as we limit the working of the Holy Spirit to certain times like Pentecost, it will remain an unsolved riddle to us.

I praise You, Spirit of God, for being my life's companion.

When Jude says, "Pray in the Spirit and keep in the love of God," he expresses the same thought as Paul, namely that the Holy Spirit wants to cherish us in God's love in the same manner that the sun warms us each day.

The Temple of God

*Don't you know that you yourselves are God's temple
and that God's Spirit lives in you?
God's temple is sacred, and you are that temple.*
1 CORINTHIANS 3:16–17

Since time began, it was the desire of God to create man as a copy of His glory. Because of the fall of man, it seemed as if the plan had "failed." Through His people Israel, however, God found a way of putting His plan into practice. He would have a home in the midst of His people—first the tabernacle and then a temple in which He could dwell. This would only be the shadow of the true indwelling of God in the redeemed person who would be His temple to eternity. In the words of Paul, the ideal would be that His children would be "built up as a spiritual home in which God lives" (Ephesians 2:22).

*Lord God, thank
You that I may be
the temple of
Your Spirit.
Build me into a
spiritual house.*

Since the outpouring of the Holy Spirit, He has His home in every heart that has been purified and restored by the Holy Spirit. The message is for every believer: "Do you not know that you are the temple of God and that the Spirit of God lives in you?"

In another passage, Paul declares that Christ lives in him. It was the abundance of the gospel that he was preaching: the mystery of God in us. He earnestly prayed that God's Spirit would inwardly strengthen his fellow believers, and that Christ would live in their hearts by faith (see Ephesians 3:16–17). Christ Himself promised that He would come to us and make His home with us (see John 14:23).

Through the Holy Spirit you will become a temple of God, and you will find that Christ with the Father dwells in you.

The Fellowship of the Holy Spirit

*May the grace of the Lord Jesus Christ, and the love of God,
and the fellowship of the Holy Spirit be with you all.*
2 CORINTHIANS 13:14

In this verse we find one of the main characteristics of the Holy Spirit. It is by the Holy Spirit that the Father and the Son are one, and through whom they have fellowship with each other, because the Holy Spirit is the true life of the Godhead.

As children of God, we have fellowship with one another through the Spirit. In the child of God there should be no selfishness or self-interest, which merely seeks its own benefit. We are members of one body, and the Spirit must preserve the unity of this body. One reason why the Spirit is not more powerfully at work in the church today is because there is no serious striving after the unity of the Spirit. After Jesus' ascension to heaven and ten days of unified prayer, one hundred and twenty people gathered as one body to receive the Spirit of God in fellowship with one another.

We have fellowship with one another in the bread and wine at the communion table; we also have fellowship with one another in the trials of other members of the body. In heaven there is an eternal fellowship of love between the Father and the Son through the Spirit. Do you desire to be filled with the Spirit of God? Offer yourself to God, praying that He will bestow on you, and all the members of Christ's body, the unity and the fellowship of the Spirit.

Lord, thank You for fellowship with Your Spirit, and through Your Spirit, with other members of Your body. I pray that You will make us a powerful witness for Your name.

With Your Whole Heart

You will seek me and find me when you seek me with all your heart.
JEREMIAH 29:13

It is often said that the secret of success is to apply yourself heart and soul to your work. This is also true in the spiritual realm, especially when praying for the Holy Spirit to be present.

I cannot emphasize it enough, that the Holy Spirit desires to possess you completely. He cannot be satisfied with less if He wishes to let His great power work in your life. He has the right to this because He is the almighty God.

When you pray for the Holy Spirit, you are praying for the tri-une God to take possession of you. You cannot expect God to bring about just one or two changes and for the rest leave you free to further your own will. The Holy Spirit wishes to take complete possession of you.

Lord, You know me through and through. You know of my desire and that I love You. You also know where I still hold back. Forgive me for this. Take full possession of my life and work in it with Your power.

Perhaps you feel that this is the problem: You do not have such a burning desire for this as you should have. You do not see this as a reality in your life. Fortunately, God is aware of your inability and has therefore arranged it so that the Holy Spirit will work in you for everything that you need. What God expects of you, He will Himself bring to pass. On your part, there must just be an earnest prayer to the Father each day and acceptance of the Holy Spirit as your leader and guide.

The Holy Spirit longs to take possession of you. Take time to answer Him and rely in complete confidence in His Word, that His power will work in you.

The Love of God in Your Heart

And hope does not disappoint us, because God has poured out his love into our hearts by the Holy Spirit, whom he has given us.

ROMANS 5:5

God the Father pours out the Holy Spirit into your heart, and the Holy Spirit pours out God's love into your heart. As surely as God gives His Spirit, He will also bestow His love.

Why do we so seldom experience this truth? Simply because we do not believe. It takes time to believe in the mighty work of the Holy Spirit, through whom we are filled with the love of God. We need time to withdraw from the world and its interests, time to revel in the love of God so that His great love can take possession of us. If we believe in the great love of God and its power, we will receive what we ask.

God wants you to love Him with your whole heart and with all your strength. He knows your shortcomings. That is why He gave you His Spirit, who knows about the deep secrets of eternal love with which He desires to fill you.

If this is what you want, seek God and spend time with Him in quiet worship and praise, and you will find the love of God in Christ that goes beyond all understanding. The Holy Spirit will teach you each day what it means to remain in the Father's love like a cherished child. He will teach you what it means to remain in the love of Christ each day and how to show this love to a broken world. He will make your heart a fountain of eternal love, to be a blessing to all around you.

Lord, let me be a blessing to all with whom I come into contact. Help me to make more time to be in Your glorious presence.

Walking in the Spirit of God

*Since we live in the Spirit,
let us keep in step with the Spirit.*
GALATIANS 5:25

A Christian should experience the leadership of the Holy Spirit in his everyday life and conversations. That will be the sign of the spiritual man, who serves God in the Spirit and does not trust in the flesh.

People think of the Spirit of God as though He is only needed during prayer, or for our service in the kingdom of God. But to reason in this way is a mistake. God gives us His Spirit to accompany us throughout the day. We need him most in our daily work, since the world has the ability to draw us away from God. We need to ask God every morning for the assistance of His Spirit during the whole day.

Abba, Father, I submit myself once again to the leadership of Your Spirit, so that I will not succumb so easily to the world and the things of the flesh.

Paul often reminds us of this: "You received Jesus Christ, so walk in Him" (see Colossians 2:6). Just as we put on our clothes before going out, so a Christian should "put on" Jesus Christ and show by his behavior that Christ lives in him, and that he is clothed in the Holy Spirit. As long as we don't live according to the leadership of the Holy Spirit, the world and things of the flesh will have us in its grip.

Let us as children of God know this: The Spirit is given to us so that we will, at all times, be aware of His presence. Thank God continually for this Leader, who daily renews us and enables us to walk and to remain in Christ.

The Promise of the Spirit to Those Who Are Obedient

If you love me, you will obey what I command.
I will ask the Father, and he will give you another
Counselor to be with you forever.
JOHN 14:15–16

After the ascension of Christ, the Holy Spirit became our intercessor: He prays ceaselessly on our behalf. The continual fellowship with the Spirit of God comes from the Son. In today's verse, Jesus sets the prerequisite for the gift of the Spirit: *If you love me and follow my commands, I will ask the Father.* The Holy Spirit is given to us so that we can do the will of the Father.

The conditions are reasonable: As long as we obey God's commands, the Spirit will be given to us in abundance. As we accept the truth and submit to the leadership of the Holy Spirit, we will receive His Spirit from day to day. Let us then tell God that we accept the condition with our whole heart and strive to abide by His commands. Let us also pray for strength to obey those commands.

Do not listen to the whispers of Satan that this is impossible; do not lose faith or become lazy. Give yourself unconditionally to God, who says that if you love Him you will obey His commands. He gives you the strength and grace to declare that it is your pleasure to do His will. Trust Him with childlike faith. Give yourself completely so that His Spirit can renew you each day.

Lord, I love You. I accept Your condition and will strive to obey Your commands with the help of the Holy Spirit. Thank You that I may live by Your grace every moment.

Spiritual or Worldly?

Brothers, I could not address you as spiritual but as worldly—
mere infants in Christ.

1 CORINTHIANS 3:1

Paul uses certain expressions to describe the spiritual condition of people. He says there is the natural man, one who does not accept the things of the Spirit of God (see 1 Corinthians 2:14). Then there are those who are spiritual and judge all things spiritually (see 1 Corinthians 2:15). Between those two, there is the worldly person, who is guilty of jealousy, strife, and division (see 1 Corinthians 3:3).

Am I a worldly Christian who is guilty of sinful and worldly desires? Because I often think that it cannot be otherwise, I allow that which is wrong into my life.

When Jesus Christ promised the Holy Spirit to His disciples, it was in the expectation that they would give themselves wholly to be led by the Holy Spirit. Once I give myself unconditionally to be led by the Holy Spirit in my daily life and conversations, the Holy Spirit will control my life every day.

Many Christians pray for the Holy Spirit, but often with some reservation, because they still intend to make their own decisions about certain issues. When you pray, give yourself totally to the Holy Spirit. If you are willing, the Holy Spirit will take possession of you and will guide and control all facets of your life. Do not serve God half-heartedly. Pray that the Holy Spirit will lead you to the wonder of a life wholly surrendered to God's service.

Lord, forgive me my stubbornness. You gave Your Spirit to control every aspect of my life. I ask that You lead me.

The Spirit of Wisdom

I keep asking that the God of our Lord Jesus Christ,
the glorious Father, may give you the Spirit of wisdom and revelation,
so that you may know him better.
EPHESIANS 1:17

In the Word of God, we find a wonderful combination of the human and the godly. The language is that of a human—anyone with insight can understand the words and the truths locked within. But that is as far as it goes.

There is also a divine side in which the holy God expresses His deepest thoughts to us. The worldly man cannot understand these thoughts, because such thoughts must be evaluated spiritually. Only through the working of the Holy Spirit can a Christian take possession of the truths locked away in God's Word.

Too much of our so-called religion is powerless because people try to understand God's truths with their intellect, and then they have trouble putting them into action by their own power. Only the Holy Spirit can reveal divine truth to us. A young theology student may understand these truths intellectually, but the Word of God itself has little power to lead him or her to a life of joy and peace in Jesus Christ.

Paul teaches us to pray for the Spirit of wisdom and revelation to enable us to understand God better. When you do that, you will discover that the Word of God is alive and powerful and that God's commands will change to promises. The Holy Spirit will teach you to obey His commands lovingly and joyfully.

Thank You that Your Spirit enlightens and guides me when I read from Your Word. Thank You that through Your Word, You work so powerfully in my life.

Sanctified by the Spirit

*To God's elect…who have been chosen according to the foreknowledge
of God the Father, through the sanctifying work of the Spirit,
for obedience to Jesus Christ and sprinkling by his blood.*

1 PETER 1:1–2

In the New Testament, the Spirit of God is described as the Holy Spirit. Christ made Himself holy for us, that we can be made holy through Him. The important work of the Holy Spirit is to glorify God within ourselves so that we can become more like Him.

Has this truth ever struck you that the most important task of the Holy Spirit is to sanctify you, so that you are able to become obedient to Jesus Christ, and to grow more and more like Him? If you do not understand this truth, the Holy Spirit cannot carry out His purifying work. If all you require is for the Holy Spirit to "make you a slightly better person," you will not get very far. But if you recognize that the Holy Spirit means to pass on God's holiness to you, and that the Spirit lives within you, you will start to realize that He wants to totally possess you.

This is a deep, eternal truth. Even if you were willing to accept the truth and think about it every day, it will have no impact if you do not wait upon God to grant you the Spirit of heavenly wisdom that God wants to give you. You need to envisage what God plans for your future by sanctification through the Spirit. Therefore, say slowly and calmly each morning, "Abba, Father, renew within me the gift of your Holy Spirit for this day."

Thank You, Spirit of God, that You set me apart to belong to the Father. The more I think about it, the greater becomes the wonder of Your provision.

Rivers of Living Water

Whoever believes in me, as the Scripture has said,
streams of living water will flow from within him.
JOHN 7:38

Jesus said in his conversation with the Samaritan woman, "Everyone who drinks this water will be thirsty again, but whoever drinks the water I give him will never thirst" (John 4:13–14). In today's text the promise is even greater: Rivers of living water will flow from his heart, bringing life and blessing to others.

John says that this refers to the Holy Spirit who, while Christ lived, had not yet been poured out. Christ first had to be sacrificed to God by the eternal Spirit and, by virtue of the resurrection, be declared by the Holy Spirit as the Son of God (see Romans 1:4).

Then only would the Son of God receive power from the Father to pour out the Holy Spirit, for the children of God to be able to declare, "The Holy Spirit of Christ lives in me."

What does one need to be able to experience the promise of the streams of living water? Only one thing: an intimate clinging to Christ—an undivided submission to Him and the assurance that His Spirit will do the work within you that you yourself cannot do. You need a faith which trusts Him from day to day to let the living water flow from you.

If the water from a reservoir is to flow into a house every day, the connection must be perfect; then the water will pass through the pipes of its own accord. This is how the connection between you and Christ should be. You need to accept Christ through faith and trust Him to sustain your new life.

Lord, I pray to receive those rivers of living water, to have them flow from within me to a world where it is very dry. Thank You for the promise of Your Word.

Joy in God

*May the God of hope fill you with all joy and peace as you trust in him,
so that you may overflow with hope by the power of the Holy Spirit.*
ROMANS 15:13

Shortly after his conversion a man said to me, "I always thought that if I became religious it would become impossible for me to run my business. The two things just seemed too diverse to me. It seemed to me like a man trying to dig a vineyard with a bag of sand upon his shoulders. However, when I found the Lord, I was so filled with joy that I could cheerfully do my work from morning till night. The bag of sand was gone! The joy in the Lord was my strength and power."

This is an important lesson. Many Christians do not understand that the joy of the Lord equips them for their task. Even subordinates, when filled with the love of God, can testify to this truth.

Lord, thank You for the big difference You have made in my life. Please transform me to be the joyful person that You meant me to be.

Today's text testifies to the joy and peace available to us through the power of the Holy Spirit. For many the thought of the Holy Spirit may mean heartache, regret, disappointment, or something too distant and too "holy." But this is a foolish thought! This great gift of the Father, which was meant to keep us in the joy and peace of Christ, should never be a source of self-reproach and worry!

Read Galatians 5:22–23 once more about the fruit of the Spirit. Listen attentively to the voice of the Holy Spirit, who refers to Jesus Christ, who gives us the gift of love, joy, and peace. Pray earnestly to the Holy Spirit while believing with your whole heart that He will lead you into the joy of the Lord.

I Want to Praise You Every Day

Every day I will praise you, and extol your name for ever and ever.
PSALM 145:2

It is a big step forward in the life of believers when they decide to seek fellowship with God through His Word every day, without fail. Their perseverance will be rewarded with success if they are serious about it. Their experience may be more or less as follows.

When they wake up in the morning, God will be the first thing on their mind. They will allocate time for prayer and will give God time to reveal Himself to them. Then they may voice all their desires to God and expect an answer.

Later, during the course of the day—even if only for a few minutes—they will take time once more to strengthen this fellowship with God. Then again in the evening, a quiet time is needed to think about the events of the day. This is a time for confessing sins and for renewed commitment to God and His service.

As time goes by, these believers will learn what is lacking in their life. They will be ready to say not only "every day" but also "all the day." They will realize that the Holy Spirit is with them all the time, uninterrupted, like breathing. In their quiet place they will aim to gain the assurance through faith that the Holy Trinity will be with them all through the day.

Thank You, Lord, that I have the privilege of being conscious of Your presence every moment of the day

Therefore, you should seek to trust the Holy Spirit to guide you all of the day. You need not worry about tomorrow. He who guides you today will also lead you tomorrow.

The Spirit and the Cross

How much more, then, will the blood of Christ,
who through the eternal Spirit offered himself unblemished to God,
cleanse our consciences from acts that lead to death,
so that we may serve the living God!

HEBREWS 9:14

There is a secure and meaningful bond between the cross and the Spirit of God. The Spirit brought Christ to the cross and enabled Him to die there. The cross gave Christ the right to pray for the Holy Spirit because He had there made reconciliation for sin. The cross gave Christ the right to bestow on us the power of the Spirit, because it was there that He freed us from the power of sin.

To summarize: Christ would not have been able to inherit the heavenly glory, nor been able to pour out the Holy Spirit, had He not first died for the sins of the world. He died for our sins in order that He could live for God.

In this way the Holy Spirit brings the cross into your life as well. Only the people who have been crucified with Christ can receive the full power of the Spirit. It is because we do not realize how necessary it is to die to all earthly things that the Spirit cannot gain full possession of us.

You must pray that the Spirit of wisdom gives you insight into the close relationship between the cross and the Spirit of God. This is a divine truth which only the Spirit of God can teach you.

Ask God today to give you insight into the fellowship of the cross of Christ, and how to die to the world and to sin, so that everything will be renewed. Then you will live, work, and pray in the Spirit, to the glory of God.

Spirit of God, I pray that You give me insight into the fellowship of the cross, which is also fellowship with You. Enable me to die fully to sin and to the world.

The Spirit of God and the Blood

For there are three that testify: the Spirit,
the water and the blood; and the three are in agreement.

1 JOHN 5:7–8

Water is the external sign that baptism is the renewal and purification of rebirth. The Spirit and the blood of Christ are two divine powers that work together in this rebirth—the blood for the forgiveness of sin, and the Spirit for the renewal of the person as a whole.

Through the blood you receive the Spirit and are saved and purified to receive the Spirit. That is why you as a Christian may have the confidence to trust the Spirit to lead you. Let your faith in the precious blood of Christ be strong and sure.

The blood of Jesus Christ cleanses us from all sin. The only way to approach God is through the blood of the Lamb. Approach through the blood with every conscious and unconscious sin and plead the blood of Christ as your only claim to forgiveness.

Do not be satisfied with only the redemption of sin, but also accept the work of the Spirit, whom you may approach through the blood of Christ. In the Old Testament the priest entered into the Holy Place, and the high priest into the Most Holy Place, by blood sacrifice. Through His blood, Christ entered the heavenly realm, from where He poured out His Spirit. Through His blood you have a right to the abundance of the Spirit.

Thank You, Lord, for the blood of the Lamb, which covers all my sin. Thank You that I may live because of Your forgiveness.

The Spirit Within as Preacher and Listener

*Our gospel came to you not simply with words,
but also with power, with the Holy Spirit and with deep conviction.*
1 THESSALONIANS 1:5

Paul reminds us more than once that the power of his preaching lies in the supernatural power of the Holy Spirit. The Holy Spirit was so much a part of his audience that they accepted the Word with a joy which comes from the Holy Spirit (see 1 Thessalonians 1:6).

We are so used to being attentive only to hear what we can learn from the sermon that we forget the blessings of church attendance consist of two parts. First, we must pray for the preacher that he should preach with the power of the Holy Spirit. Second, we must pray for the congregation, that they will receive the Word with the conviction that it is the Word of God, and not the words of man (see 1 Thessalonians 2:13).

Too often the preaching of—and the listening to—the Word are purely a matter of human communication. Too often there is no power which deepens faith or gives greater spiritual insight.

That is why you should pray earnestly that God would give the preacher and the congregation the Spirit of wisdom and revelation. As Christ promised, "You shall receive power when the Holy Spirit comes on you" (Acts 1:8).

Thank You, Lord, that I can pray that Your Word will work with power everywhere it is read and preached today.

The Whole Gospel

Peter replied, "Repent and be baptized, every one of you,
in the name of Jesus Christ for the forgiveness of your sins.
And you will receive the gift of the Holy Spirit.
ACTS 2:38

John the Baptist had announced the coming of Jesus, who would baptize in the name of the Holy Spirit and with fire. Jesus Himself said that some would not taste death till they had seen the kingdom of God come with power (see Mark 9:1). That is what happened when the Holy Spirit was poured out.

Peter, on the day of Pentecost, preached the whole gospel of repentance and forgiveness, as well as the gift of the Holy Spirit. The last point is most important in the preaching of this passage because only then is the Christian able to live within the will of God and please Him in all things. The kingdom of God is the absolution in Christ and joy in God through the Holy Spirit. The continual joy of which Christ speaks can only come to pass through the power of the Holy Spirit.

Often the full gospel is not preached—only conversion and forgiveness of sin. People are not guided toward the full knowledge and possession of the Holy Spirit within us. No wonder then that Christians often do not know that they need to rely on the Spirit of God all day for the joy which is also their strength.

Thank You, Lord,
that I can rely
upon guidance
from Your Spirit
and that He
renews me daily.

You must remember that a life of daily guidance by the Spirit of God is essential for a joyful life of faith. If your spiritual life feels dull, pray to God the Father to renew you daily with His Spirit.

The Ministry of
the Spirit

You show that you are a letter from Christ, the result of our ministry,
written not with ink but with the Spirit of the living God,
not on tablets of stone but on tablets of human hearts.

2 CORINTHIANS 3:3

The church at Corinth was a letter of commendation for Paul, show-ing how much he had done for them. He did not claim anything for himself. God had helped him to write upon their hearts with the Spirit of the living God, and God would equip them as preachers of the New Covenant.

This is a wonderful example of the work of a pastor for his people. The preacher, a servant of the Spirit of God, is equipped with the power to write on the hearts of people. If Moses' face gleamed as he came down from the mountain, how much greater would be the glory of service through the Holy Spirit! We all mirror the glory of the Lord, because the veil is removed from our faces. We are being changed more and more to become equal to the image of Christ (see 2 Corinthians 3:18).

Lord, I pray for the powerful preaching of Your Word. Strengthen our preacher with power from above.

If only God could restore this power to the ministry of the gospel today! If only preachers of the Word and church members would pray together that when Christ is preached, they will see the glory of the Lord as though looking in a mirror and be changed into the same image by the Spirit of the Lord!

This is a call to persevere in prayer, which will restore the Holy Spirit to His rightful place in the ministry of the Word.

Sent from Heaven

It was revealed to them that they were not serving themselves but you,
when they spoke of the things that have now been told you by those who
have preached the gospel to you by the Holy Spirit sent from heaven.

1 PETER 1:12

Our Father in heaven wants to bless His children on earth. Jesus Christ was taken into heaven and we were promised that we would be kept with God in Christ. The Holy Spirit descends from heaven and bestows on us the heavenly light, the love, the joy, and the power of God as gifts.

Those who are truly filled with the Holy Spirit carry the heavenly life within them. They walk with the Father and the Son every day; their lifestyle and conversations confirm that. They seek the things of God, because their life is with God, kept in Christ. Their most important feature is that they are focused upon the Father. They already bear the signs of their heavenly destination.

How can you nurture a heavenly disposition? By allowing the Holy Spirit to work in your life and let the fruit, which the Spirit has grown in God's paradise, reach full potential. The Spirit will daily feed your fellowship with God and teach you to abide in His presence.

Lord God, thank You that You are my Father. Thank You for all the blessings in which I so undeservedly share. Teach me through Your Spirit what true thankfulness is.

Make time each day to receive from the Father the continual guidance of the Holy Spirit. Allow Him to overcome the world for you and to strengthen you as a heavenly child to walk daily with God and Jesus Christ. You will learn to speak to others with such heavenly joy that they will be inspired to wholeheartedly submit themselves to the guidance of the Holy Spirit.

The Spirit and Prayer

I tell you the truth, my Father will give you whatever you ask in my name.
JOHN 16:23

In His final talk to His followers, Jesus described a new dispensation to them—the dispensation of the Holy Spirit in all its power. One of the great blessings of this dispensation would be that His children would now be able to pray down from heaven the power of God to bless the world. This promise is repeated several times (see John 14:13–14, 15:7, 16:23–26).

In the power of the perfect redemption which Christ accomplished, in the power of His glory with the Father, and in the power of the outpouring of the Holy Spirit, believers would have the inexpressible privilege of asking what they desired from the fullness of God, and they would receive it. Everything is summarized in the promise, "You may ask me for anything in my name, and I will do it" (John 14:14).

Thank You, Lord, that I can ask You to equip my loved ones, friends, and me with the power to be loyal witnesses in the world.

During the ten days before Pentecost, the disciples put this promise to the proof. In answer to their incessant united prayer, the heavens were opened and the Spirit of God descended to earth to dwell within them. They were filled with life-giving power, which they in turn imparted to thousands. That power is still the guarantee of what God can do.

Remember that you are living in the dispensation of the Holy Spirit. That means that the Holy Spirit, with heavenly power, lives within you and enables you to witness for Him. It also means that you can unite with other children of God to pray for even greater things than you ever thought possible.

With One Accord in Prayer

They all joined together constantly in prayer.
ACTS 1:14

Jesus commanded His disciples to go into the world and teach His Word, and He added that He would be with them always (see Matthew 28:19–20). We can be certain that this command and promise are also meant for us.

Just before His ascension to heaven, Christ gave His final command with a promise attached to it. The command was that the disciples wait until the Holy Spirit was poured out. The promise was that they would receive power from the Holy Spirit to become His witnesses in all the furthest corners of the earth.

For ten days the disciples pleaded for the promise to be fulfilled, then their prayers were answered. Likewise, wait upon the promise of the Holy Spirit until you receive it and then preach the gospel.

Often churches today preach the gospel, but they forget about the promise of the Holy Spirit. Every believer should answer the call to pray for the gift of the Holy Spirit daily, as though speaking from one mouth and one heart. Many Christians pray only for themselves and forget to pray for the church of Christ. The power of the first disciples lay in the fact that they forgot about themselves and prayed as one body for the Holy Spirit to descend upon humanity.

Daily prayer in fellowship with God's children is indispensable. Do not pray only for yourself or your church, but pray for the all-encompassing love of Christ for all His children and for the coming of His kingdom on earth.

Lord, I dedicate every one of Your children to You. I do not know their names or who they are. Nevertheless, let Your kingdom come in all its glory.

The Secret to Fellowship with God

Many Christians experience an anti-climax following the month of Pentecost. A sure way to maintain the experience of the spirit of Pentecost is continued fellowship with God.

The purpose of redemption is not only to ensure our place in heaven. In fact, God's name is honored when we understand that He wants us to live in fellowship with Him daily. A hasty prayer or superficial reading of a few verses from God's Word cannot obtain this. We must make time to be quiet in God's presence and to wait upon His Holy Spirit to renew our hearts and minds. Only then can we expect to remain in the power of Christ throughout the day with all its temptations. It is thus clear that our daily quiet time in the presence of God is not negotiable.

The powerless state of many believers may be ascribed to the fact that they do not faithfully practice fellowship with God each day. I therefore want to urge you to consider the matter seriously. May this month's daily writings help you achieve this fellowship with the Lord.

Day by Day

Though outwardly we are wasting away, yet inwardly
we are being renewed day by day.
2 CORINTHIANS 4:16

All Christians should learn the importance of fellowship with Jesus each day. We have to realize that to be accepted as God's children, to receive forgiveness of our sins, and to experience the joy in the Holy Spirit, we need to be renewed in fellowship with Jesus Christ daily.

Many Christians regress and have difficulty resisting temptation because they have not learned this. They don't understand the great truth that Jesus will continue His work with His children daily, if only they will set aside time for Him each day to share His love and His mercy. A prerequisite for growth and strength is the daily time spent alone with Jesus Christ.

In Matthew 11:29, Jesus says, "Take my yoke upon you and learn from me, for I am gentle and humble in heart, and you will find rest for your souls." Jesus will teach you how humble He is. Kneel before Him, tell Him how you long for Him, and He will comfort you in His love. This is an important thought for all those who love the Lord. For Christ's sake, as well as your own, you need to learn to spend time each day—without exception—in fellowship with the Lord. In this way the inner man will be renewed from day to day.

God, I pray that You will renew my spirit daily, so I will be able to withstand temptation. I want to grow spiritually and that is why I will remain close at Your feet. I long for Your presence.

Fellowship with God

As the Father has loved me, so have I loved you.
Now remain in my love.
JOHN 15:9

God reveals Himself to us as a Person—somebody whom we can have a relationship with and talk to. God greatly desires this fellowship with man, but sin has come between man and His God. Even among Christians who think that they know God, there is often great ignorance and even indifference to this personal relationship of love.

People do believe that their sins can be forgiven by repenting, that God will accept them and have them enter into heaven, and that they should try to do God's will. But the thought that God would want to commune with man, as a Father with His child, is unfamiliar to them.

God gave His Son in order to draw us closer to Him. This can only be achieved by having fellowship with Jesus Christ. Our relationship with Jesus is based on His deep and tender love for us. We ourselves cannot render Him this love, but the Holy Spirit will do the work in us. For this we need to separate ourselves from the world daily and focus our faith on Jesus. He will pour out His love into our hearts and fill us with it.

Ponder the words of today's passage and take time for fellowship with Him. Tell Him you know He loves you and that you desire to love Him.

Thank You, Jesus, for Your unconditional love. Thank You for proving that love with Your Supreme Sacrifice, that I can experience it from day to day. I confess that I love You, too, and pray my love will increase in honesty and depth.

Jesus

And you are to give him the name Jesus,
for he will save his people from their sins.
MATTHEW 1:21

As our Lord was born a child, He had His own name: Jesus. His mother, His disciples, and His friends called Him by that name. Very few Christians know what a treasure is contained in the name *Jesus*. It means, *He will save His people from sin.*

Many people think of Jesus' death on the cross, or of His role as mediator in heaven, but they seldom think of Him as a living Person who thinks of us constantly, longing to reveal Himself to us. He also wants us to glorify and praise Him every day.

It is through a personal encounter that we are freed from our sins. I need to bring my sinful heart to Jesus—to my personal Redeemer in whom God's holiness dwells. As He and I commune in the expression of common love and longing, His love will, by the working of the Holy Spirit, conquer all sin in me.

May you experience the joy of fellowship with Jesus every day. Soon you will begin to look forward to this as the highlight of your day. You will be aware of the presence of Jesus throughout the day and discover the secret of a life dedicated to Him.

Thank You, Jesus, that a sinner like me can have fellowship with You, the holy and mighty God. I pray that I will experience the presence of Your Spirit throughout the day.

The Inner Sanctuary

But when you pray, go into your room,
close the door and pray to your Father, who is unseen.
Then your Father, who sees what is done in secret, will reward you.
MATTHEW 6:6

Have you ever thought what a privilege it is to be able to go to a quiet place at any time of the day, asking for God's presence and listening to what He has to say? Of course, to go to your room and close the door means that you must also exclude all worldly thoughts, as well as that with which you are busy. You must be alone with God and pray to Him only. If you do this, your Father whom you cannot see will reward you. Let this be the main purpose of your quiet time: to sense the presence of your heavenly Father. Take time to pray to Him. He knows how you long to be in His presence, and He will listen to you.

Then follows the great promise: Your Father who sees what is done in secret will reward you openly. All through your busy, active day, God will answer your prayer. The prayer said in your sanctuary will be followed by the secret working of God in your heart.

Jesus, who shows you the way to the inner sanctuary, will teach you to pray. It is through Him that we have access to the Father. Be child-like and trustful in your fellowship with Christ. Confess each sin and make your every need known to Him. Offer your prayer to the Father in the name of Christ. Prayer in fellowship with Jesus cannot be in vain.

Thank You, Jesus for my inner sanctuary. Thank You that I may meet You there every day and that I can be aware of Your presence throughout each day. Please remove the dividing walls which may still exist between us.

Faith

Don't be afraid; just believe.
MARK 5:36

In this verse we find an extremely important message: When we are alone with God in our sanctuary, we need to make our needs known, trusting implicitly in the love of God and the power of the Holy Spirit. Ask yourself, *Do I have unwavering trust in God?*

If this is not the case, do not begin praying immediately. Faith does not come naturally. Think about how impossible it is for God not to speak the truth. He *wants* to bless you. Take a passage from the Word that reveals God's power, faithfulness, and love. Appropriate these words and say, "Yes, Lord, I will pray with firm faith in you and your great love."

Do not limit your faith merely to the forgiveness of your sin and your acceptance as a child of God. Faith is far more than that. You must have faith in all that God is willing to do for you. You need to have faith according to your particular needs. God is infinitely great and powerful, and Christ has grace for the need of every day.

Upon entering your sanctuary ask yourself, before commencing your prayer, whether you believe that God is with you, that Jesus will help you pray, and that you can expect to have a blessed time of close fellowship with Him.

Jesus, it is in anticipation that I come before You. I pray that You will strengthen my faith and let it grow, so that Your wonderful promises will become a reality to me.

Jesus taught His disciples the importance of faith when praying. He will teach that to us, too. Remain in fellowship with Him, and ask Him to strengthen your faith.

The Word of God

Man does not live on bread alone,
but on every word that comes from the mouth of God.
MATTHEW 4:4

This illustration, where the Word of God is compared to our daily bread, is most instructive.

Bread is indispensable to life. However strong a person may be, if he takes no nourishment, he will grow weaker and die. It is the same with the Word of God: It contains a heavenly principle and works powerfully in those who believe.

Bread must be eaten. I may know everything about bread. I may even give it to others. I may have more than enough in my house and on my table. But if I do not eat, I will die. So the mere knowledge of God's Word, and even the preaching of it, will be of no use to me. Just thinking about it is not enough. I must feed on His Word and absorb it into my life and heart. I have to apply God's Word to my life and allow it to possess my heart. Then it is the gospel of life.

Bread needs to be eaten daily. This holds true for God's Word as well. The psalmist said, "Oh, how I love your law! I meditate on it all day long" (Psalm 119:97). For a vibrant spiritual life, the Word of God is a daily necessity.

If you seek fellowship with God, you will find Him in His Word. Christ will teach you to communicate with the Father through His Word, as was His custom. In this way you will learn, like Him, to live solely for the glory of God and the fulfillment of His Word.

Heavenly Father, I thank You for the spiritual diet that You prepared for me in Your wisdom. Make me study Your Word faithfully every day. Empower me through Your Spirit also to live by Your Word.

How to Read God's Word

Blessed is the man...(whose) delight is in the law of the LORD.
PSALM 1:1–2

Here are a few guidelines by which to read the Bible.

Read God's Word with reverence. Remember that these words come from almighty God Himself. Kneel in reverence and be still before God. Allow Him to reveal His Word to you.

Read with undivided attention. If you read the words superficially and think you will understand it by human insight only, you will not grasp the true depth of their meaning. God's thoughts are higher and deeper than ours, as the heavens are higher than the earth. With devoted attention, you need to try to understand the deeper meaning.

Expect to be led by the Holy Spirit when reading. Only God's Spirit can make the Word come alive in our hearts and lives. Read Psalm 119 and see how seriously David prays that God will teach him, open his eyes, give him insight, and turn his heart toward God. Never forget that God's Word and Spirit are inseparable.

Thank You, Lord, for Your precious Word that You entrusted to me.

Read with the intention of keeping His Word day and night in your heart and life. The Word must influence your entire life. Think of David, who often cried out, "I love your law!" We need to think about this all day long and cherish God's Word in our hearts.

Read Psalm 119 and pray that God may teach you to understand and obey His Word.

The Word and Prayer

Preserve my life, O LORD, according to your word.
PSALM 119:107

Prayer and the Word of God are inseparable and should always go together in our quiet times. In His Word, God speaks to me; in prayer, I speak to God. If there is to be true fellowship, God and I must both take part.

If I pray without involving the Word of God, I tend to use my own words and thoughts. What makes prayer more powerful is when I take God's thoughts from His Word and present them before Him. Then I am praying according to His Word. God's Word is indispensable for all true prayer.

When praying, you should strive to get to know God. It is through the Word that the Holy Spirit will teach you about Him. The Word teaches you how sinful you are, yet it will also reveal to you all the wonders that God will do for you, and the strength He will give you to do His will. The Word teaches you how to pray—with enthusiasm, with faith, and with perseverance. The Word teaches what you can become with God's grace. It reminds you that Christ is the mediator and teaches you to pray in His name. Above all, prayer makes you receptive to what God wants to tell you through His Word and His Spirit.

On the other hand, you need prayer when reading the Word. You need to pray that, through the Holy Spirit, you will understand God's Word, and use it correctly. Pray that you will know that Christ is everything to you, and that you may walk in His love every day.

Thank You, God, that through Your Word and Spirit I have the privilege of renewing my strength each day and so be able to pray according to Your will.

Obedience

Obey me and do everything I command you,
and you will be my people, and I will be your God.
JEREMIAH 11:4

God gave this command to Israel when He gave them the law, but they were unable to keep the law. Then God made a new everlasting covenant with them to enable them to live a life of obedience. In Jeremiah 31:33 we read, "I will put my law in their minds and write it on their hearts." In Jeremiah 32:40, God adds, "so that they will never turn away from me." In Ezekiel 36:27, God says, "And I will put my Spirit in you and move you to follow my decrees and be careful to keep my laws." These promises hold the assurance that obedience will bring great joy.

What does Jesus say about obedience? "Whoever has my commands and obeys them, he is the one who loves me" (John 14:21). "If you obey my commands, you will remain in my love" (John 15:10). In faith we can trust Christ to enable us to live such a life of love and obedience.

No father can teach his children unless they are obedient, and no teacher can impart knowledge to a child who will not listen. No general can lead his soldiers to victory without prompt obedience. Allow God to teach you that a life of faith is a life of obedience. Just as Christ was obedient to the Father, so we also need obedience for a life in the love of God.

Maybe you think it impossible to be obedient, but think about these words and pray that God, through His spirit, will teach you to live in obedience to Him.

Heavenly Father, thank You for Your Spirit that enables me to be obedient. Thank You for the joy of a life in Your love.

Confession of Sin

If we confess our sins, he is faithful and just and will forgive us our sins and purify us from all unrighteousness.

1 JOHN 1:9

Often the confession of sin is superficial or even completely neglected. Christians do not always realize how necessary it is to confess sin. When we walk with Jesus, it is important to honestly confess every sin, for each is a stumbling block in the way of our growth. Hear what David says: "Then I acknowledged my sin to you and did not cover up my iniquity. I said, 'I will confess my transgressions to the LORD'" (Psalm 32:5).

But David also speaks of a time when he was unwilling to confess his sin: "When I kept silent, my bones wasted away through my groaning all day long" (Psalm 32:3).

Thank You, Lord Jesus, that Your sacrifice upon the cross bought forgiveness for me.

Confession does not only mean that I confess my sin in shame, but also that I give it to God, trusting Him to take it away. A confession of this kind implies that I cannot rid myself of sin, but by an act of faith I can trust God to deliver me. This means in the first place I know my sins are forgiven and, second, that Christ undertakes to purify me from my sin and keep me from its power.

If you seek sincere fellowship with God, confess each sin and be assured that you will be forgiven. Jesus saves from sin. Believe that there is power through the confession of sin, and that sin is borne by Jesus Christ our Lord and Savior.

The First Love

Yet I hold this against you:
You have forsaken your first love.
REVELATION 2:4

In Revelation 2:2–3 the good works of the Ephesians are listed. But then something less commendable follows. "Yet I hold this against you: You have forsaken your first love."

Today the same accusation can be leveled at the church of Christ. There is an eagerness for truth; there is continuous and persevering labor; but the intimate love for Him, which the Lord values most, is often lacking. A church, a community, or a Christian can set an example with good deeds but still not have the love for Jesus Christ that grows quietly in the inner sanctuary. If there is no personal, daily communion with Him, all the countless daily activities are in vain.

Christ came to earth to love us just as the Father loved Him. He suffered and died to win our hearts for this love. His love cannot be satisfied by anything other than a personal love from our side.

Many spiritual workers confess in shame— no matter how conscientious their other work for Him—that their prayers leave much to be desired. Write on a piece of paper: My love for You, Jesus Christ, is most important to me—in my quiet place, in all my work, and in my daily life.

Lord, You saw what I wrote. That is truly the prayer and confession of my heart. Make it a daily reality through Your Holy Spirit.

The Holy Spirit

*He will bring glory to me by taking
from what is mine and making it known to you.*
JOHN 16:14

When Jesus Christ spoke to His disciples for the last time, He promised to send the Holy Spirit to comfort them. Even though Jesus' physical body would not be with them anymore, they would constantly be aware of His presence within them. The Holy Spirit would reveal the exalted Christ.

This truth is often misunderstood. Pastors would be neglecting their duty if they encouraged people to love Jesus Christ, without at the same time warning them that it is not a "duty" they can perform in their own strength. They need the assistance of the Holy Spirit who alone can fill their hearts with love and teach them to love.

Thank You, Lord, for Your Spirit that works in my life. I pray that all I do shall be to the glory of Your name.

Through the Holy Spirit we may experience the presence and love of Jesus Christ throughout the day. For this, however, He must possess us entirely. He claims our whole heart and life. He gives us inner strength to enable us to have fellowship with God, obey His commands, and remain in His love.

Once we fully understand this truth, we will realize how dependent we are on the Holy Spirit and will pray to the Father to send Him with power into our lives. The Spirit will teach us to love the Word, to meditate on it, and to keep it. He will reveal the love of Christ to us so that we can love Him with pure hearts in the midst of a busy life, with all its distractions.

Christ's Love for Us

As the Father has loved me, so have I loved you.
Now remain in my love.
JOHN 15:9

Relationships between friends and family depend entirely on their love for one another. What value is there in riches when there is no love between a husband and his wife, or a parent and his child? And what value is there in the knowledge and fervor of God's work without the knowledge and experience of God's love? The one thing you need when you are practicing fellowship with God is to know by experience how much God loves you, and to learn how to remain and continue in that love.

Think about the words of Christ: "As the Father has loved me, so have I loved you. Now remain in my love." What godly, everlasting, wonderful love! The same love that He had for the Father, Jesus now gives as a gift to His children. He longs to see that this everlasting love shall rest upon us and work within us, so that we may remain in it day by day. Do you realize that in your fellowship with Christ you are surrounded by this love? May you reach out to this love. Christ longs to fill you with it.

Read what God's Word says about the love of Christ. Think about it and let it sink into your heart. In time you will begin to realize that the greatest happiness of your life is to know that Christ loves you and that His Spirit will help you to remain in His love.

Thank You, Lord, for the wonderful and everlasting love that You have for me. I praise Your name for the love with which You have filled my heart. Teach me how to remain and continue in that love.

Our Love for Christ

Though you have not seen him, you love him;
and even though you do not see him now,
you believe in him and are filled with an inexpressible and glorious joy.

1 PETER 1:8

The verse speaks of people who had not yet seen Christ, but nonetheless loved Him and believed in Him. They were filled with inexpressible joy.

The most important feature of the Father and the Son is their love for each other and for mankind. This should also be the most important characteristic of a true Christian: The love of God fills one's heart and becomes a fountain of living water flowing toward others.

This love for Christ is not merely an emotion; it is a working principle. It finds pleasure in doing the will of the Lord. It is a joy to obey His commands. Christ showed us how much He loved us by His death on the cross. We must show our love for Him with unselfish and self-sacrificing lives. In the Christian life, our love for Christ is everything.

Great love invokes great faith—faith in His love for us, faith in the powerful revelations of His love in our hearts, and faith that His love will bring forth the best within us.

This faith and love will fill you with unspeakable joy. The joy of the Christian is a witness to the world of the power of Christ to change hearts.

You should therefore make time for fellowship with God every day so that you can be filled with His love. Love, joy, and faith will fill your life by the grace of our Lord, Jesus Christ.

Lord, thank You that through the working of the Holy Spirit You are a reality to me, even though I cannot see You. Fill my life with love and faith.

Love for Others

A new commandment I give you: Love one another.
As I have loved you, so you must love one another.
JOHN 13:34

Jesus told His disciples that He loved them as much as His Father loved Him, and this is how they should love one another. If they will love one another, everyone will know that they are His disciples (see John 13:35). Jesus prayed fervently for their unity (see John 17:21). If we show the world the love that was in God for Christ and in Christ for us, the world would experience Christianity as being genuine.

This is exactly what happened. There was no love lost among all the nations of the world. The Greeks, Romans, Jews, and the heathens all hated one another. The idea of self-sacrifice was strange to them. When the heathens saw that Christians from various nations became one through the power of the Holy Spirit, with self-sacrifice in times of need and illness, they were amazed and exclaimed, "See how these people love one another!"

Among professing Christians there are feelings of unity and brotherhood, but the heavenly love of Jesus is often lacking. We do not bear one another's burdens—or is it rather that we do not love others?

Pray that you may love your fellow believers in the same way as Christ loves you. If you remain in Christ's love, and let that love fill your heart, you will receive the power to love all God's children. The bond of love between all God's children should be as close as the bond between the Father and the Son, and between Christ and His followers.

Thank You, Lord Jesus, for demonstrating Your love for me in such a practical way. Help me to love my neighbor just as much.

Save a Sinner

*Whoever turns a sinner from the error of his way will
save him from death and cover over a multitude of sins.*
JAMES 5:20

What a wonderful thought—rescuing someone from death! This call
to save sinners does not only go out to spiritual workers but also to
every believer.

When Christ and His love took possession of our hearts, He gave
us a love to lead others to Him. In this way His kingdom is extended.
Thus, everyone who has the love of Christ within his or her heart has
to share it with others.

This was the way in the early Christian church. After the events
of Pentecost, people went out and told others of the love of Christ that
they had personally experienced. According to some non-Christian
writers, this was the reason for the rapid spread of
the gospel in the first century.

*Thank You, Lord,
that You want to
use me to convey
Your love to
others. Make me
Your faithful
witness.*

But today the love of many Christians is so
weak that they have no desire to help others.
During a revival in Korea at the beginning of the
previous century, the converts were filled with
such a love for Christ that they could not help but
tell others of His love. Whether you had led someone to Jesus was even used as a test for admission
as a member of the church.

Therefore, examine yourself. Do not think
only of yourself. Pray that you become so filled
with His love that you, in submission to Him,
will win others for His kingdom.

The Spirit of Love

But the fruit of the Spirit is love.
GALATIANS 5:22

When we think of what Christ's love demands from us, we may think that it is impossible for a Christian to live this life of love. And because we think it is unattainable, and because of our unbelief and lack of faith in God's promises, we make little progress along the road of love.

We need to remind ourselves continually that it is not in our own strength, or through deep meditation, that we attain the love of Christ. No, it is a gift from God, which is renewed daily by the Holy Spirit in our lives. The more we let ourselves be guided by the Holy Spirit, the more we will live according to God's will.

We can make the prayer of Paul for the Ephesians our own: "I pray also that the eyes of your heart may be enlightened in order that you may know the hope to which he has called you, the riches of his glorious inheritance in the saints, and his incomparably great power for us who believe" (Ephesians 1:18–19). To be founded in love means to receive inner strength from the Spirit of God so that Christ can live in us.

Unless you kneel daily to receive strength from the Holy Spirit, you cannot grow in this love. A life of prayer makes this love a reality.

Thank You, Lord Jesus, that I can live close to You every day and be filled with Your love by the Holy Spirit. Help me to show the same love to others.

Perseverance in Prayer

*Then Jesus told his disciples a parable to show them
that they should always pray and not give up.*
LUKE 18:1

One of the biggest obstacles to prayer is that God's answer does not come as speedily as we expect. We may become discouraged and think that it is because we did not pray correctly.

When we stop to think about it, however, we realize that there could be a good reason for the delay and that the waiting may bring its own blessings. Our desire needs to grow deeper and stronger, and we should learn to ask with all our heart. God places us in a training school for persevering prayer in order to strengthen our weak faith. Believe that there is a great blessing in the delayed answer to prayer!

*Thank You, my
Father, that I can
feel free to leave
my life in
Your hands.*

In this way God also wants to draw us into closer fellowship with Him. When our prayers are not answered immediately, we learn that the fellowship and closeness and love of God are more important than our requests. Just think of the rich blessing Jacob received after having waited so long for an answer to his prayer! He saw God face-to-face and, with power, continued his work as the chosen one (Genesis 32:22–32).

Therefore, do not be disillusioned when the reply does not come immediately. Persevere and pray ceaselessly. You will learn to question whether your prayer is according to the will and Word of God, and if it is offered in the right spirit. The delayed answer may be one of the richest blessings of grace that God has granted you. You will learn that those who persevere the longest and keep reminding God of His promises have the greatest power with God in prayer.

Prayer Meetings

They all joined together constantly in prayer.
ACTS 1:14

Prayer meetings are of the greatest importance. There God's children meet, not as in church to listen to one speaker, but to unite in front of God. This draws Christians closer together. Weaker members are strengthened and encouraged by the witnessing of older, more experienced members. Even young Christians have the opportunity to express their joy in Christ.

Prayer meetings can become a great power for good in a congregation and a spiritual help to both minister and members. Through prayer, God's blessing is poured out on the congregation.

There are some dangers to be aware of, however. Many attend prayer meetings, but never learn to pray themselves. Others attend enthusiastically because of a social or religious drive, but never know the hidden power of prayer. Without sincere prayer alone in the inner chamber beforehand, the attendance of prayer meetings can become a mere formality.

Furthermore, there needs to be a sincere love and fellowship between members. Remember that you do not live for yourself alone. You are part of the body of Christ. Prayer must therefore include God's children all over the world, as well as His church. Just as the roots of a tree are hidden deep in the earth and the branches spread out to heaven, so the secret prayer in the inner chamber is bound to united prayer.

Thank You, Lord, for the privilege of praying together with Your children, and also of praying for them. Unite us in love.

Intercession

And pray in the Spirit on all occasions with all kinds of prayers and requests.
With this in mind, be alert and always keep on praying for all the saints.
EPHESIANS 6:18

There is much blessing in prayers for others. To pray for heavenly gifts for oneself is grace, but to pray for blessings to be bestowed upon others is a far greater privilege.

Does this mean that God's blessing of others is dependent upon our prayers? Yes, because He makes those who remind Him of His promises His coworkers. If we fail in doing our part, others will suffer, as will His work.

To intercede on behalf of others is a way whereby people are saved and spiritual workers become stronger in their faith. Yes, the entire world is blessed through our prayers.

Thank You, Lord, that I may kneel before You with all my needs. I plead that You will equip Your children to work together for the coming of Your kingdom.

You need to view prayer as a source of blessings for yourself and others. Pray for your neighbors. Pray for others that they may be won for Christ. Pray for your pastor, other ministers, missionaries, and spiritual workers. Pray for your country and its people, for rulers and subordinates. Pray for all people.

Once you commit yourself to be guided by the Holy Spirit and live a life that is dedicated to God, you will realize that prayer is an offering that pleases God. It brings blessings upon yourself and strength to the lives of those for whom you pray.

Pray often, for this is the most important way in which you can lead others to God and glorify Him.

The Spirit of Prayer

And he who searches our hearts knows the mind of the Spirit,
because the Spirit intercedes for the saints in accordance with God's will.
ROMANS 8:27

Praying is not our task but rather that of God, which He works within us through His almighty power. Therefore, we should pray in expectation that the Holy Spirit will help us in our weakness and pray with us, often in wordless groaning.

What a wonderful thought! When I find my own prayers to be lacking and discover that I have no power, I may kneel before God, trusting that His Holy Spirit will teach me how to pray. My desire is a guarantee that God will hear me. God awakens the desire within us and the Holy Spirit completes the work in spite of our weakness.

Think about the story of Jacob. The same One with whom he wrestled also strengthened him; and the One who withheld blessings from him also encouraged him to persist in prayer.

Prayer is the work of the Trinity:

The Father, who will awaken the desire in us and give us all we may need.

The Son, who through His prayer on our behalf teaches us to pray in His name.

The Holy Spirit, who in secret strengthens our weak desires, dwells in our hearts, and teaches us to pray.

We should therefore listen to the leading of the Holy Spirit. Obey His voice in everything. You will then realize the glory of your calling as intercessor, asking great things of God for those around you, for your church, and for the world that does not know Him yet.

Thank You, Lord, for the calling I received to become an intercessor. Thank You for the Spirit through whom my life can be one of continual prayer.

For Christ Alone

For Christ's love compels us, because we are convinced that one died for all,
and therefore all died. And he died for all, that those who live should no longer
live for themselves but for him who died for them and was raised again.
2 CORINTHIANS 5:14–15

Here we have life described at three levels.

First, the life of a Christian who lives only for himself.

Second, the life of a true Christian who lives for Christ.

And third, the life of Christ in heaven, living for us.

Many Christians still need to realize how unwise they are, living only for themselves. At conversion, they think more of their own salvation, and much less of the glory of God and the purchased right Christ has to their lives. Blessed is the one who realizes the importance of total devotion to God.

Thank You, Lord Jesus, that I may love You and serve You wholeheartedly. It is my desire to tell the world about You and Your love.

It is lack of faith that says such devotion is impossible. But once the truth strikes you that Christ lives for you and enables you to live for Him, you will be able to say, "Let my prayer from now on be total devotion to Christ."

Let this then be your greatest desire, your prayer, and your expectation: *Christ died for me, and lives in heaven in order to keep me more and more devoted to Him. I am His most precious possession.*

Think about how Christ will preserve you as part of His body, to work and live for Him alone. Take time every day to become one with Christ; pray for grace to be totally devoted to Him, in seeking souls for Him and serving His people.

The Cross of Christ

I have been crucified with Christ and I no longer live,
but Christ lives in me.
GALATIANS 2:20

The cross of Christ is also His greatest triumph. Because He humbled Himself to the death on the cross, God elevated Him. The cross was the power which overcame Satan and sin.

Christians share in Christ and His cross. The crucified Christ lives in us through the Holy Spirit, and the spirit of the cross inspires us. As we make the power of the crucifixion more and more our own, we live as though we died to the world, and the power becomes a reality in our lives.

Jesus told His disciples to take up their cross and follow Him. Did they understand that? They had seen men carrying a cross and knew that it meant a painful death.

Throughout His life, Christ bore His cross— the death sentence that He should die for the world. In this way every Christian should bear His cross, believing that He was crucified with Christ, and that the crucified Christ lives within Him. Christians should confess, "I was crucified with Christ, as were my sinful desires. Together with Paul, I say that I have pride solely in the cross of Christ."

Ponder this and the Holy Spirit will teach you. Let the disposition of Christ on the cross— His humility, His aversion to all worldly honors, and His refusal to assert Himself—take possession of you. The power of His death will work within you, and you will become one with Him in His death. You will get to know Him and the power of His resurrection.

Heavenly Lord,
I pray that
through the
working of Your
Holy Spirit, I will
display the image
of our Lord Jesus
more and more.

Things of the World

Do not love the world or anything in the world.
If anyone loves the world, the love of the Father is not in him.
1 JOHN 2:15

John clearly explains what he means by *the world*: "For everything in the world—the cravings of sinful man, the lust of his eyes and the boasting of what he has and does—comes not from the Father but from the world" (1 John 2:16).

The world is that disposition or power under which man has fallen through sin. And the god of the world hides himself so well. This world, with its pleasures and temptations, surrounds the Christian every day.

The desires of the sinful person were evident in the first human couple. Eve desired the forbidden fruit. Desire possessed Adam. Today the world still approaches us with its desirables and with so much that is aimed at satisfying the desires of the flesh. That which the eye sees, man desires: riches and earthly beauty and luxury. In his pride, man thinks he knows and understands all. Our life is full of danger with the allure of things of the flesh, the desires of the eye, and worldly knowledge and cunning.

Lord, protect me from the world each moment and focus all my love on You.

That is why John warns against loving the sinful world. Once that happens, the love of the Father is no longer in us. Jesus calls us to leave everything and follow Him.

The world in which you live is dangerous. Keep hold of Jesus Christ. As He teaches you not to love the world, you will become more devoted in your service to Him. Then, however, there needs to be daily fellowship with Jesus.

Clothe Yourself with Christ

For all of you who were baptized into
Christ have clothed yourselves with Christ.
GALATIANS 3:27

In the original text, the verb that describes the life of a Christian who is united with Christ has the meaning of *putting on clothes*. He is now a new person—he dons the new nature like an item of clothing by which everyone can see who and what he is. When the believer acknowledges Christ through his baptism, Paul says, he is clothing himself with Christ. By his entire life and character he exhibits Jesus Christ. Just as he puts on clothes every day, the Christian needs to "clothe himself" with Christ each day. Then he will no longer live for the desires of the flesh but rather strive to become an image of his Master.

Clothe yourself with Christ! This must be done daily in your quiet times in fellowship with Him. But for that you need time. Just as clothing protects you from the wind and the sun, Jesus will be your pride, your protection, and your joy. When you come to Him in prayer, He will share more and more of Himself with you. He will strengthen you to behave as one who is permanently attached to Him.

Thank You, Lord, for the most wonderful clothing I have to wear every day.

Think about this—just as you have to put on clothes when you go out into the world, you have to clothe yourself with Jesus Christ to remain in Him and walk with Him all day long. This cannot happen in a hurry or superficially. Spend more time in fellowship with Jesus. Your reward will be great.

The Power of Christ

Finally, be strong in the Lord and in his mighty power.
EPHESIANS 6:10

The Christian needs strength—strength which he or she does not possess naturally. This strength is to be found in the Lord.

Paul spoke of this in his letter to the Ephesians. He prays that God, from the riches of His glory, would give them the power to be strengthened from within. He refers to God's "incomparably great power for us who believe. That power is like the working of his mighty strength, which he exerted in Christ when he raised him from the dead and seated him at his right hand in the heavenly realms" (Ephesians 1:19–20).

The same strength works in every believer. We hardly dare to believe or experience it! That is why Paul prays that God, through His Spirit, will teach Christ's followers to believe in His almighty power; that He will grant them wisdom, through His Spirit, to truly know Him (see Ephesians 1:17).

Father, grant me the Spirit of wisdom so that I may experience Your immeasurable power in my life. Teach me to live from it every day.

Paul cried out, "Now to him who is able to do immeasurably more than all we ask or imagine, according to his power that is at work in us, to him be the glory in the church and in Christ Jesus throughout all generations, for ever and ever!" (Ephesians 3:20–21).

The power that is at work in us. Read this over and over and ask that God's Spirit enlighten the eyes of your understanding. Believe in the power of God working within you. Pray that the Holy Spirit will reveal it to you, so that you can appropriate God's promise that His power is within you and will take care of all your needs.

With All My Heart

I seek you with all my heart; do not let me stray from your commands.
PSALM 119:10

Time and again the psalmist speaks of doing something with "all my heart" (Psalm 119:2, 34, 69, 145). When he seeks God, when he lives by the law, when he cries out to God—each time it is with all his heart.

When we want to succeed at something, we put our whole heart into it. Should it not be even more so in the service of the holy God? Is He not worth that? Does not His holiness and the natural aversion of our hearts to God demand it?

Remind yourself constantly, while praying, reading, or seeking His will, to do it with all your heart. Repeat the words of today's text, "I seek you with all my heart," and also say, "I call with all my heart; answer me, O LORD, and I will obey your decrees" (119:145).

Think about this. Pray about it. Talk about it to God until you feel that you really mean what you say, and that you are sure God will hear your prayers. Repeat this each morning when you start to pray: *I seek You with all my heart.* In time you will realize the need to wait quietly upon God, for Him to take possession of your whole heart. You will learn to love Him with all your heart and all your strength.

Lord, thank You for the blessing that I may wait upon You. I seek You with all my heart. Make me of service in Your kingdom.

United with Christ

It is because of him that you are in Christ Jesus,
1 CORINTHIANS 1:30

The idea that God's Spirit lives in His children is often seen in the Gospels and letters. It is difficult for the Christian to understand God's Word correctly if he or she does not have the assurance of being united with Christ.

"On that day"—that is, when the Holy Spirit is poured out—"you will realize that I am in the Father, and you are in me, and I am in you," said Jesus (John 14:20). He also said, "If anyone loves me, he will obey my teaching. My Father will love him, and we will come to him and make our home with him" (John 14:23). Every Christian should take these words to heart, in prayer.

Paul says in his letter to the Romans, that our old self is crucified with Christ (see Romans 6:6) and that there is no judgment for those who are in Jesus Christ.

We are united with Christ and the Holy Spirit will make this our experience. Pray seriously about this and follow the guidance of the Spirit. You can, for example, use Ephesians or Colossians to direct your thoughts. These words will take root in your heart, and you will experience something of the heavenly power. It must be cultivated in a spirit of love by devoting some time every day to fellowship with Christ. Then Christ will become a reality within you.

Lord Jesus, thank You that I may be united with You as the branch to the vine. Feed me and prune me so that I may bear more fruit to glorify Your name and win the world for You.

Christ in Me

Do you not realize that Christ Jesus is in you?
2 CORINTHIANS 13:5

Paul wants every Christian to live in the assurance that Christ is in them. What a difference it would make to our lives if we could wake up every morning filled with this thought: *Christ in me.*

The evening before His crucifixion and death, Jesus put it clearly to His disciples: "On that day you will realize that I am in my Father, and you are in me, and I am in you" (John 14:20). *You in me—* through the power of God, everyone who believes was crucified with Christ and was also resurrected with Him. That is why Christ is in us.

This knowledge, however, does not come easily. You need to accept it through belief in God's Word, and then the Holy Spirit will lead you to the whole truth. Take time every day to think about this and claim it for your own.

It is, as written in Ephesians 3:16–17, a special revelation of God's love and power to be strengthened "with power through his Spirit in your inner being, so that Christ may dwell in your hearts through faith.'" Christians may experience this love and may be "filled to the measure of all the fullness of God" (v. 19)!

But remember that abiding in God is a matter of the heart; it must be cultivated in a spirit of love. The only way to receive this blessing is to bow before the Father in prayer (see Ephesians 3:14). Only when we take time in fellowship with God every day will our inner being be renewed from day to day.

Lord, I humbly bow before You in prayer. Please strengthen my inner being through the power of the Holy Spirit from day to day.

Christ Is All

But Christ is all, and is in all.
COLOSSIANS 3:11

The whole purpose of God's eternal plan, of the redemption on the cross and of the King upon the throne in heaven and on earth, is that Christ be all, and in all! In the salvation of sinners, in the absolution and sanctification of the redeemed, in the building of the body of Christ, in the caring for people, even in the most sinful of all people, it is these words of Paul which have authority: "Christ is all, and is in all!"

Maybe while reading the daily passages during the last thirty days, you have wondered whether complete salvation, as I have spoken about it, is perhaps not meant for you. You feel too weak, too unworthy, too unreliable. But the fact is, when you accept Jesus Christ in childlike faith, you will have a Leader and Guide to take care of all your needs. Believe with all your heart that Jesus said He will always be with you. Accept His presence every day. It does not matter how you *feel*. However sinful you are, meet with the Lord Jesus in your inner sanctum and He will reveal Himself to you. Tell Him how unworthy you are, and trust Him to help you and support you. Wait in faith for Him until you can rejoice in Him.

Lord Jesus, I have a deep desire for You to be everything in me. Be everything in my actions and thoughts as well.

If necessary, read through this month's devotions one more time, bearing this in mind: *Christ is all, and is in all!*

Think about these words all day long. Let them become your motto. Let us praise God through all eternity for this.

The Secret of the Throne of Grace

Christians often say that they do not really meet God in prayer; that they do not experience the warmth of His presence in fellowship with Him. No matter how hard they try, they only feel guilt and shame during their quiet times with God. The reason for this is that in our own strength we do not have the ability to love God or even our neighbors. It is only through the working of the Holy Spirit in us that we learn to love God and our fellow beings.

We must, however, always remember that God's love for us is so great that He sent His Son to die for our sins on the cross. Through the blood of Christ we received the liberty to enter into the holiest place and to ask and receive abundant grace. Our heavenly Father longs to fill you with His love. He wants you to have fellowship with Him so that He can reveal His countenance to you.

In our daily readings this month we are going to concentrate on the intimate connection between the throne of God and of the Lamb and the abundant grace that is bestowed on us when we pray.

When you approach the throne of grace, remember to pray for others beside yourself that they, too, may receive this grace. Encourage them to accept the grace that God is so ready to bestow on them.

The Word of God is living and active and sharper than a two-edged sword!

The Throne of Grace

To him who sits on the throne and to the Lamb be praise
and honor and glory and power, for ever and ever.
REVELATION 5:13

In the book of Revelation we are shown the difference between the throne of God the Creator and the throne of grace. In chapter four, John sees "a throne in heaven, with someone sitting on it. And the one who sat there had the appearance of jasper and carnelian" (Revelation 4:2–3). There was no definite form, but the shining light of precious stones. Surrounding the throne were four living creatures that sang God's praises night and day. The twenty-four elders also fell down before Him and worshiped Him. Without doubt we have here the throne of God, the almighty Creator!

In chapter five, John sees a Lamb, looking as if it had been slain, standing in the center of the throne. The four living creatures and the elders fell down before the Lamb and they sang a new song of praise: "You are worthy to take the scroll and to open its seals, because you were slain, and with your blood you purchased men for God from every tribe and language and people and nation" (5:9). Then every creature in heaven and on the earth and under the earth and in the sea praised God: "To him who sits on the throne and to the Lamb be praise and honor and glory and power, for ever and ever" (5:13). Here we have the throne of grace, of God and the slain Lamb. And the threefold song that we hear is the heavenly chorus that is sung at the dedication of the throne of grace to the glory of God and the Lamb.

Lord, please teach me the secret of true praise and worship—not only with words, but with my whole style of living.

When you draw near to the throne of grace, think of what it cost Christ to found that throne, and what assurance it gives that you will find grace to help in times of need. In deepest humility and with all your heart, worship the Lamb on the throne of grace.

The Lamb in the Middle

Since we have a great high priest…Jesus the Son of God…
let us then approach the throne of grace with confidence.
HEBREWS 4:14, 16

Can you imagine a better way by which the Father could have given us access to Him than by giving His only Son as a Lamb to be slain for us? After Jesus had given Himself on the cross as ransom for our sins, God placed Him in the middle of the throne, so that we as sinners might have the liberty, through His blood, to have full access to the Father. In this way we can pray through the Son with the assurance that He will make our prayers acceptable to the Father. Truly, the holy God has done His utmost to draw us to Himself.

With this vision of the Lamb on the throne before you, take time to worship Him in the deepest humility and childlike faith, and with all the love of which your heart is capable, as your Surety and Intercessor and great High Priest. Once the Holy Spirit has imprinted that vision of the Lamb on the throne in your heart, it will indeed become a throne of grace to you. Then you will do nothing less but kneel before Him in adoration and praise, giving Him the glory to all eternity.

Your heart will then become a true temple of God where, day by day and hour after hour, this song of praise will arise: "Salvation belongs to our God, who sits on the throne, and to the Lamb" (Revelation 7:10).

Holy, holy, holy is the Lord God Almighty, who was, and is, and is to come.

When your heart is filled with love for the Lamb, then you will have the joy and the faith to expect a speedy answer to prayer.

Abundant Grace

The grace of our Lord was poured out on me abundantly,
along with the faith and love that are in Christ Jesus.
1 TIMOTHY 1:14

In the Word of God the meaning of grace is described with meaningful words like "the riches of grace," "the glory of grace," "the abundance of grace," and the "manifold riches of grace." Paul speaks of the gift that was given by the grace of one man, Jesus Christ, but overflowed to the many (see Romans 5:15). How much more will those who receive God's abundant provision of grace and of the gift of righteousness reign in life through the one man, Jesus Christ (5:17). But where sin increased, grace increased all the more (5:20).

In Corinthians the apostle Paul says, "But by the grace of God I am what I am, and his grace to me was not without effect. No, I worked harder than all of them—yet not I, but the grace of God that was with me" (1 Corinthians 15:10).

Thank You, Lord,
for the abundance
of grace that I
receive from You
every day.

In the same vein there are many other passages in the Word that speak of grace. In Him we have redemption through His blood, the forgiveness of sins, in accordance with the richness of God's grace (see Ephesians 1:7). "For it is by grace you have been saved, through faith—and this is not from yourselves, it is the gift of God" (Ephesians 2:8).

What treasure is contained in these words! Let the Holy Spirit write them in your heart, that you may receive the full impression of the "exceeding riches" and the abundance of grace that you will receive at the throne of grace.

With All Your Heart

*Love the Lord your God with all your heart and with all your soul
and with all your mind and with all your strength.*

MARK 12:30

In this great command the Lord our God teaches us to trust Him
above all else. Our love, our prayers, our consecration, our trust, our
obedience—in all these there must be an unreserved surrender to
God's will and service.

With all your heart—with its longings, its affections, its attach-
ments, its desires. *With all your soul*—with its vital powers and the will
as a royal master in the soul. *With all your mind*—with its faculties of
thought, of knowledge, of reasoning, and its powers of memory and
imagination. *With all your strength*—this is nothing less than the sacrifice of everything. All for God and for God alone.
Our greatest desire must be to love and serve God.

God has the right to expect so much from us!
For He is the Creator who made us to reflect His
glory, and for this purpose He must possess us
wholly. He is perfect and glorious and worthy that
we should forsake all to follow Him. He is the
everlasting love and goodness and mercy, and He
longs to pour out blessings upon us. He is indeed
worthy of being loved and honored by us with all
our strength and all our heart!

God will work in our hearts that which He
has promised in this command. He will, through
His Spirit, pour out His love in our hearts. Let us
earnestly desire an answer to our prayers and approach the throne of
grace confidently, where this grace may be received.

*Lord, I love You
with all my heart.
I pray that Your
Holy Spirit will
work within me a
true and ever
growing love.*

Song of the Lamb

*Because you were slain, and with your blood you purchased men for
God from every tribe and language and people and nation*
REVELATION 5:9

The Song of the Lamb from Revelation tells us that the redeemed shall come from all the different tribes and nations. The many languages into which the Bible has been translated will give us some idea of how devotedly missionaries in many countries are proclaiming Christ and His gospel.

Christ came as propitiation not only for *our* sins, but also for the sins of the world, and to complete the great work of the redemption of mankind. When He had accomplished His share of the work on earth, He entrusted the rest of the work to His people. As holy and divine as was Christ's part, so equally holy is the second part of the work—to bring souls everywhere to know of and accept His great salvation.

In the Song of the Lamb we find this twofold truth: The Lamb upon the throne has brought salvation to all the nations and tribes of the earth, and the church of the Lamb has been entrusted with the distribution of the message of salvation by the power of the Holy Spirit to all people.

We shall only be able to truly understand this when we can visualize the great multitude before the throne crying out, "Salvation belongs to our God, who sits on the throne, and to the Lamb" (Revelation 7:10).

May the Holy Spirit imprint deeply in our hearts the wonder of missionary work! The message of salvation must reach all those who have not heard it. Let us offer ourselves wholly and without reserve that souls may be led to join in the Song of the Lamb before the throne of God.

*Lord Jesus Christ,
thank You for the
message of
salvation that You
entrusted to me.
Thank You for
every opportunity
that You give me
to convey this
message to others.
Make me faithful
to do Your work.*

Worshipers of the Lamb

*You have made them to be a kingdom and priests to serve our God,
and they will reign on the earth.*
REVELATION 5:10

As priests we worship God and the Lamb, and with hearts full of adoration we may approach the throne of the Lamb for ourselves and also on behalf of others. As kings we receive the abundance of grace to reign over sin and the power of the world, so that we may bring liberty to the captives. To those that overcome, Christ will give the right to sit on His throne (see Revelation 3:21).

You must remember, however, that you do not only approach the throne of grace for your own sake, but also for others. How can the Lamb make known the glory of the throne of grace to those who sit in darkness? (See Romans 10:14.) Only by means of those who know the throne of grace and are willing to share their experience with others. If we do this, the throne of grace will become more precious to us, and the abundance of grace that we receive will increase and will work within us in greater power. Remember that the Lamb has chosen you to make Him and His love known to others. He demands it from you and His grace will strengthen you with heavenly power and joy.

Then the Song of the Lamb will acquire a new meaning for us. "To him who loves us and has freed us from our sins by his blood, and has made us to be a kingdom and priests to serve his God and Father—to him be the glory and power for ever and ever!" (Revelation 1:5–6). We shall realize that it is worth the while to live as men ready to fulfill a heavenly calling.

Lord, let Your grace strengthen me with power and joy when I approach the throne of grace, so that I can fulfill my heavenly calling.

The Lamb and the Spirit

Then I saw a Lamb, looking as if it had been slain,
standing in the center of the throne.... He had seven horns and seven eyes,
which are the seven spirits of God sent out into all the earth.

REVELATION 5:6

In the fourth chapter of Revelation, John sees seven lamps of fire burning before the throne, which are the seven spirits of God. In our text we see that these spirits have been taken up into the life of the Lamb; they are His eyes and through them He works in all the earth.

When the Lamb was on earth, He was obedient to God's Spirit in all things. This is why the Father gave Him unlimited power to pour out the Holy Spirit in full measure on whom He chooses.

From this we first learn that the Lamb on the throne has power to fill us with the Holy Spirit, which enables us to follow Him. In this way He prepares us to commune with God in the power of His blood and become more than conquerors.

Second, we learn that it is only through the Spirit that we shall understand the glory of the Lamb and be filled with His love, and so stand firm in the faith of that which He can do in us and for us and through us.

Let the Song of the Lamb ring in your ears continually. The Lamb who was slain is worthy to receive the power and the glory. God has exalted Him to the throne and has put all things under His feet. Give Him the place of honor in your heart, and submit all that you have to Him and His service. Take time to become quiet before the throne of the Lamb and enjoy His presence. Only then will you be ready to conquer the world.

Thank You, Lord, that You include me in Your plan for the world. To You who sit on the throne and the Lamb belong the praise and honor and glory and power!

The Lamb and Prayer

The twenty-four elders fell down before the Lamb.
Each one had a harp and they were holding golden bowls full of incense,
which are the prayers of the saints.
REVELATION 5:8

We learn here that the prayers of the saints in the Old Testament concerning the promised redemption were preserved in heaven. These prayers are offered as incense at the throne of the Lamb, so that He may lay them before the Father. Later, in Revelation 8 we also read of the angel who stood at the altar before the throne with a golden censer filled with the prayers of all the saints.

What profound and heavenly thoughts do these words awaken within us! The prayers of the saints are not answered at once. Just as men on earth accumulate money and allow it to increase as capital for greater undertakings, so the prayers of the saints are stored up in heaven until the measure is full and the answer can descend.

Remember this: You do not pray alone. God's children all over the world are also praying to the Lamb with perseverance and faith. In His own good time God will graciously send the answer. Do not think your prayer is in vain because you do not receive the answer at once. The Lamb on the throne keeps our prayers in safety to lay them before the Father at the right time.

Persevere in wholehearted prayer. Pray for the church of God all over the world, pray for preachers and teachers, pray for all believers. Pray in love and fellowship with others who are also praying. By means of daily fellowship with God and the Lamb you will receive abundant grace for your own need and the needs of those around you in the church and the world.

Here, before the throne of grace, I am again aware of the power of prayer. Give me the strength to persevere in prayer and to faithfully seek fellowship with You.

The Blood of the Lamb

They have washed their robes and made them white in the blood of the Lamb.
Therefore, they are before the throne of God and
serve him day and night in his temple.

REVELATION 7:14–15

If I am to be presented to a king in his palace, my garments must be in accordance with the rules of the court. What I wear helps to give me liberty to approach an earthly monarch. If I am to appear before God and serve Him day and night in His temple, I must wear a robe "made white in the blood of the Lamb."

What a close relationship to the Lord Jesus it gives me when I know that He has bought me with His blood—paid so great a price for me! It gives me the assurance that He places a great value upon me and will preserve me so that I may appear in His presence and serve Him day and night in His temple.

Lord, thank You that, through Your blood, You made it possible for me to gain access to the presence of God at the throne of grace.

The Lamb of God lives each day to make me acceptable to the Father, and I receive the abundant grace that I need to abound in good works. How attractive the inner chamber becomes when we love and honor the Lamb on the throne and ask to be fitted for His service!

You must each day put on the white robe that has been washed in the blood of the Lamb. You then become one of the royal priesthood who serve God and intercede for lost souls and for the whole world. The precious blood of the Lamb gives us the liberty to access God's presence with confidence. It links us closely to the Lord Jesus and gives us the power to be a blessing to others. That is why you "are before the throne of God and serve him day and night in his temple."

Following the Lamb

They follow the Lamb wherever he goes.
They were purchased from among men and offered as
firstfruits to God and the Lamb.
REVELATION 14:4

The Lamb is the leader of whom it was written He will bring His children to glory and perfection through suffering (see Hebrews 2:10). He is "the author and perfecter of our faith…who endured the cross" (Hebrews 12:2). Let us therefore remember that the Lamb is our leader and example and His redeemed ones follow Him wherever He goes.

The Lamb in His great humility says, "Learn of me, for I am meek and lowly of heart." The Lamb is innocent and pure. The Lamb is patient and silent. The Lamb offered Himself to God as a burnt offering and sweet-smelling incense. He is the leader of our salvation whom the Father gave us to bring others to Him, and in whose footsteps we seek to walk.

The Lamb on the throne is my advocate with the Father, the One who lives to intercede for me. The Lamb on the throne has the power to lead me and mold me according to His own image. The Lamb on the throne also lives in me, and He is willing and able to replicate His own meekness and self-sacrifice within me. The Lamb at the center of the throne is also my shepherd and He will lead me to springs of living water (see Revelation 7:17).

Follow the Lamb! Let this be your watchword and prayer every day.

Lord, I so often still want to follow my own will and make my own decisions. Please give me the strength to follow You wherever You lead me.

The Victory of the Lamb

They overcame [the accuser] by the blood of the Lamb and by the word of their testimony; they did not love their lives so much as to shrink from death.
REVELATION 12:11

The Lamb is the victor over every enemy; and those who are with Him, the called, the chosen and faithful, reign with Him. They conquered the enemy through the blood of the Lamb. Faith in the power of Christ and His blood is the assurance that every foe has been vanquished. The blood now makes each one a conqueror in the power of God. The daily fellowship with Christ in the sprinkling of the blood makes us triumph daily. There is victory through the blood of the Lamb!

Do not seek only your own salvation, however. The message of God's love must be carried to the ends of the earth according to Christ's last command before His ascension. As we make known the love of God, witness to the power of the blood, and strive to win souls for Him, the enemy will be overcome and souls will be rescued from His power.

Revelation says that Christ's followers did not love their lives so much that they were unwilling to die for Him. This was the way the Lamb that was slain gained the victory and won his place in the middle of the throne. Those who follow the Lamb must dedicate themselves wholly to His service and count no task too great or too small in His service.

If you desire to be crowned as a conqueror in life, be a faithful follower of the Lamb. Live as He did. Let your trust in the wonderful life-giving power of the blood, and the remembrance of all the Lamb has done for you, inspire you to offer your whole life to Him.

Lord, it might be easier to die for You than to live a life wholly dedicated to You. Make me willing to sacrifice everything for You.

The Marriage of the Lamb

Then the angel said to me, "Write: 'Blessed are those who are invited to the wedding supper of the Lamb!'"

REVELATION 19:9

All who rejoice in salvation are invited to the marriage of the Lamb, not merely as spectators, but as the bride of the Lamb. The angel refers to the Holy City, the New Jerusalem, coming down from heaven as the bride of Christ. All the nations that are saved walk in her light. The time of the marriage feast of the Lamb will be when Christ presents His redeemed people as one body to the Father, and they are taken up to sit with Him on the throne eternally.

When the prodigal son returned to his home, his father prepared a feast, where all rejoiced over the return of the son who had been dead and was alive again. What joy there will be when the Lamb, who died for us on the cross, celebrates His triumph and the glory of God!

When we are invited to the wedding of a distinguished person we take great care to wear suitable clothes. What concern then, mingled with joy, should there be in the hearts of those who are called to the marriage supper of the Lamb! If you really cherish the joyful hope of sitting at the marriage feast of the Lamb, will you not each day make use of the unspeakable privilege of approaching the throne of grace? Will you not entrust yourself in loving surrender to Him, and pray for grace that each day the way may be made more ready for the great heavenly marriage feast of the Lamb? Do not only prepare yourself, but also seek for the grace to win others to partake of the feast of Everlasting Love.

Thank You, Lord, that You have chosen to invite me to the marriage of the Lamb. Thank You that we can join You as Your bride at the wedding supper.

The Throne of God and of the Lamb

*Then the angel showed me the river of the water of life,
as clear as crystal, flowing from the throne of God and of the Lamb.*
REVELATION 22:1

What does the river of the water of life signify? Nothing less than the Holy Spirit, who was not given until the Lamb was on the throne. Now the water of life streams from the throne of the Lamb to those who believe in Him fully, giving to each according to His faith and desire that which Christ has promised: a fountain springing up to eternal life. The water of life surrounds us all, but because of laziness and worldliness we are unable to grasp it and enjoy it.

Perhaps I may make this clear by means of an illustration. When Marconi discovered how the radio worked, he realized that he could send messages throughout the whole world by means of radio waves. When he sent his first message from England to Italy, it passed through France, where there were millions of people who had no idea that such a message was passing. The message was heard and understood only when it reached the reception station that had been prepared for it in Italy.

Just so are we surrounded by the stream of eternal life without being aware of it. Yes, waves of heavenly grace, of life and power, love and joy, surround us and we do not even know it. As Marconi spent years trying to master the secret of wireless telegraphy, we must also seek with undivided hearts to see the waves of life-giving water flowing from the throne of the Lamb, and realize that the water is for our daily use.

God, I worship You and the Lamb at the throne. Let Your glory fill me with streams of living water that can flow through me as a blessing to others.

The Heavenly Life

The throne of God and of the Lamb will be in the city,
and his servants will serve him. They will see his face,
and his name will be on their foreheads.
REVELATION 22:3–4

Many Christians approach the throne of grace with the purpose of finding sufficient grace for their immediate needs. When they find this grace, they are satisfied, and they do not wait for enough grace to fill their entire life and enable them to walk in its light night and day. The result is that they never experience the full glory of God.

The promises of today's text is fulfilled to those who have faith in the unseen, and know that they have come to the heavenly Jerusalem, the city of God, and received the sprinkled blood of Jesus (see Hebrews 12:22–24). To them the earthly life becomes an actual experience of preparation for the heavenly life. Note the wonderful promises given to those who linger at the throne of God:

His servants will serve Him—at first without seeing His glory.

They shall see His face—when they become aware of His omnipresence.

His name will be on their foreheads—when they obey His commands and walk in the light of His countenance all day long, the likeness of His image can be seen in them and His name will be visible on their foreheads (see Colossians 3:17).

> Lord, I pray that something of the heavenly life will become visible to me, and in me, here on earth.

It is a great privilege to approach the throne of grace and an even greater privilege when we see the face of God and of the Lamb and walk in their light each day. When the name of Christ is engraved upon our hearts and our foreheads, we are changed to His image, from glory to glory, as by the Spirit of the Lord.

The Reign of Grace

Those who receive God's abundant provision of grace and of the gift of righteousness reign in life through the one man, Jesus Christ.
ROMANS 5:17

The grace that reigns through the blood of Jesus Christ, and the power of the Holy Spirit, enable us to gain victory over sin.

Salvation does not, as many think, mean a life of falling and rising again. No, it is God's will that His children should be conquerors in their life on earth. There is, however, one condition and that is that they should live day by day in the abundance of grace that is to be obtained at the throne of grace.

In Romans 5:20, Paul says that where sin increases, grace increases all the more. Is it not wonderful that although sin abounds, grace is always greater and more abundant than sin can ever be? I may, by reading God's Word, have an overpowering sense of the great power of sin, but I also have the assurance that grace—the life-power of God within me—is far more abundant and powerful.

Lord, thank You for the abundant grace You bestow on me. Remind me always that Your grace is stronger than the power of sin.

Just as sin reigned in death, grace reigns through righteousness unto eternal life through Jesus Christ our Lord (see Romans 5:21). Remember that God's grace is stronger than the power of sin and that you are more than a conqueror through Him that loves you. This is a sure word. They that receive the abundance of grace reign already in this life through Jesus Christ.

I am sure that by this time you have noticed how important it is to approach the throne of grace every day with a deep sense of need, but fully assured that you will receive the power to conquer sin. Daily fellowship with God will lead to a rich life full of good deeds—a life that will bear witness to the abundant grace of God.

Face to Face

So Jacob called the place Peniel, saying,
"It is because I saw God face to face, and yet my life was spared."
GENESIS 32:30

In these words of Jacob, uttered after he had become *Israel,* we find expression of that which prayer meant to him. The words show us what each child of God, through the grace of God and the power of the Holy Spirit, may experience every day. God will cause His face to shine upon us, and we shall see Him face-to-face and be delivered.

How often Christians complain that they have little experience of what it means to meet with God in prayer and feel the light of His countenance upon them. They have tried their best, but it seems to no avail. Their thoughts in the inner chamber bring only self-reproach and shame.

And yet your Father in heaven is not only willing but strongly desires that the light of His countenance shall rest upon you. Perhaps the words of this text may help to assure you of God's desire. Yes, your inner chamber can also be called *Peniel,* because it is the place where God wants to meet you face-to-face. Only there will you realize what it is to meet with God, to see His face, and to feel how certain and blessed it is that His love rests upon you.

Begin with this prayer: "Restore us, O LORD God Almighty; make your face shine upon us, that we may be saved" (Psalm 80:19). Meditate on the words. Believe firmly that you may know their power and truth. Remember how Jacob refused to let go of God before God blessed him. Persevering prayer is needed to convince us that God will indeed make Himself known to us.

Lord, I thank You for the great privilege that You want to meet with me, a sinner, face-to-face.

The Lord Is One

"The most important [commandment]," answered Jesus, "is this:
'Hear, O Israel, the Lord our God, the Lord is one.'"
MARK 12:29

The law may command us to love, but it cannot *make* us love; it is powerless to force us to love God. Love for God can only be born of the knowledge of Him as the one true God, in His excellent greatness and glory and in His unspeakable love and compassion. When Moses said that the Lord our God is one God, He was making known the supreme right that God has to our love. The love of God enters our hearts when we are reminded of his words, "The LORD, the LORD, the compassionate and gracious God, slow to anger, abounding in love and faithfulness, maintaining love to thousands, and forgiving wickedness, rebellion and sin" (Exodus 34:6–7).

Lord, forgive me for placing my trust in other things. Reveal Yourself to me every day so that I can love and serve You with all my heart and all my strength.

We cannot love God as we should unless we realize that He is worthy to be loved wholeheartedly. It is no wonder that Christians are afraid of the command to love God with all their heart and all their strength. Without true confession of sin it is impossible for anyone to understand how abundantly God forgives, and how rich He is in mercy. The heart filled with a burning desire to serve God will say, "God is indeed worthy of my love; I will love him with my whole heart!"

Meet God in prayer each day. Live in the light of His love and draw near to Him in absolute surrender to His will. You will find that this love works two ways: God gives Himself wholly to you, and you surrender yourself and everything you own to Him.

The Abiding Presence of God

The LORD is near to all who call on him, to all who call on him in truth.
PSALM 145:18

You long to continually experience the nearness of God. Here is the secret: Pray. Pray without ceasing. Then you will have the assurance that the Lord is near to those who call upon Him. Prayer has the wonderful power of drawing us nearer to God and keeping us in His presence. God is everywhere and He is ready and able to grant us unbroken fellowship with Him.

What does it mean to pray without ceasing? The answer is clear. Realize first that God is near you, within you, and then you will feel how natural it is to talk to Him each moment about your needs and desires. It is this kind of prayer of which Paul says, "Night and day we pray most earnestly" (1 Thessalonians 3:10)

It is only the person who lives a life independent of God that says, "I must take time to first find God before I can pray." But to the true Christian, life is a constant abiding with the Father. Interaction between you and the Father should be a daily activity, like breathing or sleeping, instead of something that happens only once a day. The principle of complete dependence on the unseen God, and the holy habit of claiming His presence with us each moment of the day, is the secret to a life of true godliness.

God is always near, so that you may call upon Him at all times. We must make all our needs and requests known to God through prayer and the peace of God will be with us.

Thank You, Lord, that You are always near to me and that I can call on You at any time. Thank You that I can experience Your presence all day long.

Take Time with God

There is a time for everything,
and a season for every activity under heaven.
ECCLESIASTES 3:1

It should be the aim of every Christian to set aside a little time each day for quiet communion with God. There is a time for everything. Shall there be no time to spend in the presence of the Creator of all things? No time to contemplate His will and purpose for us? The holy, loving God is indeed worthy of the *best* of our time. We should live in constant fellowship with Him, but each day there should be a special time of quiet when we are with Him alone.

We need a period daily for secret fellowship. Time to turn from daily activities and search our hearts in His presence. Time to study His Word with reverence and godly fear. Time to seek His face and ask Him to reveal Himself to us. Time to wait until we know that He sees and hears us so that we can make our needs known to Him in words that come from the depth of our hearts. Time to let God deal with our special needs, to let Him shine in our hearts, to let ourselves be filled with His Spirit!

What do you think: Will a quarter of an hour each day be sufficient for this purpose? If you are unwilling to make such an arrangement you must not be surprised if your spiritual life becomes ineffective. Fellowship with God should be your first priority. If you do this regularly, you will learn to value it more and more. Soon you will feel ashamed that there was ever a time when you thought that fifteen minutes would suffice.

Think of the hours a child spends at school to prepare Him for life. How much longer then should we spend to prepare ourselves for the eternal life?

Lord, it is so easy to find time for my own interests. Thank You that You not only gave me a little of Your time, but that You gave me Your life.

The Will

All Judah rejoiced about the oath because they had sworn it wholeheartedly.
They sought God eagerly, and he was found by them.
So the LORD gave them rest on every side.

2 CHRONICLES 15:15

The will is the royal faculty of the soul; it rules over the whole man. Many people become the slaves of sin because they do not decide with a firm will to listen to the voice of conscience. Many Christians make no advance in their prayer life, because they do not have the courage to decide with a strong purpose of will to take time to listen to God's Word and their own conscience.

In the practice of prayer it is essential not to give way to wandering thoughts, or the temptation to say rushed, superficial prayers. Call upon God with all your heart and strength. This is not an easy task. Of course, you can go on praying without any real zeal or enthusiasm. The other possibility is to ask God's help through the Holy Spirit. Ask Him to help you spend time with Him with an undivided heart. Keep on, even though you might find it difficult. It will become easier each time you seek God with an undivided heart.

All Judah sought the Lord with their whole desire, or will, and they found Him. God is longing to bless you, but is unable to do so as long as you are not willing to give yourself unreservedly, and with all the strength of your will, to let him work out His will in you. Therefore, tell the Father out loud, "Father, I will seek You with all my heart and will." He will allow Himself to be found by you!

Thank You, Lord, that through the Holy Spirit I can pray for an undivided heart. I pray with all my heart that You will bend me to Your will.

Christ's Love for Us

As the Father has loved me, so have I loved you.
Now remain in my love.
JOHN 15:9

The Lord gave His disciples a new commandment, that they should love one another, as He loved them. To this end He wanted them to know how much He loved them. He loved them with the same everlasting, unchangeable, and divine love that the Father had loved Him. It is with a love such as this that they were to love one another.

This thought is so overwhelming that it takes time to grasp its full meaning. Pray about it and let God's Spirit make it a blessed reality in your life: *We must love one another in the same way that the Father loved His Son.*

God sent His Son to earth to manifest this love. God loves you and all human beings with the same love that He loved His Son. This is also the same love that Jesus exercised toward His disciples. This love was given them when the Holy Spirit was poured out on the Day of Pentecost, that they might love one another and more— even love those who were the enemies of Christ.

This love is not merely a feeling or a blessed experience, but a living divine power, flowing from the Father to the Son to the hearts of His disciples, and so streaming forth to the whole world. Meditate on this truth until you believe it, and you will receive the courage to confidently approach the throne of grace to receive the love that passes all understanding.

Thank You, Lord, for the love with which You atoned for my sin. Work within me a love that overflows to the people around me and to those who do not know You.

Our Love for Christ

If you love me, you will obey what I command.
JOHN 14:15

Six times in the Gospel of John, our Lord Jesus Christ mentions the fact that our love for Him depends on the doing of His will (see John 14:15, 21, 23; 5:7, 10, 14). It is not enough to read these words once. Go over them again carefully and notice how in each verse there is a wonderful promise. Then you will begin to realize the blessedness of the life of the one who loves Christ, obeys His commands, and remains in His love.

Notice this striking promise: "If anyone loves me, he will obey my teaching. My Father will love him, and we will come to him and make our home with him" (John 14:23). The Father and the Son dwell in the hearts of those that love Jesus and obey His commands. Thus Paul can say, "Do you not realize that Christ Jesus is in you?" (2 Corinthians 13:5.)

Christians seldom think about this, or about the love of Christ for them. If we are strengthened through the Holy Spirit, Christ will dwell in our hearts by faith and we shall be rooted and grounded in love. The divine power will work within us, and we shall learn to love Him as He loves us.

If you remain in His love and obey His commands, He will enable you to love. The measure of His sacrifice for you will be the measure of your willing surrender to Him in all things.

Lord Jesus Christ, thank You that You love me with an everlasting love. Strengthen me through Your Holy Spirit so that I can prove through my obedience how much I love You.

Our Love for Others

My command is this: Love each other as I have loved you.
JOHN 15:12

Many people think it is quite impossible to keep this command; therefore, they do not even attempt to obey it. But the Lord has indeed made provision for the fulfillment of His command.

The great love with which the Father loved the Son is the same love with which Christ loves us. The love of the Father worked powerfully in the Son. This same relationship—between Father and Son—exists between the Lord Jesus and us. As He loves us, His love comes to abide in us, because He Himself dwells within us.

Even the world agrees that if a man says he loves God, but hates his brother, he is a liar. Hatred toward a brother is a sign that a man does not love God; love toward a brother is an indication that he loves God.

Thank You, Lord, that You never ask anything from me for which You have not made provision. Let Your Holy Spirit work within me, so that I can be a witness of Your love wherever I go.

Let us try to understand what the Lord really means by His command to love one another. Jesus came to earth to reveal God's love to us. Then He returned to His Father, and His disciples had to carry on this love, with the assurance that the Holy Spirit would dwell within them and would enable them to love one another. As they loved others in the power of Christ's love, they would also grow strong to love. And that would be a powerful sign to the world that His love was in them.

As a child of God you must bow humbly at the feet of your Lord and worship Him. He will dwell within you and enable you to love others. In this way you will convince the world that God is truly in our midst.

Love Demands All

This is how we know what love is: Jesus Christ laid down his life for us.
And we ought to lay down our lives for our brothers.
1 JOHN 3:16

It was not only on the cross that Christ gave His life for us; the cross was the consummation of a life of service and healing. His example demands from us that we be willing to give our entire life to the service of others.

The strength of God's love in Christ enabled Him to give up His life wholly for us. The same strength is available to us, and as we yield ourselves wholly to it, we shall be able to make the welfare of others the central object of our lives. Those who give themselves wholly into the keeping of God's love will experience His power and all-sufficiency.

One sometimes finds that the love of Christ works within the hearts of even uneducated people an unquenchable desire to pray and work for others. I have read the story of a young girl who began leading others to Jesus when she was only nine years old. A few years later when she went to boarding school, she prayed every day for people to meet God and to know and love Him. This continued until her nineteenth year, when she became a regular worker among soldiers, giving all her time and energy to the work. The Lord blessed her with such a spirit of love and prayer that she continued the work for many years. She was a living example of how God enables one to spend life in the service of others, and especially in winning hearts for Christ.

Because Christ gave His life for you, you are now a debtor who owes your life to others. The love of Christ constrains you and will supply all the power and strength you need.

Lord, I pray that I will grow to be more and more like You every day. Fill me with Your love and let Your power motivate me to win over souls for You.

A New Command

A new command I give you: Love one another.
JOHN 13:34

This command to love one another as God loves us differs from the law that was given on Sinai. This command was accompanied by the gift of power to obey it. Christ promised that through His Holy Spirit He would remain within us and that He would give us the strength to love others. It is in the power of this indwelling that He makes our hearts the dwelling place of His love for His people.

Christ prayed to the Father that the love with which His Father had loved Him may also be in His disciples and that He (Jesus) will remain in them. He will indeed dwell in our hearts, bringing the love of God and manifesting His love to His children. As He dwells in our hearts with His divine love, He teaches us to love others at all times and in all circumstances. He is the vine, and we are the branches; He that dwells in Him as a branch in the vine bears much fruit—chiefly love to fellow human beings.

Lord, thank You for the new command of love and that You gave me Your Holy Spirit to enable me to love sinners and to show them Your love.

Let us say to ourselves, *The world cannot see the Lord Jesus; therefore, it is my duty to show the love of Christ to the world. I am commanded by my love to show forth His love as manifested when He was on earth. Christ has given His love in my heart towards others in order that I may help them. Christ loved me while I was yet a sinner, and He gives me His own love towards a wandering brother. This will bring blessing to the Lord Jesus, to my brother, and to myself.*

Receive Christ into your heart to abide there with His heavenly love, and let us have faith to reveal this love to our fellow human beings.

Do You Love Me?

Peter was hurt because Jesus asked him the third time,
"Do you love me?" He said, "Lord, you know all things;
you know that I love you."
JOHN 21:17

The Lord comes to us, time after time, with the question, "Do you love me?" until we are made to cry out, "You know that I love you!" But at the same time we have to confess how little this love is manifested in our hearts and lives.

What are the signs of true love? How can you be sure that it is the love the Bible speaks of? First, it is a *sincere longing for fellowship with the loved one.* We see in daily life how friends and relations like to be together. Our love for Christ can be tested by the joy we experience in his presence when we meet with Him in the inner chamber.

Second, love seeks *to please the loved one.* Love strives to bring happiness to the object of its love. The extent of our love to the Lord is shown by the way we obey His commands. Love does all that it can to make the loved one happy.

Third, love seeks to *become entirely one with the loved one,* and so attain spiritual unity.

"Do you love me?" is the test question that needs to be answered. If you fall short on any point, humbly confess it to our Lord, and receive from Him on the throne of grace the power to love Him with all your heart.

We read that when Peter was grieved the Lord gave Him power to tend to His sheep. By the same love that Jesus sought and found you, He will constrain you to win souls for Christ and His service.

Lord, my only answer is that of Peter: You know everything; therefore, You know that I love You.

The Love of Christ for the World

By this all men will know that you are my disciples, if you love one another.
JOHN 13:35

I pray…that all of them may be one, Father, just as you are in me and I am in you. May they also be in us so that the world may believe that you have sent me.
JOHN 17:20–21

The great power on which our Lord built His hopes of winning the world to Himself was a wonderful love with which all people and nations would be melded, so that even the heathen would say, "Behold how these Christians love one another!"

The Lord has not saved us merely to make us happy. His great object is to use everyone who receives His love as a witness to win others to His service. It is not only a witness in words that is needed, but also the power of a heavenly love by which selfish people may be renewed into a life like that of Jesus Christ—a life of self-sacrificing love that embraces all.

Lord, give me the power to put my love into action. I love You with all my heart!

Do you realize why some preaching holds little power for conversion? The world wants proof that Christians are better than other people. The proof is that Christ can change selfish people into models of love and self-sacrifice. It is a matter of deep concern for the church and for the world that Christians should manifest this heavenly love. What the world needs most today is a revival of love in the hearts of men and women through the Holy Spirit. This would bring untold blessing to every believer, to the church, and to all those who accept what the love of God can do in hearts fully yielded to Him.

Love for Souls

He who wins souls is wise.
PROVERBS 11:30

"Come, follow me," Jesus said, "and I will make you fishers of men."
MATTHEW 4:19

When Jesus Christ taught Peter the great lesson about love (see John 19:15–17), He gave him the right and the power to tend to the Lord's sheep. The Lord expects that each one who receives into his heart His wonderful love will use that love to win souls for Him. If we are in the right relationship with God, we have the liberty to pray and expect God's blessing on our personal witness and work.

The principle is so simple that every Christian, old or young, rich or poor, may have a share in it. A healthy spiritual life in the church and in the individual members can be preserved only when each one takes part.

Everywhere there are souls in need of help. Eminent ministers and evangelists agree that it is not so much in the preaching of the Word, but in work for individual souls, that the best results are to be found.

Personal witnessing and reaching out to others mean more love to our Lord and more joy in His service. This work does not only consist of speaking to individuals about their souls, but in speaking to God for souls. It is a great privilege to be a soul-winner, a work that angels might envy us. God sent His only Son into the world to win souls for the kingdom. Surrender your lives to the Everlasting Love, that through that love, you may bring God's wandering children home to their Father. A life consecrated to the winning of souls will bring joy to the heart of Christ and glory to His name.

Lord, please give me the love to reach out to those who do not know You and to win their souls for the kingdom.

Not I, but the Grace of God

But by the grace of God I am what I am,
and his grace to me was not without effect. No, I worked harder than
all of them—yet not I, but the grace of God that was with me.
1 CORINTHIANS 15:10

The word *grace* may be used in two senses. First, it points to the free and undeserved blessings bestowed on us by God, upon which we can always reckon and for which we should thank Him daily. Second, the word may be used of the divine power with which this compassionate love works within us. Grace is not merely an attribute of God, but a life power which works in us every day and every hour, giving us the power to do God's will.

Paul speaks of the goodness of God that made him, all undeserving, what he was. The grace that God bestowed on Paul was not in vain, because Paul worked "harder than all of them" in the service of the Lord. The divine power within him enabled him to do the work.

Lord, I humbly kneel before You in great gratitude for the grace You bestowed on me. I pray that Your grace will never be in vain.

Let us hold fast to these truths when we approach the throne of grace. God will receive us and use us and bestow His grace upon us, not according to what we deserve, but according to the great love that He has for us. We will then be able to do what God requires each moment of the day. Grace is the power that enables us to abound in good works (see 2 Corinthians 9:8).

Not I, but the grace of God that is in me. Make these words your motto for the day. Cultivate large thoughts of what God will do for you. Bow before the throne of grace fully assured of what His grace can and will do. Be strong and of good courage, and He will strengthen your heart.

The God Who Performs Miracles

And I pray that you, being rooted and established in love, may have
power to grasp…and to know this love that surpasses knowledge.
EPHESIANS 3:17–19

The gift of love is not bestowed separately, but comes to us when our hearts are filled with Christ. Our love for God will be sustained if we seek daily fellowship with Him. Paul, in Ephesians 3:14, refers to a kneeling position: "For this reason I kneel before the Father." When we bow before the throne of grace and humbly wait and worship there, we shall receive the indwelling Spirit and our hearts shall be filled with the love of Christ.

We must not seek only the forgiveness of sin, but we must also seek the abundant grace that will help us to be victorious over sin and enable us to be fitted for the continual indwelling of the Spirit. We must earnestly pray that the love of Christ that surpasses knowledge will be our first priority in life. At the throne of grace we shall be rooted and grounded in that love. And having come to love God, that love will radiate from us and will reach and enrich the hearts of those who do not as yet love Him.

Such a state of blessedness will be obtained only in answer to much faith and prayer. Pray that the Father may strengthen your faith. It is only as we see the wonderful power of God and learn to know the love of Christ that we shall be able to love others.

Lord, thank You that I may live in Your everlasting love, even though I do not deserve it. Teach me to radiate this love to those who do not yet know You.

Grace and Love

Grace to all who love our Lord Jesus Christ with an undying love.
EPHESIANS 6:24

I have already emphasized the relationship between faith and love. Today we are going to concentrate on the relationship between grace and love, which are closely linked.

It is by faith that the sinner first experiences the forgiveness of sins. Together with the free grace of our Lord Jesus, the new believer also receives the sincere, fervent love for God and his fellow man. When we approach the throne of grace, it is in answer to the eternal love of God and of the Lamb. Paul calls it an "undying love" (Ephesians 6:24). This is the description of a special quality of love—a love that you can also have within you!

Lord, I beg You to pour out the power of Your love into my heart through the Holy Spirit. Enable me to witness in word and deed that God is love!

We should strive to live in the incorruptible, unbroken love of Jesus as the Father desires of us. If we open our hearts to the Holy Spirit, the pure love of God will enter and we shall find that His grace is exceedingly abundant.

There is no need for you to despair that this love is not meant for you. The wonder-working almighty God is able to do immeasurably more than you ask or imagine, according to the power that is at work in you (see Ephesians 3:20). Therefore, the praise and the glory and the honor belong to Him who sits on the throne. To Him be the glory and the power for ever and ever.

The Secret of Intercession

During this month we shall become aware of the solemn
duty, the great privilege, and the wonderful power of
intercessory prayer.

What a place intercession has in God's plan for the extension
of His kingdom! We will pay particular attention to God's
plan for the strengthening of the life of His children, so that
they may receive His heavenly blessings and impart them to
others. We are also going to look at the special blessings that
the Lord has promised for those who intercede on behalf of
others.

Intercession is not always an easy task, and it demands
sacrifices from us. Therefore, we will give special attention to
how Christians can foster the spirit of devotion and prayer
that is so essential for intercession.

Intercession

Therefore confess your sins to each other and pray for each other so that you may be healed.
JAMES 5:16

What a mystery of glory is locked in prayer! On the one hand, we see God in all His holiness and love and power, waiting and longing to bless man. On the other side we see sinful man, a worm of the dust, bringing down from God, by prayer, the very life and love of heaven to dwell in His heart. How much greater the glory of intercession when you boldly tell God what you desire for others and, through prayer, call down upon them the power of eternal life with all its blessings!

Intercession is the greatest privilege and the greatest joy God's children can experience. It is closely connected to our daily fellowship with God; it is an instrument God uses for His great work to reveal His glory. Because intercession is one of the most powerful means of grace available to the church, the church should therefore seek above everything to cultivate in God's children the power of an unceasing prayerfulness on behalf of the perishing world.

One would expect that believers would realize what strength there is in unity, and how God will certainly avenge His own elect who cry out night and day to Him. Christians should cease looking to worldly sources and, rather, aim at being bound together at the throne of God by an unceasing devotion to Jesus Christ, in continuous prayer for the power of God's Spirit. Only then will the church put on her beautiful garments and receive the power to overcome the world.

Lord, teach me what blessings intercession holds for me, for others, and for the church.

The Opening of the Eyes

And Elisha prayed, "O LORD, open his eyes so he may see"
2 KINGS 6:17

How wonderfully Elisha's prayer for his servant was answered! The young man could suddenly see the mountain covered with horsemen and chariots of fire—a heavenly host sent by God to protect Elisha from the Syrian army arrayed against him. Immediately thereafter, Elisha prayed that the Syrians would be struck with blindness and, so, led into Samaria. There the prophet prayed for the opening of their eyes, only for them to discover that they were prisoners in the hand of the enemy. We can apply Elisha's prayers in a spiritual sense.

First of all, we can ask that our eyes may see the wonderful provision that God has made for His church, in the baptism with the Holy Spirit and with fire. All the powers of heaven are now at our disposal in the service of the kingdom. How little the children of God live in the faith of this heavenly vision—the power of the Holy Spirit on them, with them, and in them, for their strengthening as witnesses for their Lord and His work!

We need to utter Elisha's second prayer, too, that God may open the eyes of those of His children who are unaware of the grip our sinful world has on them. The church must become aware of its weakness in winning souls for Christ and its alarming inability to build up believers for a life of holiness and fruitfulness. Let us pray, therefore, that God may open our eyes to see that the great and fundamental need of the church is the power of the Holy Spirit to work within the church and all its members.

Lord, open my eyes so that I can see myself, my friends, and my church as You see us. Make me aware of the abundant strength and power that You long to bestow on us.

Man's Place in God's Plan

The highest heavens belong to the LORD, but the earth he has given to man.
PSALM 115:16

God created heaven as a dwelling for Himself—perfect, glorious, and most holy. The earth He gave to man as his dwelling; initially it was good, but it needed to be kept and cultivated. The work that God had done was to be continued by man. It was left to man to discover and use all the wonders that were hidden in the earth. What the earth is today, with its cities and habitations, its cornfields and orchards, it owes to man. The work that God began and prepared was continued by man in fulfillment of God's purpose. And so nature teaches us of the wonderful partnership to which God calls man for the carrying out of the work of Creation to its destined end.

This law holds equally good in the kingdom of grace. In this great redemption God has revealed the power of the heavenly life and the spiritual blessings of which heaven is full. But He has entrusted to His people the work of making these blessings known, and making men partakers of them.

What diligence the children of this world show in seeking for the treasures that God has hidden in the earth for their use! Shall not the children of God be equally faithful in seeking for the treasures hidden in heaven, to bring them down in blessing upon the world? It is by the unceasing intercession of God's people that His Kingdom will come, and His will be done on earth as it is in heaven.

Blessed Lord, how wonderful is the place that You have given us to live. Thank You that You trust me to continue with the work that You have started. Bless the work of my hands.

Intercession in the Plan of Redemption

O you who hear prayer, to you all men will come.
PSALM 65:2

When God gave the world He created into the hands of man, it was His plan that Adam should do nothing but with God and through God, and God Himself would do all His work in the world through Adam. When sin entered the world, the whole human race was brought under the curse of sin.

When God made His plan of redemption, His object was to restore man to the place from which he had fallen. God chose His servants who, through the power of intercession, could ask what they would and it would be given to them. When Christ became man, it was as *man*—both on earth and in heaven—that He could intercede for man.

Before Christ left the world, he imparted this right of intercession to His disciples in His great farewell discourse (see John 15–17). Whatever they should ask He would do for them. God's intense longing to bless seems, in some sense, to be graciously limited by His dependence on the intercession that rises from the earth. He seeks to rouse the spirit of intercession that He may be able to bestow His blessings on mankind. God regards intercession as the highest expression of His people's readiness to receive and to yield themselves wholly to the working of His almighty power.

Thank You, Lord, that You gave me the privilege of intercession. Please bestow Your blessings on my family and me.

Christians need to realize their unique power to claim and expect that God will answer their prayers. It is only when God's children begin to see what intercession means in regard to God's kingdom that they will realize how great their responsibility is.

God Seeks Intercessors

He saw that there was no one,
he was appalled that there was no one to intervene.
ISAIAH 59:16

From the earliest ages God had among His people intercessors to whom He listened and through whom He gave deliverance. Here we read of a time when He searched in vain for an intercessor. And He was "appalled that there was no one to intervene." Think of what this means: God could not find even one who loved the people enough to intercede on their behalf, or who had sufficient faith in His power to deliver. If there had been an intercessor He would have given deliverance; without an intercessor His judgments came down (see Isaiah 64:7; Ezekiel 22:30, 31).

Our Father, thank You for the invitation to take part in the extension of Your kingdom by unceasing prayer and intercession.

Of what infinite importance is the place the intercessor holds in the kingdom of God! Is it not indeed a matter of wonder that God should give men such power, and yet that there are so few who know what it is to take hold of His strength and pray down His blessing on the world?

After Christ had taken His place on the throne, the work of the extension of His kingdom was given into the hands of men. Christ lives to pray. God rules the world and His church through the prayers of His children. That God made the extension of His kingdom largely dependent on the faithfulness of His people in prayer is a stupendous mystery and yet an absolute certainty. God calls for intercessors, and in His grace He has made His work dependent on them. He waits for us.

Christ as Intercessor

Therefore he is able to save completely those who come to God through him,
because he always lives to intercede for them.
HEBREWS 7:25

When God saw that there was nobody to intercede, He Himself provided the true intercessor in Jesus Christ, His Son, of whom it had already been said, "He bore the sin of many, and made intercession for the transgressors" (Isaiah 53:12).

In His life on earth, Christ began His work as intercessor. Think of the high-priestly prayer on behalf of His disciples and all those who should through them believe in His name (see John 17). Think of His words to Peter, "But I have prayed for you, Simon, that your faith may not fail" (Luke 22:32). This shows how intensely personal His intercession is. Even on the cross He spoke as intercessor: "Father, forgive them" (Luke 23:34).

Now that Christ is seated at God's right hand, He continually intercedes for us as our great High Priest. But with the difference that He gives His people the power to take part in it. Seven times in His farewell discourse Jesus repeated the assurance that He would do what they asked.

The power of heaven was to be at the disciples' disposal. The grace and power of God waited for their bidding. Through the leading of the Holy Spirit they would know the will of God. They would learn in faith to pray in His name. He would present their petition to the Father, and through His and their united intercession the church would be clothed with the power of the Spirit.

Blessed Redeemer, what wonderful grace that You call me to share in Your intercession! I pray that all believers will be aware of their calling and of the rich blessings that they can bring down on this earth through their prayers in Your name.

The Watchmen

I have posted watchmen on your walls, O Jerusalem;
they will never be silent day or night.
You who call on the LORD, give yourselves no rest, and give him no rest.
ISAIAH 62:6–7

Watchmen are usually placed on the walls of a city to warn rulers of imminent danger. God appoints watchmen not only to warn men, but also to summon Him to come to their aid whenever they feel threatened. Intercessors should not rest, nor give God any rest, until He sends deliverance. In faith they may count upon the assurance that God will answer their prayer: "And will not God bring about justice for his chosen ones, who cry out to him day and night?" (Luke 18:7).

Father, I pray that You will call and equip intercessors, such as You would have. Let the Holy Spirit teach us how to pray.

From all over the world the complaint is heard that the church of Christ, under the influence of the world, is losing its power. There is but little proof of God's presence in the conversion of sinners or the holiness of His people. The great majority of Christians ignore Christ's call to take a part in the extension of His kingdom, and they do not experience the power of the Holy Spirit.

Amid all the discussions as to what can be done to interest young and old in the study of God's Word, one hears but little of the indispensable necessity of the power of the Holy Spirit in the ministry and the membership of the church. One seldom hears that it is because of a lack of prayer that the workings of the Spirit are limited. If ever there was a time when God's elect should cry out to Him day and night, it is now.

Will you not offer yourself to God for this blessed work of intercession, and learn to count it the highest privilege to become a channel through which God's blessing can be brought down to earth?

The School of Intercession

*During the days of Jesus' life on earth, he offered up prayers and petitions
with loud cries and tears to the one who could save him from death,
and he was heard because of his reverent submission.*

HEBREWS 5:7

Christ, as our head, is our intercessor in heaven; we, as the members of His body, are His coworkers on earth. Do not think that it cost Christ nothing to become an intercessor. He could not be our example without sacrifice.

Prayers and petitions offered up with loud cries and tears. This is truly the divine meaning of intercession. Nothing less than this was needed if His sacrifice and prayer were to have power with God. This giving of Himself to save the perishing was a revelation of the spirit that has power to prevail with God.

Do you wish to be a helper and coworker of Jesus Christ and share in His power of intercession? Then you will have to give up your life and its pleasures and distractions to pray for others. Intercession must not be a passing interest; it must become an ever-growing object of intense desire, for which above everything we long for and live. It is a life of consecration and self-sacrifice that will give power to intercession (see Acts 15:20, 20:24; Philippians 2:17; Revelation 12:11).

The more we think of what it means to exercise this power for the glory of God and the salvation of men, the deeper our conviction will grow that it is worth giving up everything to join with Christ in His work of intercession.

Blessed Lord Jesus, teach me to unite with You in prayer to intercede for those whom You purchased with Your blood. Fill our hearts with love, so that the power of the Holy Spirit may be revealed to us.

In the Name of Jesus

Until now you have not asked for anything in my name.
In that day you will ask in my name.
JOHN 16:24, 26

During Christ's life upon earth, the disciples knew very little of the power of prayer. In Gethsemane, Peter and the others utterly failed. They had no conception of what it was to ask in the name of Jesus and receive. The Lord promised that when He was no longer with them, they would be able to pray with power in His name. Anything they asked would be given to them.

Blessed Savior, I pray for the courage to approach the throne of grace with confidence and with the assurance that my prayers will be heard.

Unfortunately, the great majority of Christians know so little of their oneness with Christ Jesus and with the Holy Spirit as the Spirit of prayer that they do not even attempt to claim the wonderful promises Christ made to them. However, when God's children learn to abide in Christ and yield to the teaching of the Spirit, they will begin to realize that their intercession avails much and that God gives the power of His Spirit in answer to prayer.

It is faith in the power of Jesus' name and the privilege to pray in His name that will give us the courage to become intercessors. Jesus sent His disciples out into the world with the promise that everything they asked for in His name would be given to them.

You must learn that unceasing prayer is essential to a healthy spiritual life, and that the power of intercession is an inextricable part of those who yield themselves wholly to Jesus Christ and His service.

The Work of the Spirit

Because you are sons, God sent the Spirit of his Son into our hearts, the Spirit who calls out, "Abba, Father."
GALATIANS 4:6

When Christ prayed in Gethsemane He was ready for any sacrifice, even to the yielding of His life. In this prayer the heart of Him who sits at the right hand of God is revealed to us. We see the wonderful power of intercession that He exercises there, and the power to pour out the Holy Spirit.

The Father has bestowed the Holy Spirit to breathe the very Spirit of His Son into our hearts. Our Lord would have us yield ourselves as wholly to God as He did; to pray like Him that God's love should be made manifest on earth at any cost. As God's love is revealed in His desire for the salvation of souls, so also the desire of Jesus was made plain when He gave Himself for them. And He now asks that His people be filled with that same love, too, so that they may give themselves wholly to the work of intercession and, at any cost, pray down God's love upon the perishing.

And lest anyone should think this is too high and beyond our reach, the Holy Spirit is actually given into our hearts that we may pray in Christ's likeness, in His name, and in His power. Those who yield themselves wholly to the leading of the Holy Spirit will feel the need to pray. They will know that God is working in them.

Now we can understand why Christ gave such unlimited promises to His disciples. They were first going to be filled with the Holy Spirit. The Spirit breathes God's own desire into us and enables us to intercede for others.

Lord Jesus, according to Your example I want to intercede for the world that is perishing. Give Your children the vision of the blessedness and the power which come to those who yield themselves to this high calling.

Christ Our Example

He will divide the spoils with the strong...for he bore the sin of many,
and made intercession for the transgressors.
ISAIAH 53:12

Jesus made intercession for transgressors. He poured out His soul as an offering for sin. Think what moved Him to sacrifice Himself to the very utmost! It was His love for the Father—that God's holiness and His love for others might be manifested, that His children might be partakers of His holiness.

Think of the reward Christ received! As conqueror He is now seated at the right hand of God, with the power of unlimited and assured intercession. And He would see a generation of those whom He could train to share in His great work of intercession.

And what does this mean for us, when we indeed seek to pray for the transgressors? That we, too, yield ourselves wholly to the glory of the holiness and the love of the Father; that we, too, say, "May Your will be done, cost what it may"; that we, too, sacrifice ourselves, even unto death.

Lord, give me the strength to pray unceasingly for others—even for my enemies—cost what it may.

The Lord Jesus has taken us into a partnership with Himself to carry out the great work of intercession. He in heaven and we on earth must have one mind, one aim in life: that we should, out of love for the Father and for the lost, consecrate our lives to intercession for God's blessing. The burning desire of Father and Son for the salvation of souls must be the burning desire of your heart, too.

What an honor! What a blessing! We receive the power to do this work from Him who lives within us and, by His Spirit, pours out His love into our hearts!

God's Will and Ours

May your will be done.
MATTHEW 26:42

It is the prerogative of God that everything in heaven and earth is to be done according to His will and as the fulfillment of His desires. When He made man in His image it was, above all, with the purpose that the desires of man would be in harmony with the desires of God. This is the high honor of being made in the likeness of God—that we are to feel and wish just as God. In human flesh man was to be the embodiment and fulfillment of God's desires.

But God created man with a will of his own and the power to choose and make decisions for himself. And after man had fallen and yielded himself to the will of God's enemy, God in His infinite love set about the great work of winning man back, that man would make the desires of God his own once more. As in God, so in man, desire is the great moving power. And just as man had yielded himself to a life of desire after the things of the earth and the flesh, God had to redeem him into a life of harmony with Himself.

And so the Son came into this world to reproduce the divine desires in His human nature. Jesus yielded Himself to the perfect fulfillment of all that God wished and willed. He was even prepared to be forsaken by God, so that the power that had deceived man might be conquered and deliverance procured. It was in the wonderful and complete harmony between the Father and the Son, when the Son said, "May your will be done," that the great redemption was accomplished.

Lord, it is my desire that Your will may be done in my life. For that reason I am praying for the need of the world and for those who are lost. Bless them, O Lord.

The Privilege of Intercession

You who call on the LORD, give yourselves no rest, and give him no rest till he establishes Jerusalem and makes her the praise of the earth.
ISAIAH 62:6–7

It is an unspeakable grace to be able to pray for others! What a blessing, in close union with Christ, to take part in His great work as intercessor and mingle my prayers with His! What an honor to pray to God in heaven to bestow His blessings on people and to obtain more for them than they could ever imagine. What a privilege, as a steward of the grace of God, to bring to Him the state of the church of individual souls, of ministers of the Word, of workers in His kingdom, and plead on their behalf till He entrusts me with the answer!

What a blessing it is, in union with other children of God, to strive together in prayer until the victory is gained over difficulties here on earth and over the powers of darkness. God wants to use you as intercessor to receive and dispense His heavenly blessings and the power of His Holy Spirit to others. It is the love of Jesus Himself that urges you to pray for others.

Too long have we thought of prayer as a means of supplying for our own needs. May God help you to see what place intercession takes in His divine counsel and in the service of His kingdom. There is no greater honor or glory on earth than the privilege of intercession.

Thank You, Lord, for the privilege that I may intercede for others. Let Your love and blessings flow down to earth and fill the hearts of all Your children.

The Place of Prayer

They all joined together constantly in prayer, along with the women.
ACTS 1:14

The last words that Christ spoke before He left the world contain the four basic principles that mark His church: they are united in unceasing prayerfulness; they are filled with the power of the Holy Spirit; they are witnesses for the living Christ; they carry a message for all human beings, from Jerusalem to the ends of the world (see Acts 1:4–8). Such are the marks of the true gospel, of true ministry, and of the true church of the New Testament. Such is the church that went out to conquer the world.

When Christ ascended to heaven, the disciples were commanded to continue with one accord in prayer and supplication. They were to be bound together by the love and Spirit of Christ into one body. That is what gave them their wonderful power in heaven with God and on earth with men.

Their first duty was to wait in united prayer for the power of the Holy Spirit as endowment from on high for their task as witnesses to the ends of the earth. A praying church, a Spirit-filled church, a witnessing church, with the entire world as its sphere and aim—such is the church of Jesus Christ.

As long as the church maintained this character, it had the power to conquer. But alas, under the influence of the sinful world, it lost its power. Unfaithful in prayer, weak in the working of the Spirit, its witness to Christ a mere formality, and unfaithful to its worldwide mission—such are the marks of a powerless church.

Lord, have mercy on Your church. Make us faithful in our mission and give us the power to conquer the world, so that Your name may be glorified.

Paul as Intercessor

For this reason I kneel before the Father. I pray that…he may strengthen
you with power through his Spirit in your inner being.
EPHESIANS 3:14, 16

We think of Paul as the great missionary, the great preacher, the great writer, and the great apostle. We do not often think of him as an intercessor, who sought and obtained by his supplication the power that rested upon all his other activities and brought down blessing on the churches that he served.

Paul wrote to the churches in his charge, "Night and day we pray most earnestly" (1 Thessalonians 3:10). He constantly remembered them in his prayers (see Romans 1:9). He prayed for them with joy (see Philippians 1:4). He prayed for them unceasingly (see Colossians 1:9, 2:1). Day and night he cried out to God in his intercession for them, that the light and the power of the Holy Spirit might be in them.

Lord, teach me
how to pray.
Thank You that
the Holy Spirit
intercedes for me
at Your throne
of grace.

As earnestly as he believed in the power of his intercession for them, he also believed in the churches' intercession for him. He asked them, "Join me in my struggle by praying to God for me" (Romans 15:30). "Be alert and always keep on praying for all the saints" (Ephesians 6:18). "I know that through your prayers…what has happened to me will turn out for my deliverance" (Philippians 1:19).

The relationship among the members of the church depends on united and unceasing prayer. This relationship is spiritual and can only be maintained by unceasing prayer. When ministers and their flocks fully understand this truth, the church will again become like the first church on the day of Pentecost.

Intercession for Workers

"The harvest is plentiful but the workers are few. Ask the Lord of the harvest,
therefore, to send out workers into his harvest field."
MATTHEW 9:37–38

At first the disciples understood very little of what these words meant. Christ gave them as a seed-thought to be lodged in their hearts for later use. At Pentecost, however, they could see how the ten days of united, unceasing prayer brought the blessing of more workers as fruit of the Spirit's outpouring. However few the workers, prayer is the best, the surest, and the only means of supplying the need.

Hudson Taylor, a missionary to China, initially asked God for eighteen missionaries, two for every province. God granted his request. When there were two hundred missionaries, a conference was held. There was a strong feeling that even more missionaries were needed to reach more districts. After much prayer they felt free to ask God to give them an additional hundred workers within a year. They agreed to continue in prayer day by day throughout the year. At the end of that year they had found a hundred suitable men and women and the funds to meet their expenses.

Churches complain of the lack of workers and of funds to meet the need of the world. Does not Christ's voice call us to the united, unceasing prayer of the first disciples? God is faithful, by the power of His Spirit, to supply our every need. Let the church kneel together in prayer and supplication. God hears prayer.

Lord, please forgive me my disobedience and help me to truly believe in the power of prayer. Teach me to be a faithful intercessor.

Intercession for Souls

And you, O Israelites, will be gathered up one by one.
ISAIAH 27:12

In the human body every member has its appointed place. This is also true of society and the church, where any work must always aim at the welfare and the highest perfection of the whole, through the cooperation of every individual member.

People often think that the salvation of mankind is the work of the minister, whereas he generally only deals with the crowd and very seldom reaches the individual. This is the cause of a twofold evil: The individual believer does not understand that it is necessary for him to witness to those around him—for the nourishment and the strengthening of his own spiritual life, as well as for the gathering of souls—while unconverted souls suffer unspeakable loss because believers do not speak to them about Christ.

Thank You, Lord, that I can pray not only for those who are nearest to me, but also for those who do not yet know You.

When will Christians learn that prayer is an indispensable condition for what God wants to do on the earth? Intercession is the way by which people are converted. Without the power of the Holy Spirit given in answer to prayer, all our efforts are in vain. When spiritual leaders and believers unite in a covenant of prayer and testimony, the church will again flourish.

What can we do to stir up the spirit of intercession? Start praying for a few individuals. Pray for your children, for your relatives and friends, and for all with whom God brings you into contact. If you feel that you do not have the power to intercede, let the discovery humble you and drive you to the mercy seat. God wants every redeemed child of His to intercede for those who do not know Him. It is the vital breath of Christian life.

Intercession for Leaders

Finally, brothers, pray for us that the message of the Lord
may spread rapidly and be honored.
2 THESSALONIANS 3:1

These words suggest that Paul believed the prayers of Christians strengthened him in his work. He was deeply impressed by the unity of the body of Christ, the interdependence of each member, and by the life that flowed through the whole body. He sought to rouse Christians, both for their own sakes and for his, and for the sake of the kingdom of God, with his call, "Be alert and always keep on praying for all the saints" (Ephesians 6:18).

The church depends upon the ministry more than we will ever realize. The calling of the minister as God's steward and as ambassador to reconcile people with God is so important that unfaithfulness or inefficiency brings a terrible blight on the church that he serves. If Paul, after having preached for twenty years in the power of God, still needed the prayer of the church, how much more does the ministry in our day need it?

The minister needs the prayers of his people. He has a right to it. He is, in truth, dependent on it. It is his task to train Christians for the work of intercession on behalf of the church and the world—and for himself. Let all intercessors who are seeking to enter more deeply into their blessed work give a larger place to the ministry, whether of their own church or of other churches.

Let them continue praying for church leaders that they may be men of power, men of prayer, and filled with the Holy Spirit. Pray for the ministry!

Our Father, I humbly pray for the spiritual leaders of our church and of all the churches all over the world. Fill them with the power of Your Holy Spirit for their service in the kingdom.

Prayer for All Saints

And pray in the Spirit on all occasions with all kinds of prayers and requests.
With this in mind, be alert and always keep on praying for all the saints.
EPHESIANS 6:18

Notice how Paul repeats certain phrases in the intensity of his desire to reach the hearts of his readers: *On all occasions. Keep on praying. For all the saints.*

Paul felt deeply for the unity of the body of Christ. He was convinced that unity could only be reached by the exercise of love and prayer. Therefore, he pleaded with the believers at Ephesus to unceasingly and fervently pray for all saints, not only in their immediate circle but in all the churches all over the world.

Unity is strength. As we exercise this power of intercession with all perseverance, we shall be delivered from the self, with all its feeble prayers, and lifted up to that enlargement of heart in which the love of Christ can flow freely and fully through us.

Father, in my mind's eye I see a host of believers whom I wish to dedicate to You. Please bless them in the name of Jesus.

When believers pray, they are often occupied with themselves and with what God must do for them. Let us realize that we have here a call to every believer to give himself without ceasing to the exercise of love and prayer. It is when we forget ourselves and pray for God's blessing on others that the church will be equipped to make Christ known to every creature.

Pray for God's children and for His church. Pray for the work in which they are engaged, or ought to be. Pray in all seasons in the Spirit for all God's saints. There is no greater blessing than that of abiding communion with God. And there is no way that leads to the enjoyment of this more surely than the life of intercession for which these words of Paul appeal so pleadingly.

Missionary Intercession

*So after they had fasted and prayed,
they placed their hands on them and sent them off.*
ACTS 13:3

The supreme question of foreign missions is how to multiply the number of Christians who will individually and collectively pray for the conversion and transformation of people. Every other consideration and plan is secondary to that of wielding the forces of prayer.

We may take it for granted that those who love this work and bear it upon their hearts will follow the scriptural injunction to pray unceasingly for its triumph. To them not only the morning watch and the hours of stated devotion, but all times and seasons will witness an attitude of intercession that refuses to let God go until He crowns His workers with victory.

Pray for the missionaries and other spiritual leaders that the life of Christ in them may be clear and strong, and that they may be people of prayer and filled with love in whom the power of the spiritual life is revealed.

Pray for all the people of the world who do not know God, that they may know the glory of God's mystery and that Christ in them is the hope of glory.

Pray that the teaching of God's Word may be in power. Pray, above all, for the church of Christ, that it may be lifted out of its indifference, and that every believer may be brought to understand that the one object of his life is to do his share in the coming of God's kingdom on earth.

Thank You, Lord, that I can in such an intimate and personal way be involved in the coming of Your kingdom in all its glory.

The Grace of Intercession

Devote yourselves to prayer, being watchful and thankful.
And pray for us, too, that God may open a door for our message.
COLOSSIANS 4:2–3

There is nothing that can bring us nearer to God, and lead us deeper into His love, than the work of intercession. There is nothing that can give us a deeper experience of the likeness of God than the power of pouring out our hearts into the bosom of God, in prayer for everyone around us. There is nothing that can so closely link us to Jesus Christ as the yielding of our lives to the work of bringing the great redemption into the hearts and lives of our fellow men.

There is nothing through which we shall know more of the powerful working of the Holy Spirit than through prayer. There is nothing that can so help us to prove the power and the trustworthiness of God's Word as when we reach out in intercession to the multitudes.

Thank You, Father, for the privilege to pray for others.

There is nothing that will do more for the unity of the body of Christ than daily and continued fellowship with God's children in the persistent plea for God's grace.

When we open our hearts to God and pray for His blessing, He is glorified and we reach our highest purpose. In this way we are praying for the coming of God's kingdom.

In heaven, Christ lives to pray. His whole intercourse with His Father is prayer—an asking and receiving of the fullness of the Spirit for His people. God delights in nothing so much as in prayer. We must believe that the highest blessings of heaven will be unfolded to us as we pray more.

United Intercession

There is one body and one Spirit.
EPHESIANS 4:4

Our own bodies teach us how essential it is for one's health and strength that every member of the body should take its full share in seeking the welfare of the whole. Even more so in the body of Christ. There are many who look upon salvation only in regard to their own happiness. Others know that they do not live for themselves and truly pray and work to make others share in their happiness. But they do not yet understand that they have a calling to intercede for the whole body of Christ.

Yet it is only when intercession for the whole church, by the whole church, ascends to God's throne that the Spirit of unity and of power can have its full sway. The desire that has been awakened for closer union between the different branches of the church is cause for thanksgiving. And yet the difficulties are so great and, in the case of different nationalities of the world, so apparently insuperable, that the thought of a united church on earth appears beyond reach.

Let us thank God that there is a unity in Christ Jesus deeper and stronger than any visible manifestation could be, and that despite our differences, the spirit of intercession can help us to achieve true unity—a means to obtain divine strength and blessing in the service of the kingdom.

When believers learn what their calling as a royal priesthood really means, they realize that God is not confined in His love or promises to their limited spheres of labor. He invites them to open up their hearts and, like Christ, pray for all those who believe or can be brought to believe.

Lord, I realize anew what great potential is locked up in united and unceasing prayer. Help me to pray faithfully.

Unceasing Intercession

Pray continually.
1 THESSALONIANS 5:17

Often Christians think only of their own personal safety in their relationship with God—they want only pardon for their sin and to live such a life as may secure their entrance into heaven.

The Bible, however, has a different norm for salvation: Christians should yield themselves wholly to the glorious God who has redeemed them, to delight in serving Him in whose fellowship heaven has already begun.

To the former Christians the command to "pray continually" is simply a needless and impossible life of perfection; they can get to heaven without it. To the true believer, however, it holds the promise of the highest happiness, of a life crowned by all the blessings that can be brought down on souls through intercession.

Father, help me to be a faithful steward in the service of Your kingdom. Give me the strength to surrender myself wholly to You.

Pray continually. In faith you must accept these words as a promise of what God's Spirit will work in you, of how close and intimate your relationship with Jesus could be, and how you could grow to be more and more like Him as He intercedes for you at the right hand of God.

Christ said, "I in them and you in me" (John 17:23). Believe that Christ, the interceding high priest, will work and pray in you just as the Father has worked in Him. Believe also that nothing can be compared with the privilege of being God's priests—to be in His holy presence without intermission and to bring the burden of others to His throne. And finally to receive from His hand the power and blessing to dispense to others.

The Link Between Heaven and Earth

"Your will be done on earth as it is in heaven."
MATTHEW 6:10

How can God's will be done on this earth, with all its sin and misery and people who have no knowledge of the one true God? Where many people are only Christians in name, utterly indifferent to God's claims and estranged from His holiness and love? How is it ever to come true?

Only through the prayers of God's children will the words "on earth as it is in heaven" be fulfilled. Our Lord teaches us to pray for it. Intercession is to be the great link between heaven and earth. The intercession of the Son began on earth, when Christ said that He had come to do the will of His Father. It continued in heaven and was carried on by His redeemed followers on earth. In Gethsemane, Christ prayed that God's will be done, and this is also what His children pray.

Every prayer of a parent for a child, of a believer for the saving of the lost, or for more grace to those who have been saved, is part of the great unceasing cry rising up day and night from the earth: "Your will be done on earth as it is in heaven!"

However, when God's children learn to pray not only for their immediate circles and interests, but for the entire world, their united supplication will have power with God and hasten the day when the prayer "Your will be done on earth as it is in heaven" will come true. The whole earth filled with the glory of God! Yield yourself to God to live with this prayer:

Our Father in heaven, hallowed be Your name. Your kingdom come, Your will be done on earth as it is in heaven.

The Fulfillment of God's Desires

For the LORD has chosen Zion, he has desired it for his dwelling:
"This is my resting place for ever and ever."
PSALM 132:13–14

Here you have the one great desire of God that moved Him to do His work of redemption: His heart longed to dwell with man. To Moses he said, "Have them make a sanctuary for me, and I will dwell among them" (Exodus 25:8). This should awaken in you the desire to encourage others to yield themselves to God so that He may dwell in them.

What an honor! What a high calling, to count my worldly business as secondary, and to find my delight in winning souls in whom God may find a dwelling! I do this through faithful intercession, asking God to pour out His Holy Spirit on the people around me. It is, after all, the will of the Father that His children prepare a dwelling for Him. This will only happen in answer to the intercession of God's children.

David said, "I will allow no sleep to my eyes, no slumber to my eyelids, till I find a place for the LORD, a dwelling for the Mighty One of Jacob" (Psalm 132:4–5). Then shall not we, to whom it has been revealed what that indwelling of God may be, give our lives for the fulfillment of His heart's desire?

Let us begin to pray as never before—for our children, for the souls around us, and for the entire world. And that not only because we love them, but also especially because God longs for them. He wants to give us the honor of serving as channels through which His blessing can flow to others.

Thank You, God, that You have opened Your heart for me to know Your desires. Thank You for using me to reach others with Your blessings.

The Fulfillment of Man's Desire

Delight yourself in the LORD and he will give you the desires of your heart.
PSALM 37:4

God is an ever-flowing fountain out of which streams the love and desire to make His creatures partakers of all the holiness and the glory there is in Himself. This desire for the salvation of souls is indeed God's perfect will, His highest glory. He shares this with His children who are prepared to yield themselves to Him. In this we are the likeness and image of God: to have a heart in which His love takes complete possession and leads us to find our highest joy in loving as He does.

Delight yourself in the Lord, and in His life of love, and He will give you the desires of your heart. Count upon it that your desire, rising up to heaven, will be answered. If we delight in what God delights in, we may be sure that God inspires our prayers and they will be answered. Then our prayer becomes, "Your desire, my Father, is mine. Your holy will of love is my will, too."

In fellowship with God we receive the courage, with all our heart and strength, to bring others to God with an ever-growing confidence that our prayers will be heard. When we reach out to others in love, we shall know that God wants to bless us and wants to give us the desire of our heart, because our desire is also His desire.

We then become, in the highest sense of the word, coworkers in the service of God. Our prayer becomes part of God's divine plan of salvation. And we learn to find our happiness in losing ourselves to save others.

Father, it is with confidence that I bring the need of the world to You. Empower me to reach out to others and to convey Your love to them.

My Great Desire

One thing I ask of the LORD, this is what I seek:
that I may dwell in the house of the LORD all the days of my life,
to gaze upon the beauty of the LORD and to seek him in his temple.

PSALM 27:4

When God's desire becomes our desire, these words also become our words: to dwell in His house, to gaze upon His beauty, and to seek Him in His temple. The more we realize God's desire to give rest and peace in our heart, and the more our desire is quickened to dwell with Him and behold His beauty, the more the spirit of intercession will grow upon us to claim all that God has promised in His New Covenant.

We will start thinking more of our church and country, home and school. We will think of saved ones and their need, or the unsaved and the dangers that threaten them. We will think of God's desire to find His home and His rest in the hearts of men. All thoughts of our weakness and unworthiness will be swallowed up in the wonderful assurance that He gave to His children: "This is my resting place for ever and ever; here I will sit enthroned, for I have desired it" (Psalm 132:14).

Lord, I pray that I might be so filled with the Holy Spirit that your desires become mine, and that this would be visible in my intercession for others.

As you begin to understand how high your calling is, you will realize how indispensable unceasing prayer is to fulfill God's purpose. Then you will devote your life to a closer walk with God, to an unceasing waiting upon Him, and to be a living testimony to others of what God will do in them. It is a divine partnership in which God commits the fulfillment of His desires to your keeping.

Day and Night

"And will not God bring about justice for his chosen ones,
who cry out to him day and night?
Will he keep putting them off?"

LUKE 18:7

When Nehemiah heard of the destruction of Jerusalem, he cried out to God, "Hear the prayer your servant is praying before you day and night" (Nehemiah 1:6). Of the watchmen posted on the walls of Jerusalem, God said, "They will never be silent day or night" (Isaiah 62:6). And Paul wrote, "Night and day we pray most earnestly" (1 Thessalonians 3:10).

Is such around-the-clock prayer really needed or even possible? Most assuredly. That is, when the heart is so entirely possessed by God's desire that it cannot rest until the desire has been fulfilled.

When a child of God gets a vision of the need of the church and of the world; a vision of the divine redemption that God has promised in the outpouring of His love to our hearts; a vision of the power of true intercession to bring down heavenly blessing; a vision of the honor of being allowed to take part in that work—it is quite natural that He would regard the work as intercessor the most heavenly thing on earth.

Let us learn from David, who said, "Zeal for your house consumes me" (Psalm 69:9). Christ, of whom these words were so intensely true, regarded nothing as important as to satisfy God's desire to find a dwelling place in the heart of man. May our hearts be so influenced by these divine truths that we will yield ourselves fully to Christ, and may our longing to satisfy the heart of God become the most important object of our life.

Lord Jesus, thank You that through the powerful working of Your Holy Spirit, I can also make Your vision mine. Let it become visible in everything I do.

The High Priest Prays

Because Jesus lives forever, he has a permanent priesthood.
Therefore he is able to save completely those who come to God through him,
because he always lives to intercede for them.
H E B R E W S   7 : 2 4 – 2 5

There was a great difference between the high priest and the priests of Israel. Only the high priest had access to the Holiest of All. He bore on his forehead the golden crown and, by his intercession on the great Day of Atonement, bore the sins of the people. The priests brought the daily sacrifices, stood before the Lord, and then came out to bless the people.

Despite the differences in their responsibilities, there was great unity between the high priest and the priests. Together they formed one body and shared the power to appear before God to receive and dispense His blessing to His people.

Lord, thank You for the responsibility You placed upon me. I feel unworthy, but through the power of the Holy Spirit, I will do as You ask me.

It is even so with our great High Priest. Jesus alone has the power through His unceasing intercession to obtain from the Father that which His people need. The blessing that He obtains from His Father, He gives to His people who pray. They dispense it to the people among whom God has placed them as His witnesses and representatives.

As long as Christians think only of their own salvation and of a life that will make that salvation secure, they will never understand the mystery of the power of intercession to which they are called. But once they realize that salvation means a powerful fellowship with Jesus Christ, an actual sharing of His life dwelling and working in us, we will find it our greatest joy to live, work, think, and will as a royal priesthood.

A Royal Priesthood

*Call to me and I will answer you and tell you
great and unsearchable things you do not know.*

JEREMIAH 33:3

God has an infinite willingness to bless. His very nature is a pledge of it. He delights in mercy. He waits to be gracious. His promises and the experience of His saints assure us of it. Why then does the blessing so often tarry?

In creating man with a free will, and making him a partner in the rule of the earth, God limited Himself. He made Himself dependent on what man would do. Man by his prayer determines the measure of God's blessing.

Think how disappointed God is when His children do not pray, or pray but little. The fading life of the church, the lack of the power of the Holy Spirit for conversion and holiness, can often be ascribed to the lack of prayer.

Lord, I am prepared to be an intercessor in Your strength.

And yet God has blessed His people according to the measure of their faith and zeal. This does not mean that we can now sit back and regard His blessing as a sign of approval. We should rather ask, "If this is how He blesses our feeble efforts and prayers, how much more would He do if we were to yield ourselves wholly to a life of intercession?"

What a call to penitence and confession that our lack of consecration has kept back God's blessing from the world! He was ready to save sinners, but we were not willing for the sacrifice of a wholehearted devotion to Christ and His service.

Take your place before His throne as intercessor. Think of your holy calling as a member of the royal priesthood. Always remember to intercede for others according to the example set by Jesus Christ.

A Divine Reality

Another angel, who had a golden censer, came and stood at the altar.
He was given much incense to offer, with the prayers of all the saints,
on the golden altar before the throne.

REVELATION 8:3

The thoughts that we discussed in this month's daily readings are a grave indictment of the subordinate place given to intercession in the teaching and practice of today's church by its leaders and members.

Intercession is, by amazing grace, an essential element in God's redeeming purpose—so much so that without it the failure of its accomplishment may lie at our door. Christ's intercession in heaven is essential to the carrying out of the work He began on earth, but He calls for the intercession of the saints in the attainment of His object.

Lord, I pray that the church will awake and start to pray without ceasing. Help us to know and fulfill our calling

Just as the reconciliation was dependent on Christ's doing His part, so intercession is needed for the completion of the work that the church was called to do.

Intercession is indeed a divine reality. Without it, the church loses the joy and the power of the Spirit for achieving great things for God. Without these things, the command to preach the gospel to every creature can never be carried out. Without them, there is no power for the church to recover from her sickly, feeble life and conquer the world. In the life of the believer, the minister, or the church member, there can be no entrance into the abundant life and joy of daily fellowship with God except if He takes His place among God's elect—the watchmen who cry to Him day and night.

The Secret of Inspiration

This month's daily readings draw inspiration from a book by William Law entitled *A Humble, Earnest and Affectionate Address to the Clergy*. What Law wrote about the three great articles of our faith—the Spirit of God, the Spirit of love, and the Spirit of prayer—is so important that I want to share it with you.

Law explains to us the way God inspires and equips us for our calling. He unfolds the great truth that the Holy Spirit does not occasionally dwell or work in the Christian. By His immediate and continual inspiration He is ever working toward bringing the Christian to the full knowledge and experience of the life of God.

He also points out how we have fallen into a life of such entire and utter selfishness and worldliness that nothing but the denial and the death of the self can prepare us for the love with which God, by His Holy Spirit, wants to fill us. Law says that perpetual inspiration is as necessary to a life of holiness as perpetual respiration of the air is necessary to human life.

My humble, loving prayer is that this month God will teach you the threefold blessing of the Spirit of God, the Spirit of love, and the Spirit of prayer.

One Thing Needed

From the first announcement I have not spoken in secret;
at the time it happens, I am there.
And now the Sovereign LORD has sent me with his Spirit.
ISAIAH 48:16

There is but one thing necessary that will make us rise from our fallen state to again become real partakers of the divine nature as we were at our creation. That one thing is the Spirit of God brought again to His first power of life in us.

Holy Spirit of God, thank You that through Your power I can become a child of God and a partaker of the divine nature.

Everything else, however glorious and divine in outward appearance, everything that churches or reformations may do for us, is dead and helpless if it is not the work of the Spirit of God breathing and living in it. The end and design of all that is written in Scripture is to call us back from the spirit of Satan, the flesh, and the world, to full dependence on and obedience to the Spirit of God.

The Spirit of God longs to pour out His power in us as before. All love and delight in Scripture, which is merely human, is but the self-love of the fallen Adam. This nature cannot change without the inspiration of the Holy Spirit. Only the Holy Spirit can bring forth a true, divine love. For if it is true that no man can call Jesus "Lord" but by the Holy Ghost, it must be equally true that no one can become like Christ in nature, or power, or goodness, unless he is led and governed by the Holy Spirit.

God's one desire is that the Holy Spirit should have the place in us that He had in Adam before the Fall. The only thing that gives value to our religion is that it is the immediate work of the Spirit of God.

Total Dependence

*Every good and perfect gift is from above,
coming down from the Father.*
JAMES 1:17

God is goodness and virtue. This is His nature and is an inseparable part of Him. Everything that can be regarded as goodness and virtue in man is nothing but the goodness of God manifested in His creature—inextricably part of the relationship between God and His creature.

If all that is glorious and good in man is a reflection of the glory and goodness of God dwelling in Him, it is clear that the true nature of all true religion is to give to the Father what belongs to Him. It is the continual acknowledging that all that man is and has, is in and from God alone.

The one characteristic that forms the basis of true religion is total dependence on God and the acceptance that all that is good comes from the Father.

The angels are ever abiding flames of pure love, always ascending up to and uniting with God, because the glory, the love, and goodness of God alone, are all that they see and know, either within or without themselves. Their adoration in spirit and in truth never ceases, because they never cease to acknowledge the omnipotence of God.

Nothing can be good of religion without the power and presence of God essentially living and working in it.

Father, I thank You for the privilege of having a close relationship with You. I am totally dependent on You and realize that all that I am and have come from You alone. Give me the strength through Your Holy Spirit to serve You faithfully.

Continual Inspiration

We love because he first loved us.
1 JOHN 4:19

True religion is the essential union and communion of the spirit of the creature with the Spirit of the Creator. Divine inspiration is also an inherent part of religion.

Self-love, self-esteem, self-seeking, and living wholly to self, is part of natural man. The natural man is not capable of doing more unless he is touched by the Word of God—the Spirit and the inspiration of God—that leads him to think about God and develop heavenly desires in his spirit.

No man can reach God with his love, or have union with Him by it. Only he who is inspired by the Spirit of love—the same love with which God Himself has loved from all eternity—will find God. No heavenly being can begin a new kind of love to God, or love Him, unless the Holy Spirit of love lives within him.

Divine love is the only love that can draw people to God. Without the eternal Spirit of love, they have no power of believing in Him or adoring Him. Therefore, the continual inspiration of the Holy Spirit is the only possible ground for our unceasing love of God.

This continual inspiration of God as our only power of goodness is our birthright. We must experience it if we are to live out God's will. The Holy Spirit is waiting to fill our lives with the love of God.

Thank You, Father, that I can cherish something of Your glorious image in me. Help me to radiate it to a world that is longing for salvation.

The Spirit of God in Adam

The LORD God formed the man from the dust of the ground and breathed into his nostrils the breath of life, and the man became a living being.
GENESIS 2:7

Divine inspiration was part of the Creation of man. Only when the Spirit of the triune God breathed into Adam did he become a holy creature in the image and likeness of God to serve as God's representative on earth.

Then came the Fall of man. The true and abundant life that God had breathed into Adam was lost after his Fall. God had a plan to restore man to his original state when he felt free to walk confidently with God in the Garden, but inspiration was necessary to make fallen man alive to God again, just as it was to first create him after the image of God. Thus the completion of man's redemption would require the work of God's Spirit in man.

Life cannot continue in the goodness of its first created or redeemed state unless under the influence of the Holy Spirit, which at first created and then redeemed it. Because we can do nothing without Christ, we ought to believe, expect, wait for, and depend upon His operation in everything that we do, through His Spirit dwelling in us.

Do you believe in the immediate, continual work of God's Holy Spirit in you? Let us pause to consider how little this inspiration of the Holy Spirit in the heart of God's child is believed or accepted. And let us, from the very beginning of our readings, make this the one object of our desire and prayer: the full experience of what the Holy Spirit is meant to be to us.

Thank you, Lord, for the working of the Holy Spirit in me that inspires me to a new life with God.

Ministration of the Spirit

Flesh gives birth to flesh, but the Spirit gives birth to spirit.
JOHN 3:6

A natural life cannot subsist unless it is immediately and continually under the working power of that root or source from which it sprang. Hence, nothing but obedience to the Spirit, faith in Him, and continual inspiration from Him can possibly keep men from sin. The truth and perfection of the gospel state could not show itself until it became a ministration of the Holy Spirit, or a kingdom controlled by the Spirit of God.

When Christ told His disciples that it would be better for them if He left, He taught them the need of their present condition and to joyfully expect the coming of a higher and more blessed state. This, however, could only happen after Christ's departure when He gave His Holy Spirit to live within them. His outward teaching in human language was changed into the inspiration and operation of His spirit in their souls.

Thank You, Lord, for Your Spirit who works within me a new life and prepares me for the service of Your kingdom.

Here, two fundamental truths are emphasized. First, that the truth and perfection of the gospel state could not take place till Christ was glorified and the continual, immediate ministration of His Spirit carried man into a real possession and enjoyment of a divine life.

Second, that no man can have any true and real knowledge of the spiritual blessings of Christ's redemption or live an inspired life without the indwelling Spirit revealing the mysteries of a redeeming Christ to them.

The immediate and continual inspiration of the Holy Spirit is absolutely needed in your life. God promised you that and He makes it possible for you.

Death and Life in Christ

The Spirit of Christ in them...predicted the sufferings
of Christ and the glories that would follow.
1 PETER 1:11

Why could not the apostles, who had been eyewitnesses to the suffering of Christ, testify with their human apprehension the truth of such things? Why did they have to wait till they were baptized with fire and born again of the Spirit? It is because the mysteries of Christ's life are revealed to us by the Spirit of God in our souls. Every man, however able in all kinds of human literature, remains a stranger to the mysteries of the gospel until Christ Himself reveals it to Him. The work of the Spirit consists in altering that which is the most radical in the soul, bringing forth a new spiritual death and a new spiritual life. It must therefore be true that no one can know or believe the mysteries of Christ's redeeming power except by an inner conviction.

Our faith is focused on this Christ who can only be our Savior through the work of the Holy Spirit. Then the words of Christ and His apostles become like a consuming fire. The flame of love is kindled and the believer longs for fellowship with Christ and the Holy Spirit.

Only when the Spirit of Christ is in your life can you become more like Him in everything He taught. We need to remember that the great work of the Holy Spirit is to reveal Christ in us. Not to the mind as a matter of knowledge, but in the heart and life, communicating to us the very death and life of our Lord. It is thus that Christ is formed in us, dwells in us, and works in us and through us all that is well pleasing to the Father. Therein lies the true secret of the Christian life.

Lord, every time I become quiet before You, I pray that the Holy Spirit will reveal more of Your mystery to me.

Humility

For the foolishness of God is wiser than man's wisdom,
and the weakness of God is stronger than man's strength.
1 CORINTHIANS 1:25

It is sad that human learning and wisdom gradually has become more important to the church than total dependence on the Holy Spirit. And with that learning has come, as a natural consequence, the exaltation of self instead of humility and total dependence on the teaching of the Spirit. Since the Fall of Adam, man's intellectual faculties have been in a much worse state than his natural animal appetites, and therefore have needed a much greater self-denial. To realize this we need only know two things.

First, that salvation also means being saved from ourselves, and from that which we are by nature. Second, that our salvation could only be achieved by the humility of God in human form. Therefore, the condition of this Savior to fallen man is this, "If anyone would come after me, he must deny himself and take up his cross daily and follow me" (Luke 9:23).

Self is the whole evil of fallen nature. All the vices of fallen men have their birth and power in the atheism and idolatry of self, for self is both atheist and idolater. It is atheist because it has rejected God; it is idolater because it is its own idol. On the other hand, all the virtues of the heavenly life are the virtues of humility.

In the life of faith, humility has a far greater place than we think. It leads us to know our absolute and entire impotence to do any good in our own strength. Humility leads us to Jesus Christ.

Lord, thank You for everything that You have prepared for me and worked within me in answer to my faith in You.

The Kingdom of Heaven

The Word became flesh and made his dwelling among us.
JOHN 1:14

The one Light and Spirit, which was there from all eternity, before angels or any heavenly beings were created, is the only light and spirit by which angels or men can ever have union or communion with God. Light and spirit—that must be reborn in man for the sake of his redemption.

The kingdom of heaven came to live among men. It asks nothing more from man but a dull denial of himself. The entire New Testament is proof of this: No one can enter the kingdom of God, but by being born in the Spirit; no one can continue to be alive in it but by being led by the Spirit. And not a thought, or desire, or action can be allowed to have any part in it, unless it is a fruit of the Spirit.

"Your kingdom come, your will be done on earth as it is in heaven" (Matthew 6:10). Where can God's kingdom be but where every other power but His is driven out of it? How can His will be done but where the Spirit that wills in God also wills it within the creature?

What does it mean that the kingdom of God comes to our hearts? To be delivered from our own natural spirit in Adam and the world. It is the birthright of the children of God's kingdom. And then through our lives only to say, and do, what the Spirit of God works within us. The kingdom of God means that God rules in our hearts just as He rules in the kingdom of heaven.

Thank You, Lord, that I may be a member of Your kingdom. Enable me through Your Holy Spirit to live a life worthy of this privilege.

The Nature of Love

For God did not give us a spirit of timidity,
but a spirit of power, of love and of self-discipline.
2 TIMOTHY 1:7

The spirit of love has its origin in God. God is the eternal will to goodness. This was the case long before anything was brought forth by Him, or out of Him.

God is the eternal, immutable God who, from eternity to eternity, has not changed. He can be neither more nor less, but an eternal will to all the goodness that is in Him and can come from Him. As certainly as He created everything, so certainly does He bless everything. He can give nothing but blessing, goodness, and happiness from Himself because he has in Himself nothing else to give.

This is the ground and origin of the Spirit of love in man: a desire for all that is good. It must be a will to all goodness, and man does not have the Spirit of love till he has this will to all goodness at all times and on all occasions. He may indeed do many works of love, and even delight in them, but the Spirit of love is not in him till he lives freely, willingly, and universally according to it. The Spirit of love knows no difference of time, place, or person; but whether He gives or forgives, bears or forbears, He is equally doing its own delightful work. For the Spirit of love is His own blessing and happiness, because He is the truth and the reality of God in the soul.

The infinitely perfect God is an unchangeable will to all goodness. Therefore, everyone who is led by anything else but goodness is a corrupt and unhappy human being.

Lord, teach us that the love with which You promised by Your Holy Spirit to fill our hearts, is as glorious and holy as Your love is for us.

The Necessity of Love

I urge you, brothers, by our Lord Jesus Christ and by the love of the Spirit,
to join me in my struggle by praying to God for me.
ROMANS 15:30

No one can be a child of God if the goodness of God is not in him. Nor can anyone have communion with God unless his life radiates the love of the Spirit. This is the most important bond between God and His children.

As the will to all goodness is the whole nature of God, so it must be the whole nature of every service or religion that can be acceptable to Him. God can delight in nothing but His own will, and His own Spirit, because all goodness is included therein. Everybody who follows his own will or his own spirit, forsakes the will to all goodness.

The necessity, therefore, of the Spirit of love is what God Himself cannot dispense within man, any more than He can deny Himself or act contrary to His own holy being. But as it was His will to all goodness that brought forth angels and the spirits of men, so He can will nothing in their existence but that they should live and work and manifest that same Spirit of love and goodness which brought them into being.

Man can have no peace but in the purity and perfection of his first created nature; nor can he have purity and perfection in any other way than in and by the Spirit of love. For as the love of God created all things, so love is the purity, the perfection, and the blessing of all created things. Nothing can live in God but as it lives in love. So that love alone is the cure of every evil; and he that lives in the purity of love is delivered from the power of evil into the freedom of the Spirit of love.

Thank You, Father of all love, that You long to fill my heart with nothing less than Your own divine, eternal love.

A New Birth from Above

If I have a faith that can move mountains,
but have not love, I am nothing.

1 CORINTHIANS 13:2

I want to draw your attention to the most delightful subject in the world, to help you to rejoice in the adorable God whose being is pure love. He is the inexhaustible source of meekness, delight, blessing, goodness, patience, and grace. These are like many streams breaking out of the abyss of the love of the Father, Son, and Holy Ghost. The triune God who is forever giving forth nothing but the same gifts of light and love, of blessing and joy, whether before or after the Fall, either for angels or for men.

No good can become part of you unless it is by way of a birth from above. Your nature must also be restored; it must be part of this new birth. It must cooperate in the production of new life before the Spirit of love can have a birth in it. For love is delight and delight cannot arise in any creature until its nature is in a delightful state, or is possessed of that in which it must rejoice. The reason why God came to earth as human was to make it possible for the Triune to dwell in you.

Now you will also understand the absolute necessity of the cross: The only way to life in God is the dying to self. You must resist and deny nature, so that a supernatural power or divine goodness may take possession of it and bring a new life into it. Goodness is only a sound and virtue a mere strife of natural passions until the Spirit of love is the breath of everything that lives and moves in the heart. You have no true religion but in and by that Spirit of love that is God Himself living and working in you.

I bow in deep humility before You, O God, to praise You for this wonderful love. Give me the grace to yield myself to the denial and the death of self.

The Twofold Life

The way of the LORD is a refuge for the righteous.
PROVERBS 10:29

No intelligent creature can be good and happy but by partaking of and having in himself a twofold life. The twofold life is this: It must have the life of nature and the life of God in it. The natural life is a life of various sensibilities and has the power of understanding, willing, and desiring. God created man in a natural state of emptiness, of want, of desire. The highest natural life, therefore, can only be a bare capacity for goodness and happiness and cannot possibly be a good and happy life but by the life of God dwelling in it and in union with it.

The only possible salvation for all the sons of the fallen Adam is the union of the divine and human life, or the Son of God incarnate in man, to make man again a partaker of the divine nature

There can be no happiness, blessing, or goodness for any creature in heaven or on earth but by having Jesus Christ to lead them to wisdom, righteousness, sanctification, and peace with God. The reason is that goodness and happiness are absolutely inseparable from God and can be nowhere but in God.

This great truth reveals the clear distinction between inward holiness and all outward practices of man. All the dispensations of God, whether by the law or the prophets, by the Scriptures or ordinances of the church, are nothing in themselves. They are only aids to a fuller life in Christ—a life of faith, hope, hunger, and thirst after that first union with the life of the God that was lost in the Fall of Adam.

Lord, my only hope is to be found in unceasing fellowship with You. Thank You for Your love that longs to take complete possession of me.

Perpetual Inspiration

"I will ask the Father, and he will give you another
Counselor to be with you forever."
JOHN 14:16

There can be no goodness or happiness in any human being, unless it is the breath, the life, the work of God within him. Goodness can only be in God and it cannot exist separate from Him. He can bless and sanctify by Himself becoming the blessing and sanctification of man. There is thus no goodness in the life of man from anything but the immediate indwelling and working of the Holy Trinity. Perpetual inspiration from the Holy Spirit is as necessary to a life of goodness, holiness, and happiness as the perpetual respiration of air is necessary to animal life.

It is a mistake to confine inspiration to particular times and occasions, or to prophets and apostles. Inspiration is for every Christian who trusts to be continually led and inspired by the Spirit of God. For though not all are called to be prophets or apostles, all are called to be holy and perfect as their heavenly Father is perfect; to be like Christ; to will only as God wills; to do all to His glory and honor; to renounce the spirit of the world; to love God with all their heart, soul, and spirit and their neighbor as themselves.

Devotion to God is not limited to certain times or occasions. It is always alive and stirring in our thoughts, wills, desires, and affections. If we are all called to this inward holiness and goodness, then a perpetual working of the Spirit of God within us is absolutely necessary.

Father, reveal to me in power that the immediate and continual leading and working of Your Holy Spirit is what You long to give, and what I may confidently claim.

Two Kinds of Knowledge

*With his wife's full knowledge he kept back
part of the money for himself.*
ACTS 5:2

Goodness and virtue may be brought to us in two different ways. First, they may be taught to us outwardly by men, by rules and principles, as was the case with Ananias and Sapphira (see Acts 5:1–11). Second, they may be inwardly born in us with the genuine birth of our own renewed spirit.

In the former way, they at best only change our outward behavior, putting our passions under false restraint. Ananias serves as a good example. This way of learning and attaining goodness by outward instruction, whether from good men or the laws of Scripture, is imperfect but absolutely necessary for salvation. It teaches us where to seek and find the source of all light and knowledge. It leads us to something better than can be found in laws and regulations. We soon realize, however, that it does not help to simply obey rules. The only real solution can be found only through faith in Christ Jesus.

From this twofold teaching there naturally arises a twofold state of virtue and goodness. If you learn virtue and goodness only from men or books, you will be virtuous or good according to time and place and outward forms. You may do works of humility, works of love, and use times and forms of prayer. But the Spirit of prayer, the Spirit of love, the Spirit of humility, is only to be obtained by the working of the light and Spirit of God inwardly bringing forth a newborn spirit within us.

*Lord, I believe
with all my heart
in the immediate
teaching and
working of the
Holy Spirit that
brings the life of
heaven as a
newborn spirit
within me.*

The Monster of Self

You must no longer live as the Gentiles do.
EPHESIANS 4:17

Until this birth of the Spirit of divine love is found in you, you cannot know what divine love is in itself. Divine love is perfect peace and joy. It is also the freedom from all disquiet, and brings a deep sense of contentment and happiness.

When people turn from God to self, they find only nature as it is in them and without God. In natural man is nothing but the working of every kind of evil. Covetousness, envy, pride, and wrath are the four elements of self, inseparably bound together. If we were more aware of what real good (or real evil) could work within us, we would be much more afraid of harboring these serpents of evil within us—even more afraid than of being cast into a dungeon of venomous beasts.

But instead we keep this monster of self well fed and alive. We are masters at hiding him behind all kinds of goodness. He can watch and fast, pray much and preach long, and often gets more life and strength from these virtues than from bad people and sinners.

The one only way of dying to self is very simple. It is equally practicable by everybody. It is always at hand. It meets you in everything. And it is never without success. What is this simple way? It is the way of patience, meekness, humility, and total surrender to God. This is the truth and perfection of dying to self.

Lord, I know that in my own strength I am unable to obey or love You. I pray that the Holy Spirit may work in me the meekness, gentleness, and humility to surrender to You totally.

Dying to Self

"Come to me, all you who are weary and burdened, and I will give you rest.
Take my yoke upon you and learn from me, for I am gentle and
humble in heart, and you will find rest for your souls."
MATTHEW 11:28–29

We have now learned that the only way of dying to self is the way of patience, meekness, humility, and total surrender to God. The reason you are trying in vain to obtain these virtues is that you are seeking them in a multitude of human rules and methods instead of in simple faith—the faith that is given by Christ to all those who ask for it.

"Come to me, all you who are weary and burdened, and I will give you rest." It is a short, simple, and certain way to peace and comfort. What has now become of your rules and methods to be delivered from self and the power of sin? What folly it would be to suppose that Christ, after His ascension, would become less of a Savior, and give less immediate help, than when He was on earth!

When I urge you to give up yourself in faith and hope to these virtues, what else do I do but turn you directly to faith and hope in the true Lamb of God? What is the Lamb of God but the perfection of patience, meekness, humility, and resignation to God? And consequently, is not every sincere wish and desire, every inclination of your heart that longs to be governed by these virtues, an immediate, direct application to Christ, a worshiping and falling down before Him, a giving up of yourself unto Him, and the very perfection of faith in Him?

Lord, thank You that my faith in You is more than the work You did for me on the cross. It is by faith and through the Holy Spirit that I can claim the grace and the virtues of Christ as my own.

Of Faith in Christ

"Take my yoke upon you and learn from me,
for I am gentle and humble in heart,
and you will find rest for your souls."
MATTHEW 11:29

Two truths are emphasized here. First, that to surrender yourself to God with patience, meekness, humility, and resignation is strictly the same thing as to learn from Christ, or to have faith in Him. Second, if you long for these virtues, you will be prepared to give up all that you are and all that you have from the fallen Adam. That means that you must leave all that you have as an act of faith to Him. You will be led and governed by His Spirit.

When you do this, you are in the very arms of Christ. Your whole heart is His dwelling place, and He lives and works in you. Yes, Christ is in you and the life that you now lead is not yours, but it is Christ that lives in you.

The Spirit of divine love cannot be born in sinful man, unless he wills and chooses to be dead to self, in a patient, meek, humble resignation to the power and mercy of God. When your own impatience or pride overcomes you, totally surrender yourself to the mercy of God. The greater your distress is, the nearer you are to the greatest and best relief, provided you have the patience to expect it all from God.

Be assured that the divine working within you will be no more or less than the degree of your faith and hope and trust in God.

Lord, it is my greatest desire to seek salvation through the mediation of the meek, humble, patient, resigned Lamb of God, who alone has the power to work these heavenly virtues within me.

The Lamb of God

Worthy is the Lamb, who was slain, to receive…
honor and glory and praise!
REVELATION 5:12

The Lamb of God, with His eternal love and meekness, left the bosom of His Father to be Himself the resurrection of meekness and love in the darkened souls of fallen men. What a comfort it is to think that this Lamb of God, who is the glory of heaven, is as near to us, as truly in the midst of us as He is in the midst of heaven.

It was for His humility that God so highly exalted the Lamb. It is only as our life becomes the unceasing expression of a longing for His humility and meekness that we shall find rest for our souls.

Oh, the sweet resignation of myself to God! It is the happy death of every self-desire and the blessed unction of a holy life. The result is that I will never utter a word or do anything to others or myself unless it is under the influence of the inspiration of God.

In meekness, humility, patience, and resignation I am freed from the struggle against self to rest in the Spirit of God. This gives me entrance to the most intimate communion that can ever exist between God and man in this life.

You will experience this communion if you follow the way of meekness, humility, patience, and total resignation to God. But if you stray, you are preparing yourself for death. You must die to all and everything that you have worked or done under any other spirit but that of the meekness of the Lamb.

Lord, please drive out all evil from my heart. Guide and govern me wherever I go. Only You can save me from myself and lead me to God.

Prayer Is the Key

When you ask, you do not receive, because you ask with wrong motives.
JAMES 4:3

Man has been sent into the world on no other errand but by prayer to rise out of the vanity of time into the riches of eternity. For poor and miserable as this life is, we all have free access to all that is great and good and happy and carry within ourselves a key to all the treasures of heaven.

God is not an absent or distant God, but is more present in and to our souls than our own bodies. We are only far from God if we are void of the Spirit of prayer that opens heaven and the kingdom of God within us. A root set in the finest soil is not as sure of its growth to perfection as the man whose spirit longs for God.

We are all of us by birth the offspring of God, more closely related to Him than we are to one another. For in Him we live and move and have our being (see Acts 17:28). The first man had the breath and spirit of the Father, Son, and Holy Spirit breathed into him, and so became a living soul. He was the image and likeness of God, not with regard to his outward shape or form, but because the Holy Trinity had breathed their own nature and spirit into him. And as the Father, Son, and Holy Spirit are always in heaven and make heaven to be everywhere, so this spirit breathed by them into man brought heaven into man along with it. And so man was in heaven as well as on earth. It is also our paradise—a heavenly state, or birth, of a new life on earth.

Thank You, Lord, for giving me the key to the treasures of heaven.

As willing as the sun is to shine its light and warmth on the earth, the living God is waiting to work in the heart of His child. That is, if we do not prevent Him by our unbelief or our surrender to the spirit of the world.

The Goodness of God

"Why do you call me good? No one is good—except God alone."
MARK 10:18

The goodness of God was the cause and the beginning of His Creation. God can communicate nothing but goodness. He made man to receive His goodness. As the sun can only give light, so the holy triune God can give nothing but the riches and goodness of His divine perfection to all those who are capable of receiving them.

This is the amiable nature of God: He is everything that is good. He is love itself—pure immeasurable love, doing nothing but from love, giving nothing but gifts of love to everything that He has made, requiring nothing of all His creatures but the spirit and fruit of that Love who brought them into being. What great motivation for man to return love for love!

View every part of our redemption, from Adam's first sin to the resurrection of the dead, and you will find nothing but successive mysteries of that first Love that created angels and men. All the mysteries of the gospel are proof of God's desire to make His love triumph in the removal of sin and disorder from all nature and creatures.

Father, teach me to believe in Your love and not to rest until my heart is filled with it!

With what joy an invalid on a winter's day yields himself to bask in the bright sunshine! And how little do God's children understand that they only have to wait in quiet before God till His light shines upon them and into them and through them. How little we understand that we need enough time with God for His light to shine into the depths of our hearts and fill our lives.

The Kingdom of Self

But because of his great love for us, God, who is rich in mercy,
made us alive with Christ even when we were dead in transgressions.
EPHESIANS 2:4–5

Man had fallen from a life in God into a life of self-love, self-esteem, and self-seeking and in pursuing the perishing enjoyments of the world. But on the day of Pentecost a new dispensation of God came forth. God's part in it was the working of the Holy Spirit and His gifts and graces upon the whole church. Man's part in it was the adoration of God in spirit and in truth.

All this was to make way for the immediate and continual working of God in man. Man, baptized with the Holy Spirit, should renounce self and give up his entire soul, with all the faculties of his mind, to the disposal of God.

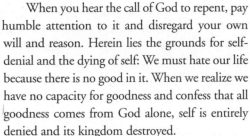

Lord, thank You that You dwell and work in me. I pray that Your redeeming love will display its power in me and bestow its blessing on me.

When you hear the call of God to repent, pay humble attention to it and disregard your own will and reason. Herein lies the grounds for self-denial and the dying of self: We must hate our life because there is no good in it. When we realize we have no capacity for goodness and confess that all goodness comes from God alone, self is entirely denied and its kingdom destroyed.

This dying of self and birth of a new life in Christ must happen daily. Cast yourself at the feet of God and pray that the seed of eternity, the spark of life that had so long been smothered under earthly rubbish, might breathe and come to life in you.

Continual Self-Denial

"When he found one (pearl) of great value,
he went away and sold everything he had and bought it."
MATTHEW 13:46

Till the end of your life every inch of the road is to be made up of denial and dying to self. To think of anything but the continual total denial of our earthly nature is to overlook the very thing on which all depends.

You might rejoice in thinking that by knowing these truths you have found the pearl of great value, but it is not yours till you sell all that you have and buy it. Self is all that you have and you have to part with it before the pearl can be yours. Self is an apostate nature, continually veering away from God, and it corrupts everything that it touches. All evil tempers are born and nourished in self. Die to this self, to this inward nature, and you will overcome all outward enemies.

Only one thing is needed. The Son of God calls us to die to this life and take up His cross. Only then will we be delivered from covetousness and sensuality, from a worldly spirit, from all self-interest and self-exaltation, from all hatred and envy.

To try to live entirely devoted to God without totally dying to the self is building castles in the air. To think of being alive in God before we are dead to our own nature is as impossible as for a grain of wheat to be alive before it dies. Spiritual life starts at the true root that grows out of death and is born in a heart deprived of its own natural life.

Lord, only You Yourself could sit in glory at the right hand of God after dying on the cross. Thank You for the new way You opened up for me through the rent veil into the Holiest of All.

A State of the Heart

*Command the Israelites to bring you clear oil of pressed olives
for the light so that the lamps may be kept burning.*
EXODUS 27:20

Although He had all wisdom, Jesus gave but a small number of moral teachings to mankind. He knew we were so focused on the pleasures of the world that only a total denial of self and a rebirth would enable us to live a new life.

True religion is a religion of the heart. The longing desire of the heart after Christ and God and heaven breaks all our worldly bonds and raises us out of the miseries of time into the riches of eternity. Once the spirit of prayer is born in us, prayer is no longer limited to certain times of the day but is the *continual* longing for God. The spirit of prayer is a state of the heart. It may possess the heart without interruption, or it may have its times of prayer, but it is never limited to certain times or ways of working.

Lord, I confess that there are many things in my life that still happen sporadically. I pray for the "continual" in my life.

It might be worthwhile making a study of the place that the word *continual* ought to have in our life. First, there is the continual streaming forth of the infinite love of God towards men. Then follows the continual, unalterable dependence on God every moment of our life. And after that, the continual receiving of goodness and happiness from God alone, as well as the continual mortification of our evil nature. This is followed by the continual and immediate inspiration of the Holy Spirit maintaining the life of Christ in us. Last, it is the continual longing of the heart expressed in prayer, and a continual love of Him that burns like the lamps in the tabernacle.

A Worldly Spirit

You are still worldly. For since there is jealousy and quarreling among you,
are you not worldly? Are you not acting like mere men?
1 CORINTHIANS 3:3

From what has been said of the first state and fall of man it plainly follows that the sin of all sin, or the heresy of all heresies, is a worldly spirit. We are apt to consider this only as an infirmity, but it is indeed the great apostasy from God and the divine life.

If you choose any life but the life of God and heaven, you choose death, for death is nothing else but the loss of the life of God. The spirit of the soul is in itself nothing else but the Spirit of God breathed into us by God, so that the life of God, the nature of God, and the working of God might be manifested in it.

The sole purpose of the redemption of fallen man is to kindle again the love of God and heaven in his heart. "For everything in the world—the cravings of sinful man, the lust of his eyes and the boasting of what he has and does—comes not from the Father but from the world" (1 John 2:16). A worldly spirit is therefore not only a sin, but also the manifestation of the kingdom of darkness in us.

Lord, I pray for Your protection against a worldly spirit. Fill me with Your love.

Scripture warns us most seriously against being conformed to the world. The Word clearly states, "Do not conform any longer to the pattern of this world" (Romans 12:2) and "If anyone loves the world, the love of the Father is not in him" (1 John 2:15). We must yield ourselves to the Holy Spirit to discover the evil and the danger of the spirit of the world, to give us the victory over it, and to fill us with the life of heaven.

The Despair of Self

What a wretched man I am!
Who will rescue me from this body of death?
ROMANS 7:24

There can be no true conversion from the life of sin and death unless people realize that they must totally deny their old nature, and yet they find themselves incapable of doing this in their own strength. This is the despair by which we lose our entire life to find a new one in God. It is at this point of despair that faith and hope and the true seeking of Christ and God are born. But till all is despair in us, faith and hope and turning to God in prayer are only practiced by rule and method. Faith and hope are not living qualities of a new birth till we have lost all trust and confidence in ourselves.

God created man so that he could live in Him. Who is God? His name is Love. He is the good, the perfection of peace, joy, the glory and the blessing of every life. Therefore, love for others must be our strongest characteristic—an irresistible divine love.

God, I believe that

You are love.

Thank You that

You wish to fill

my heart with

Your blessings.

And who is Christ? He is the healer of all evil. He is the one with unwearied compassion, patience, and unceasing mercifulness toward every want and infirmity of human nature.

Love is the Christ of God; it is the resurrection and life of every divine virtue, the mother of true humility, boundless benevolence, unwearied patience, and bowls of compassion.

Let us seek above everything to believe that God is love and, as such, longs intensely to fill every heart with His blessings. If we patiently wait on Him, that love will enter our hearts with all its gifts and graces and its unspeakable blessings.

True Religion

Religion that God our Father accepts as pure and faultless is this:
to look after orphans and widows in their distress
and to keep oneself from being polluted by the world.
JAMES 1:27

True religion is something within us—something that happens within us. It is the birth of a new life and a new love in the heart of man. It is nothing else but the power and life of God as Father, Son, and Holy Spirit, re-creating and reviving life in the fallen soul and driving out all evil from him.

Religion has no value in itself. It is no true divine service, no proper worshiping of God. It has no good in it and cannot save man from his sins. Religion has value only if the person who practices it puts his faith in the holy triune God working within him.

Keep close this idea of religion as an inward spiritual life in the soul. To the extent that you have this inward religion, you have real salvation. For salvation is nothing but a victory over nature. If you resist and renounce your own vain, selfish, and earthly nature, God will live and work within you. He is the light in you, the life and the Spirit of your soul. And in Him you are a new creature who worships Him in spirit and in truth.

Scripture teaches us that our religious services lead us to yield ourselves more and more to the working of the Spirit of God within us, so that a new nature can be formed in us. True religion is that God, through His Spirit, lives and works in us as the light and the life of our souls. This will awaken in us a continual longing for Him.

Father, I pray that through the powerful working of Your Holy Spirit, my religion will be kept pure and faultless before You.

The Practice of Prayer

No one whose hope is in you will ever be put to shame.
PSALM 25:3

Prayer makes you aware of what you are and what you should be. It fills you with the continual desire for God and the Holy Spirit.

There is only one infallible way to safely weather the numerous difficulties you will encounter in life, and that is to expect nothing from yourself, but in everything to expect and depend upon God for relief. If you cling to this truth, you will be led through all your problems to fellowship with God. Expectation comes from God alone. Once you are convinced of this, the entire spirit of your mind will become a true faith and hope and trust in the working of the Spirit of God within you. You will no more wait upon any other power to change you to a new creature in Christ than you would rely on any other power for the resurrection of your body on the last day.

Thank You, Lord, that I can expect everything from You and depend on You.

How strange then that so many regard our greatest privilege, namely to have fellowship with God in prayer, as a burden and a failure. To many more it is merely a matter of form without any inner power.

The first step to true prayer is to expect nothing from yourself. The second step is to expect everything from God with all your heart. These two thoughts lie at the root of all true prayer. Instead of focusing your thoughts on yourself and your needs, focus on God's glory and His love. Then prayer will become a joy and a power, and your trials will become your greatest blessing because they will compel you to wait on God.

A Touchstone
of Truth

Humility and the fear of the LORD bring wealth and honor and life.
PROVERBS 22:4

Whether sitting, standing, or walking, you must always pray that God in His goodness will take from your heart every kind and form and degree of pride, and that He will awaken in you the humility that will make you susceptible to His light and His Holy Spirit.

The painful awareness of what you are, kindled by the light of God within you, is the fire and light from which your spirit of prayer proceeds. In its first kindling nothing is found or felt but pain, wrath, and darkness. And so your first prayer is nothing but penitence, self-condemnation, and confession. It feels nothing but its own misery and is all humility.

This prayer of humility is met by the divine love, and the grace of God embraces it. But then it changes into songs and thanksgiving. When all worldly earthly passions and affections have melted away, leaving only the joy in God, the prayer changes again. Now you do not only pray, but you also live in God. Your prayer is not limited to certain times, words, or places, but has become the work of your entire being. You now walk in the fullness of faith, in the purity of love, in absolute resignation to do and be what and how God pleases. This is the highest form of prayer, the highest union with God in this life.

Spirit of God, give me the humility to accept everything You wish to give me.

The Prayer
of the Heart

Let us draw near to God with a sincere heart in full assurance of faith;
having our hearts sprinkled to cleanse us from a guilty conscience
and having our bodies washed with pure water.
HEBREWS 10:22

Turning to God with a sincere heart full of love, faith, and trust is the best form of prayer, even without words. A prayer that does not come from the heart is like a prayer rising out of an empty well, and you yourself are not within it.

When you really long for God, your prayer is moved by the Spirit of God. The breath, or inspiration, of God is stirring, moving, and opening itself in your heart. Surely nothing can ascend to heaven but that which was born in heaven! Therefore, every time a good desire stirs in your heart, a good prayer goes out of it that reaches God as being the fruit and work of His Holy Spirit. It is the continuity of the desire in the heart to have that which can hardly be expressed in words that is the goodness and perfection of prayer.

Lord, I pray that

my prayers will

always be sincere,

so that Your name

may be glorified

You have already taken the first step in the spiritual life by yielding yourself wholly to God to live under the light and guidance of His Holy Spirit. Your next step is to continue in this way without interruption. This second step can only be taken in the power of prayer—a prayer deep from the heart that longs for God.

Of all things, look at this prayer of the heart and consider it an infallible guide to heaven. When God alone is the object of your prayer, it will be like a man who puts everything aside for the sake of one great worldly matter. Our times of prayer are meant to lead us to a life of prayer in which the heart will continually live and rejoice in God's presence.

The Proof of
the Spirit

But if by the Spirit you put to death the misdeeds of the body, you will live,
because those who are led by the Spirit of God are sons of God.
ROMANS 8:13–14

How can you know for certain that the Spirit of God is leading you? Just as you know when you are hungry or pleased, so will you know that the Spirit of God is leading you, for the Spirit of God is more distinguishable from all other spirits than any of your natural affections are one from another.

God is unwearied patience. He is eternal grace. God is unmixed goodness and He is universal love. His delight is in the communication of Himself to everyone according to each person's capacity to receive Him. He is the Good from whom nothing but good comes, and He resists all evil with goodness.

If it is your greatest desire to be merciful as He is merciful, to be full of His unwearied patience, to dwell in His unalterable meekness, to love as He loves, and to communicate with others in love, you can be sure that the Spirit of God lives, dwells, and governs in you. However, if you lack these virtues, any pretence to try to be like Him will be vague and groundless.

The Spirit of God Himself assures us of His presence and His leadership. Anybody who yields himself in childlike faith will know that the Spirit of God is leading him. And he will grow more and more to be the person God wants him to be.

Thank You, Lord, for Your Spirit who leads me every day and enables me and motivates me to be like You.

The Secret of United Prayer

As a Christian, you are a member of the body of Christ and have the calling to intercede for others. The strength that is drawn from unity within the body is something inconceivable. The power of each individual member is increased to an unfathomable degree by fellowship with the group.

Nothing can help us toward an ever-increasing faith as effectively as being in one body and one spirit in Christ Jesus. As we have seen, the disciples were praying in unity on the Day of Pentecost when they were filled with the Holy Spirit and the church was born.

This unity is what we need in the church today. We also need enthusiasm for God and his kingdom, so that His name shall be made known to every human being. Our prayers should rise up every day, pleading for the power of the Holy Spirit on all its members.

United prayer brings answer to prayer!

The Lost Secret

*"Do not leave Jerusalem, but wait for the gift my Father promised...
in a few days you will be baptized with the Holy Spirit."*
ACTS 1:4–5

The Lord's command to preach the gospel to all people not only applied to the disciples, but also to all followers of Christ. The very last command Jesus gave to His disciples, namely not to preach until they had received the power from on high, also applies to us.

The church appears to have lost sight of this great secret. We seem to have forgotten that it is only by living in the power of the Holy Spirit that we can preach the gospel. This might be the reason why so much preaching and so much working bear so little fruit. The church lacks the much-availing prayer that brings down the power from on high.

The secret of Pentecost is that the disciples continued with one accord in prayer and supplication until they were filled with the Holy Spirit. They then proved what the mighty power of God could do through them.

Let us all seek the grace of the Holy Spirit, who alone can reveal to us that which the eye has not seen, the ear has not heard, and the heart of man has not conceived—the things that God has done and loves to do for those who wait on Him. Let us pray that the lost secret may be found: the sure promise that the power of the Holy Spirit will indeed be given in answer to fervent prayer.

Thank You, Lord, that You want to give me more than I could ever think of. Teach me to wait on the power of the Holy Spirit to fill my whole being.

The Kingdom of God

*He appeared to them over a period of forty days
and spoke about the kingdom of God.*

ACTS 1:3

The teaching of Jesus during the forty days after the resurrection dealt primarily with the kingdom of God. It is remarkable that Luke, in the last verses of Acts, sums up the teaching of Paul at Rome in the same words: "He explained and declared to them the kingdom of God" (Acts 28:23) and "He preached the kingdom of God" (Acts 28:31).

Christ had entrusted to His disciples the announcement of the coming of the kingdom—a kingdom of righteousness and peace and joy. The rule of God in heaven came down in the power of the Spirit, and the disciples were full of the one thought—to preach the coming of the Spirit into the hearts of men. The good news was that the kingdom of God was ruling and dwelling within men, even as in heaven.

In the last command our Lord gave to His disciples (see Acts 1:4–8), we will find the great truths of the gospel:

The King is the crucified Christ.

The disciples are His faithful followers.

The power for their service lies in the work of the Holy Spirit.

Their work is to be Christ's witnesses.

Their aim is to reach people to the ends of the earth.

Their first duty is to wait on the Holy Spirit in united, unceasing prayer.

If we are to take up and continue the work of the disciples, it is essential to have a clear and full impression of all that Christ spoke to them, and what it meant for their inner life and all their service.

Thank You, Lord Jesus, that through the power of the Holy Spirit, I may sit at Your feet to learn more about the kingdom of God.

Christ as King

"I tell you the truth, some who are standing here will not taste death before they see the kingdom of God come with power."
MARK 9:1

The first truth of the gospel is that Christ is King of His church. According to Jesus, the Holy Spirit would reveal the kingdom of God in the hearts of the disciples. And in the kingdom of heaven, God's will is always put first. In the power of the Holy Spirit, Christ's disciples would do His will on earth even as it was done in heaven.

Any kingdom is as good as its king. Christ reigns as God on the throne of the Father. On earth there is no embodiment or external manifestation of the kingdom; its power is seen in the lives of those in whom it rules. It is only in the church, the members of Christ, that the united body can be seen and known. Christ lives and dwells and rules in their hearts. Our Lord Himself taught how close this relationship is to be: "I am in my Father, and you are in me, and I am in you" (John 14:20).

This must be our first lesson if we are to follow in the steps of the disciples and share their blessing. We must know that Christ dwells and rules in our hearts as King. We must know that we live in Him, and in His power are able to accomplish all that He would have us do. Our entire life is to be devoted to our King and the service of His kingdom.

Lord, I thank You for the privilege to be Your child and to share in the riches of Your kingdom.

This blessed relationship to Christ will mean, above all, a daily fellowship with Him in prayer. Our prayer life is to be a continuous and unbroken exercise. Only then may we rejoice in our King and be more than conquerors in Him.

Jesus Crucified

"God has made this Jesus, whom you crucified,
both Lord and Christ."
ACTS 2:36

Christ the King is none other than the crucified Jesus. All that we have to say of Him will not teach us to fully know Him, unless we keep in mind that our King is the crucified Jesus. God placed Him in the center of His throne as a slain Lamb, and it is thus that we worship Him as King.

Christ's cross is His highest glory. It is through this that He has conquered every enemy and gained His place on the throne of God. We need to understand this if we want to know what victory over sin really means. When Paul wrote, "I have been crucified with Christ and I no longer live, but Christ lives in me" (Galatians 2:20), He taught us that the crucified Christ rules in our hearts and that the cross will lead us to victory.

Thank You, Lord Jesus, that I may know You as the crucified King. Make me a worthy servant in Your kingdom.

This was the disciples' deepest preparation for receiving the Holy Spirit: With their Lord they were crucified to the world. Their lives were hidden with Christ in God.

Each one of us needs to experience this fellowship with Christ on the cross if the Spirit of Pentecost is to take possession of us. It was through the Eternal Spirit that Christ gave Himself as a sacrifice and became the King on the throne of God. It is when we conform to His death, surrender our will, and deny our old nature that we become worthy servants of the crucified King, and our hearts the worthy temples of His glory.

The Apostles

On one occasion, while he was eating with them,
he gave them this command: "Do not leave Jerusalem,
but wait for the gift my Father has promised,
which you have heard me speak about."
ACTS 1:4

The second truth of the gospel is that the disciples were prepared to receive His Spirit and to be His witnesses.

What was there in these men that fitted them for such powerful, effectual prayer and the wonderful fulfillment of the promise that came to them? These were simple, unlearned men with many faults whom the Lord had called to forsake all and follow Him. They had done this, as far as they could; they followed Him in the life He led and the work He did.

Though there was much sin in them, and they did not have the power to fully deny themselves, their hearts clung to Him in deep sincerity. Despite their stumbling, His disciples followed Him to the cross. They shared with Him His death. They died with Him to sin and were raised with Him in the power of a new life. It was this that fitted them for prayer, and they were clothed with power from on high.

Lord, thank You
that You consider
me worthy
of receiving
Your blessing.

Let this be the test by which we try ourselves, whether we have indeed surrendered to the fellowship of Christ's suffering and death; whether we have hated our own life and crucified it and have received the power of Christ's life in us. Like the disciples, we must be willing learners in the school of Jesus and seek, above everything, that intimate fellowship with Him that will fit us for praying the prayer of Pentecost and receiving its answer.

Not of This World

"They are not of the world,
even as I am not of it."
JOHN 17:16

In His last conversation with His disciples before His final suffering and death, Jesus took pains to explain the impassable gulf between Him and the world and between them and the world. He said of the Spirit, "The world cannot accept him, because it neither sees him nor knows him" (John 14:17). Jesus also said of His disciples that the world hated them because they were not of this world, even as He was not of it. This separation from the world is to be the mark of all disciples who long to be filled with the Spirit.

How is it that faith in the Holy Spirit is so little preached and practiced in the church of Christ? Surely it is because the world rules too often in the life of Christians. Believers seldom live the heavenly life to which they are called in Christ Jesus. The love of the world, all that sinful man desires, his love for his possessions (see 1 John 2:15–16), sexual immorality, impurity, lust, greed (Colossians 3:5), delight in all that the world offers, the vainglory of life, the self-exaltation of what man has accomplished—all these things rob the heart of its susceptibility and desire for the self-denial that fits man for receiving the Holy Spirit.

Lord, give me the strength to deny the old nature in me that still delights in the pleasures of the world.

Examine yourself to find out whether love of the world is the reason for the lack of prayer in your life. Prayer is absolutely necessary for those who plead for the power of the Holy Spirit. May the Lord engrave these words in your heart: *I do not belong to this world!*

Obedience

If you love me, you will obey what I command.
I will ask the Father, and he will give you another
Counselor to be with you forever—the Spirit of truth.

JOHN 14:15–17

Christ was everything to His disciples. Even after His resurrection, He was their life, their only thought, and their only desire. Was their devotion to Christ something special? Or was it something that the Lord asks from all those who desire to be filled with the Holy Spirit?

God indeed expects this devotion from His children even today. The Lord wants to give the Holy Spirit to all His children. He wants His children to link the world to the throne of God through intercession.

What is Christ to you—something, nothing, or everything? For the unconverted, Christ is nothing. For the half-converted, the average Christian, Christ is something. For the true believer, Christ is everything. Everyone who prays for the power of the Spirit must be ready to say, "I yield myself with all my heart this day to the leading of the Spirit." Total surrender is an absolute necessity, a question of life or death.

Lord, I pray in the power of your Spirit for total surrender every moment of my life.

You must yield yourself totally to Christ, remain in Him, and obey His commands. This is the mark of discipleship. Children of God must know that the Father's love and Spirit will rest on them when they long with all their heart to do His will. This will be the secret of power in our intercession for the church and for the world.

The Holy Spirit

*"But you will receive power when
the Holy Spirit comes on you."*
ACTS 1:8

The third truth of the gospel is that Christ's disciples will receive *power for service through the Holy Spirit*. Since the Fall of Adam, the Holy Spirit had no permanent home in man. But Jesus broke the power of sin by his death and resurrection; now the Holy Spirit could take possession of our heart and make it a dwelling for God.

The Holy Spirit alone was the power in the disciples of the early church, and He is also the power in us by which sin can be overcome and the prisoners of sin set free. The Old Testament refers to this Spirit as the Spirit of God. But in the new dispensation the Spirit of God descended to dwell in men and, as the Spirit of the Son, took possession of each Christian as His temple (see Isaiah 61:1; Luke 4:18).

On earth He first led the Son into the desert to be tempted by Satan, and then to the synagogue in Nazareth to proclaim Himself as the fulfillment of what the prophets had spoken. And so on to the cross where Christ yielded Himself implicitly to the leading of the Spirit.

Amazing mystery! The Spirit of God, our life. The Spirit of the Son, our light and strength. As men and women who are led by this Spirit, we shall have the power to pray the effectual prayer of the righteous man that avails much.

*Lord, thank You
for the privilege to
have Your Spirit in
my life. May my
lifestyle and
witness be proof
that the Spirit
dwells in me.*

The Power from On High

"But stay in the city until you have been clothed with power from on high."
LUKE 24:49

Why did Jesus choose impotent, helpless men to conquer the world for Him? The reason was that in their helplessness they might yield themselves to Him, so that His power could work through them. As the Father had worked in Christ when He was on earth, so Christ in heaven would become the Great Worker and prove to them that all power in heaven and on earth had been given to Him. The disciples had only to pray, believe, and yield themselves to the mighty power of Christ.

The Holy Spirit would not be in them as a power of which they could take possession. But He would possess them and their work would be the work of the almighty Christ Himself. Their whole posture each day had to be that of unceasing dependence and prayer and of confident expectation.

The apostles had indeed learned to know Christ intimately. They had seen His mighty works; they had received His teaching; they had gone with Him through all His suffering, even to the death of the cross. They had known Him in the power of His resurrection and in the experience of His resurrection in their own hearts. Yet they were not capable of making Him known until He, through His Holy Spirit, had taken possession of them.

Thank You, Lord, that I need not be Your witness in my own strength.

As witness of Christ, you must not be content with anything less than the indwelling life and power of the Holy Spirit. It is the Holy Spirit that reveals Jesus in the hearts of men as the only power of the gospel. Nothing less than having Christ speaking through us in the power of His omnipotence will make us able ministers of the message of salvation.

My Witnesses

"And you will be my witnesses."
ACTS 1:8

The fourth truth of the gospel is that Christ's followers are to be His *witnesses*, ever testifying of His wonderful love, of His power to redeem, of His continual abiding presence, and of His wonderful power to work in us. Every one of us is called to be living proof and witness of what Jesus can do, not only by His words, but also by His life and actions. Christ's followers must tell people and bring them to the throne of grace. This is exactly what happened when the original disciples were filled with the Spirit: They immediately began to testify of the mighty things that God had done in Jesus Christ.

In this power, those who were scattered abroad by persecution went forth, even as far as Antioch, preaching in the name of Jesus, so that a multitude believed. They had no special gifts or training, but out of the fullness of the heart they spoke of Jesus Christ. They could not be silent—filled with the life and the love of Christ, they could not but speak of Him.

Lord, teach me to be Your faithful witness.

And so the gospel increased. Every new convert became a witness for Christ. A heathen author later said that if the Christians had only been content to keep the worship of Jesus to themselves, they would not have suffered. But in their zeal they wanted Christ to rule over all.

Here we have the secret of a flourishing church: *every believer a witness for Jesus*. Here we also have the cause of the weakness of the church: *so few who are willing to testify that Jesus is Lord*. What a call to prayer!

The Gospel Ministry

*"When the Counselor comes, whom I will send to you from the Father,
the Spirit of truth…will testify about me. And you also must testify,
for you have been with me from the beginning."*
JOHN 15:26–27

My witnesses. These words refer to all believers, but especially to ministers of the gospel. This is the high calling and the only power of the preacher of the gospel: in everything to be a witness for Jesus. In this may be found two great truths.

First, that the witness must place the teaching of Christ first. This is what the first disciples did. In every house they taught and preached Jesus Christ. Paul said, "I resolved to know nothing while I was with you except Jesus Christ and him crucified" (1 Corinthians 2:2). Ministers of the gospel should never forget that they have been called to be witnesses for Christ through the Holy Spirit. When they obey this calling, sinners will be saved and God's children will be sanctified and fitted for His service. This is the only way that Christ can have His proper place in the heart of His people and in the world.

*Thank You, Lord,
that I have so
much to witness
to, because You do
so much for me.*

Second, your words must be a personal testimony to who Christ is and what He can do. When this happens, the Holy Spirit carries the message as a living reality to the hearts and lives of others. This will build up believers so that they may walk in such fellowship with Jesus Christ that He can reveal Himself through them. And it is this that will lead them to the knowledge of the indispensable secret of spiritual health: the prayer life in daily fellowship, in childlike love, and true consecration with the Father and the Son.

To the Ends of the Earth

"And you will be my witnesses…to the ends of the earth."
ACTS 1:8

The fifth truth of the gospel is that we are to spread the message of salvation to *the ends of the earth.* How could Jesus Christ, who had been crucified by His enemies, speak of the ends of the earth as His dominion? And is it not foolish to dare say that a Jew whose followers had forsaken Him could conquer the world *through them?* No human mind could have formed such a conception. It is the thought of God—He alone could plan and execute such a purpose.

Jesus promised His disciples they would receive the power of the Holy Spirit, giving them assurance that the Spirit would maintain in them Christ's divine power. As Christ did His works only because the Father worked in Him, so Christ assured His disciples that He Himself from the throne of heaven would work through them. Whatever they asked of Him, He would do. In the strength of that same promise, the church can make the ends of the earth her aim.

Christians must understand that the extension of God's kingdom depends on the united, continued prayer of men and women whose lives have been totally surrendered to Christ. What they desire according to His will, He will do for them. His aim must become their aim; therefore, they must pray continually for the extension of His kingdom.

What we ask from Him, He will do.

Lord, Your aim is my aim. Help me to become an intercessor who really believes that You will do far more than I can ask or think.

Filled with His Glory

May the whole earth be filled with his glory.
PSALM 72:19

What a wonderful prospect! A world renewed and filled with the glory of God. A world wherein righteousness dwells. Although we can hardly believe it, it will surely come to pass. God's Word is the pledge of it. God's Son by His blood and death conquered the power of sin, and through the eternal Spirit the power of God is working out His purpose.

But it is a great and difficult work. Almost two thousand years have passed since Christ gave this promise and ascended the throne, and yet a large part of the human race has not even heard the name of Jesus. Others have heard His name but do not yet know Him. This great command—to make His name known to all people—has been entrusted to a church that thinks little of her responsibility and of what the consequence of her neglect might be.

You may indeed ask, "Will the work ever be done?" Blessed be His name, His power and faithfulness is our pledge that one day we shall see the whole world filled with the glory of God.

It is to this prayer that all believers are called, and they can count on the Holy Spirit to inspire and to strengthen them. Every day of our lives, with all the power there is in us, we must with one accord continually pray in the name of Jesus and the power of his Spirit.

True prayer will indeed help and be answered!

What blessing it is, Lord, to pray to You with confidence that the world may be filled with Your glory.

The First Prayer Meeting

They all joined together constantly in prayer.
ACTS 1:14

The sixth truth of the gospel is that we have to wait on the promise of the Father in *united unceasing prayer.* The first prayer meeting in the history of the kingdom was of great importance. In it we find the secret key that opens the storehouse of heaven with all its blessings.

Christ prayed that the disciples might be one, as He and the Father were one, so that the world might know that God loved them as He loved Christ. But there was strife among the disciples. At the Last Supper a dispute arose among them as to which of them was considered to be the greatest. It was only after Christ's ascension, in ten days of united supplication, that they were united in a holy unity of love and of purpose—a true body of Christ, ready to receive the Holy Spirit in all His power.

Heavenly Father, give me the strength to pray continually and to wait for Your promise.

What a prayer meeting! It was the fruit of Christ's training during the three years that He was with them. This prayer meeting gives us the law of the kingdom for all time: Where Christ's disciples are linked to one another in love, and yield themselves wholly to Him in undivided consecration, the Spirit will be given from heaven as the sign of God's approval. One of the great marks of the new dispensation is the united, unceasing prayer that avails much and is crowned with the power of the Holy Spirit. If our prayers are confined to our own churches and our own interests, we cannot expect a powerful answer.

The Unity of the Spirit

"Make every effort to keep the unity of the Spirit through the bond of peace. There is one body and one Spirit."
EPHESIANS 4:3–4

From Paul we learn that Christian communities in different places ought to remember each other in the fellowship of prayer. He points out how in such prayer God is glorified (see 2 Corinthians 1:11, 4:15, 9:12–13). There is a great need that the children of God throughout the world should be one, a holy priesthood continually ministering the sacrifice of praise and prayer. Instead, we see too little distinction between the world and the body of Christ.

What can be done to foster unity among the children of God? The separation to a life of more prayer is of the utmost importance. God's people must prove their unity in a life of holiness, love, and devotion to the Lord. That would be a living testimony to the world of what it means to live for God. When Paul wrote, "Be alert and always keep on praying for all the saints" (Ephesians 6:18), he named one of the most important differences between God's people and the world.

The one great distinctive feature of the true Christian is a life of prayer and intercession. Join with God's children who are seeking with one accord to maintain the unity of the Spirit in the body of Christ. Set aside fifteen minutes a day for meditation on some Word of God connected with His promises to His church, and to plead with Him for the fulfillment of these promises. Slowly but surely, you will see the fruit and taste the blessing of being one, heart and soul, with God's people.

Lord, I pray that my life may clearly manifest the features of a true Christian.

Union Is Strength

After they prayed, the place where they were meeting was shaken.
And they were all filled with the Holy Spirit
and spoke the word of God boldly.
ACTS 4:31

The power of union can clearly be seen in nature. A single drop of rain cannot be compared with many drops that become a stream. Speedily the stream's momentum becomes irresistible. Such is the power of true union in prayer. The world can be overcome with the power of united prayer.

In KwaZulu-Natal, owing to the many mountains, the streams often flow down with great force. The Zulu are accustomed to joining hands when they wish to pass through a stream. The leader has a strong stick in his right hand, and gives his left hand to some strong man who comes behind him. And so they form a chain of twelve or twenty and help each other to cross the current safely. When God's people reach out to others, there will be power to resist the overwhelming influence of the world. And in that unity God's children, when they have overcome the power of the world and the flesh, will have power to prevail with God.

Thank You, Lord, that our hearts can be melded together in the fellowship of loving and believing prayer.

In the ten days the disciples waited on the Holy Spirit to be poured out, they truly became one in heart and soul. When the Spirit of God descended, he not only filled each individual, but He also took possession of the whole company as the body of Christ.

Let us believe that the prayer of our Lord Jesus still applies to us today: "Holy Father, protect them by the power of your name...so that they may be one as we are one" (John 17:11).

In the Name of Christ

"And I will do whatever you ask in my name,
so that the Son may bring glory to the Father."
JOHN 14:13

How wonderful the link between our prayers and Christ's glorifying the Father in heaven. Much prayer on earth brings Him much glory in heaven. Little prayer means, as far as we are concerned, little glory to the Father. Our prayer is indispensable to the glorifying of the Father.

So deep was the desire of Christ in the last night that His disciples should learn to believe in the power of His name, and to avail themselves of His promise of a sure and abundant answer, that He repeated the promise seven times over. He knew how slow men would be to believe this wonderful promise. Yet He longs to strengthen our faith, to free our prayer from every shadow of a doubt, and to teach us that intercession is the most certain way of bringing glory to God, joy to our souls, and blessing to a perishing world.

And if you doubt again, you have only to remember Christ's promise to His disciples. When the Holy Spirit descended on them, the disciples received the power to pray. When Christ says, "Pray and you will receive," He inspires us to yield ourselves fully to the Holy Spirit. If you believe that the power of the Spirit is working in you, intercession will become the joy and the strength of your work in His service.

Lord, I love You
and want to
glorify Your name.

Paul reminds us to do everything in the name of Jesus (see Colossians 3:17), because everything in our daily life should bear the signature of the name of Jesus. When we learn to do this, we shall know that our prayers will be answered to the extent that we live in His name. When the name of Jesus rules in our life, it will give power to our prayers.

Our Heavenly Father

"Our Father in heaven…"
MATTHEW 6:9

Our Father. How simple, how beautiful, this invocation which Christ puts upon our lips! And yet how inconceivably rich in its meaning, in the fullness of the love and blessing it contains.

Just think of all the memories there have been on earth of wise and loving fathers. Just think of what this world owes to fathers who have made their children strong and happy. Meanwhile, we hear the voice of God saying, "If you, then, though you are evil, know how to give good gifts to your children, how much more will your Father in heaven give good gifts to those who ask him!" (Matthew 7:11). Then we realize how great the distance is between the earthly picture of fatherhood and the heavenly reality. What our earthly fathers are to us is but a shadow of what our heavenly Father wants to be to His children on earth.

What a gift Christ bestowed on us when He gave us the right to call His Father "our Father." *My Father!* We count it a great privilege that the Father comes so near to His earthly children, but when we pray, "Our heavenly Father," the need arises within to enter into His holy presence in heaven, to breathe its atmosphere and become truly heavenly minded. Then the words "heavenly Father" take on new meaning, and our hearts come under an influence that abides all day long.

Heavenly Father, thank You that I can call You by this name. Thank You, Lord Jesus, that You made it possible for me. Thank You, Holy Spirit, that You make it a wonderful reality.

The Power of Prayer

The prayer of a righteous man is powerful and effective.
JAMES 5:16

Prayer avails much. It avails much with God, and has availed much in the history of His church and people. Prayer is the one great power that the church can exercise in securing the working of God's omnipotence in the world.

"The prayer of a righteous man is powerful and effective" (James 5:16). This is a man who wears the righteousness of Christ, not only as a garment covering him but also as a power inspiring him to live as a new man "created in true righteousness and holiness" (Ephesians 4:24). When Christ gave His great promises regarding prayer, it was to those who keep His commands.

It is only when the righteous man stirs himself and rouses his whole being to take hold of God that his prayer avails much. Jacob wrestled with God and said, "I will not let you go" (Genesis 32:26). And through her constant pleading, the importunate widow in the parable gave the judge no rest (see Luke 18:1–8). This is proof that fervent prayer avails much.

Prayer is effective when many righteous people pray together. When two agree, there is the promise of an answer. How much more when hundreds and thousands unite with one accord to cry out to God to display His mighty power on behalf of His people.

Let us join those who have united themselves to call upon God for the mighty power of His Holy Spirit in His church. God will answer the prayer of the righteous!

Father, I have not yet experienced the powerful working of prayer in my life or in the world around me. Make my prayers effective and powerful.

Prayer and Sacrifice

I want you to know how much I am struggling for you.
COLOSSIANS 2:1

As men must prepare themselves and summon power for a great task, so Christians must prepare themselves to pray with all their heart and all their strength. The secret of powerful prayer is sacrifice—of comfort, of time, of self. It was thus with Christ Jesus, the great Intercessor. In Gethsemane He offered up prayers and petitions "with loud cries and tears" (Hebrews 5:7).

Prayer is sacrifice. Your prayer only has power if it is rooted in the sacrifice of Jesus Christ. As He gave up everything in His prayer, "Your will be done," we should also sacrifice everything to God and His service.

A pious Welsh miner had a relative whom the doctor wanted to send to Madeira because of health problems. The miner decided to take the little money he had and ventured to use it all. He procured a comfortable lodging for the invalid. The miner was content to live in a much smaller and cheaper room, and he spent much time there in prayer until he received the assurance that the invalid would recover. On the last day of the month the patient was declared healthy. When he arrived home, the miner testified that he had learned more than ever before that the secret law and the hidden power of prayer lay in self-sacrifice.

Lord, give me the strength through Your Holy Spirit to make the sacrifices needed for powerful prayer.

Are you surprised that our prayers are so powerless when we are so reluctant to make the necessary sacrifices while waiting on God? The Christ in whom we believe and in whom we live offered *Himself* as a sacrifice to God.

Intercession of the Spirit

And he who searches our hearts knows the mind of the Spirit, because the Spirit intercedes for the saints in accordance with God's will.
ROMANS 8:27

We often do not know what we should pray for, and at times we do not know *how* to pray. Then our inability to pray impedes our prayer and handicaps the faith that is essential to the prayer's success. But God's Word gives us true encouragement that at times like these the Holy Spirit intercedes for us in accordance to the will of God.

Where and how does the Spirit make intercession for the saints? In the heart that does not know how to pray, He secretly and effectually prays what is according to the will of God. This, of course, implies that we trust Him to do His work in us and that we wait on God, even when we do not know what to pray. We must have immeasurable faith in the Holy Spirit, who has been given us to cry "Abba Father!" within us.

The children of God have not only the Son of God, the great High Priest, to intercede for them; they have not only the privilege to ask in faith what they desire and the promise that it shall be given them; they also have the Holy Spirit who intercedes for them in the depths of their being.

Holy Spirit of God, thank You for interceding for me and others according to the will of God.

We are called to separate ourselves from the world and yield wholeheartedly to the leading of the Holy Spirit. He intercedes for us in a way that surpasses all our expectations. Therefore, we must surrender ourselves to silent expectation while we wait on the Lord and the Holy Spirit prays within us.

That They May Be One

"Holy Father, protect them by the power of your name...
so that they may be one as we are one."
JOHN 17:11

The Lord used the expression "that they may be one" five times over. He was on His way to the Father through the cross, and He wanted His disciples to understand that He was taking this thought with Him to heaven, where it would be the object of His unceasing intercession.

Jesus also entrusted these words to us to take them into the world and make them the object of our unceasing intercession. It would be the fulfillment of His command that we should love others as He loved us.

It seems as though the church does not regard this command as a priority anymore, as though there is a lack of love for believers, whatever their denomination might be. Should we therefore not pray more seriously that this prayer—*that they may be one*—would become the most important plea of our daily fellowship with God? How simple this would be once we connected the words "our Father" with all the children of God throughout the world, whoever they might be.

Our Father, I pray that You will protect all Your children in Your name, so that they may become one.

Christ's prayer that we may be one would then become a joy and a strength, a deeper bond of fellowship with Jesus and all His saints and an offer of a sweet savor to the Father of love.

The Disciples' Prayer

They all joined together constantly in prayer.
ACTS 1:14

However erroneous the thoughts they may have had of the Holy Spirit, the disciples believed from the words of Jesus—"It is expedient for you that I go away"—that the Spirit would give the glorified Christ into their very hearts in a way they had never known Him before. And it would be He Himself, in the mighty power of God's Spirit, who would be their strength for the work to which He had called them.

With what confidence they expected the fulfillment of this promise! Had not the Master, who had loved them so well, promised them that He would send a new Comforter to be with them always? And with what intensity and persistency the disciples pleaded! While they were praising, thanking, and worshiping their Lord in heaven, they remembered all He had taught them about constant prayer. They were sure that, no matter how long the answer might be delayed, the Lord would fulfill their desires.

Lord, forgive me that my prayers are so often selfish and center only on myself and my problems.

Let us nourish our hearts with thoughts such as these. Remember that the same promise given to the disciples was also given to us. Even if we have to pray to God day and night, we can count on the Father to answer our prayers.

Let us believe that as the disciples continued with one accord in prayer, we also may unite as one body in presenting our petitions, even though we might not be together in one place. We can claim the promise that we, too, shall be filled with the Spirit.

Paul's Call to Prayer

Be alert and always keep praying for all the saints.
Pray also for me.
EPHESIANS 6:18–19

What a sense Paul had of the deep divine unity of the whole body of Christ and of the actual need of unceasing prayer for all the members of the body!

Believers should not pray occasionally, but unceasingly, as Paul's words clearly indicate: "Always keep praying for all the saints." Paul expected Christians to be so filled with the consciousness of their being in Christ, and through Him united to the whole body, that their highest aim would be the welfare of the body of Christ. He counted on their being so filled with the Spirit that it would be perfectly natural to them to pray for all who belong to the body of Christ. As natural as it is for each member of my body to be ready to do what is needful for the welfare of the whole body, so will the joy and the love of all His members always accompany the consciousness of union with Christ.

This is just what we need in our daily lives: believers who yield themselves entirely to Christ Jesus, and always live in the consciousness that they are one with Christ and His body. Just as in times of war millions of people are prepared to sacrifice their lives for their country, so the saints of God should live for Christ their King and for all the members of that body of which He is the head. May God's people be willing to make this sacrifice of prayer and intercession at all times and for all saints!

Lord, I pray that it will become perfectly natural for me to pray for all those who belong to the body of Christ. Open my eyes and heart to the world around me.

Paul's Request
for Prayer

*Pray also for me, that whenever I open my mouth, words may be given
me so that I will fearlessly make known the mystery of the gospel.*
EPHESIANS 6:19

What light these words cast on Paul's faith in the absolute necessity
and the wonderful power of prayer! He asks the church to pray that
he may "fearlessly make known the mystery of the gospel." Paul had
been a minister of the gospel for more than twenty years when he
wrote this. One would think that by this time he was an experienced
preacher. But so deep was Paul's conviction of his own insufficiency
and weakness that he was completely dependent on divine teaching
and power to do his work. This sense of his total and unalterable
dependence on God, who was with him, teaching
him what and how to speak, was the grounds for
his confidence and the keynote of his whole life.

But there is more. During those twenty years
Paul had often been in circumstances where there
was not a single soul to pray for him and he had to
depend on God alone. And yet, such was his deep
spiritual insight into the unity of the body of
Christ and of his own dependence on prayer that
he pleaded for the church's prayers. As a wrestler
cannot afford to dispense with the help of even the
weakest member of his body, so Paul could not do
without the prayers of the believers.

*Thank You, Lord,
that Your faithful
children pray for
me, too. Let this
knowledge
strengthen me.*

We must awake to the fact that all believers here on earth are
called to intercede for the power of God's Spirit in all His servants,
that they may fearlessly make known the mystery of the gospel.

Prayer for All Saints

We always thank God...when we pray for you, because we have heard of your faith in Christ Jesus and of the love you have for all the saints.
COLOSSIANS 1:3–4

Prayer for all the saints. Time, thought, and love are needed to realize what is included in this expression. Think of your own neighborhood and the saints you know. Think of your country and praise God for all those who are His saints. Think of the Christian nations of the world and the saints to be found in each of them. And then think of all the unbelieving nations and the saints of God to be found among them in ever-increasing numbers.

Think of all the different circumstances and conditions in which these believers find themselves, and of all their needs that call for God's grace and help. Think of the many who are God's saints, and yet through ignorance or sloth, through worldliness or a heart of unbelief, are walking in the dark and bringing no honor to God. Think of the many believers who take up religion seriously and yet experience lives of failure, with little or no power to please God or bless man. Think also of those whose one aim is to serve the Lord and be a light for those around them.

Lord, thank You that I may stand before You with the needs and praise of all Your children.

Pray that these may know they are part of the body of Christ. Pray for the great promise of the Holy Spirit and the love and oneness of heart that He alone can give. This is not the work of one day or one night. It needs a heart that is willing to seriously consider the state and the need of the body of Christ. Pray constantly for the love of God and Christ to fill the hearts of His people, and for the power of the Holy Spirit to come down and accomplish God's work in this sinful world.

Prayer by All Saints

You help us by your prayers.
Then many will give thanks on our behalf for
the gracious favor granted us in answer to the prayers of many.
2 CORINTHIANS 1:11

There are many believers who almost never think of the privilege they have to intercede for the body of Christ and its members. There are many who do intercede in the power of the Holy Spirit and for whom we must thank God. Unfortunately, their thoughts may be chiefly limited to spheres of work that they are acquainted with, or directly interested in.

We are now left with a limited number of Christians who will intercede for the unity of the body and the power of the Holy Spirit. Although it is a prayer that ought to be sent up by the entire church of Christ on earth, only a small number of believers feel themselves drawn to take part in this daily prayer for the outpouring of the Spirit on all God's people.

And yet it is an unspeakable privilege to make Christ's last prayer, "that we may be one," the daily supplication of our faith and love. It may be that in time believers will bond together in small circles and help to rouse those around them to pray for the unity of all believers.

This message must be sent out as a love letter from heart to heart, so that believers will pray unceasingly for the power of His love and Spirit to be revealed to all His people.

Lord, I am praying
for the unity of
the believers
around me. Please
reveal Your
strength and love
in and through
each one of us.

The Fullness of the Spirit

"Bring the whole tithe into the storehouse, that there may be food in my house. Test me in this, and see if I will not throw open the floodgates of heaven and pour out so much blessing that you will not have room enough for it."
MALACHI 3:10

This last promise in the Old Testament tells us how abundant God's blessing will be. Pentecost was only the beginning of what God was willing to do. The promise of the Father, as Christ gave it, still waits for its perfect fulfillment.

What is it that we have to ask for, and what should we expect? Christ's great command to go and preach the gospel was not only meant for the disciples, but for us, too. Christ's last promise to His disciples, that they would be baptized with the Holy Spirit, was also meant for us. It is the grounds for the confident assurance that our prayers will be heard.

Lord, I pray for the richness of Your blessing on me and on all Your children.

Take time today to think of the needs of the church and her missionaries. Let us realize that the only solution to our problems is the supernatural, almighty intervention of the Lord Himself. He must rouse His hosts for the great battle against evil. No other matter can be so important as to pray for the ministers of the gospel, and for all His people, that God would endue them with power from on high to make the gospel the power of God unto salvation.

When you connect the prayer for the church on earth with the prayer for the power of God in heaven, you will feel the great truths of the heavenly world and the kingdom of God taking possession of you. You will ask what God is longing to give to all of His children whose hearts are entirely yielded to Him in faith and obedience.

Prayer Every Day

"Give us each day our daily bread."
LUKE 11:3

There are some Christians who think daily prayer is impossible, yet they pray to God to give them their daily bread. Surely if a child of God has once yielded his entire life to God's love and service, he should count it a privilege to appear before God daily with the needs and desires of the church and the kingdom.

Are there not many that confess that they desire to live entirely for God? They acknowledge that Christ gave Himself for them, and that He protects them and works in them. They acknowledge that the measure of Christ's love to us is to be the measure of our love to Him. If this is indeed to be the standard of their lives, they ought to welcome every opportunity to devote themselves to the interests of Christ's kingdom and to the prayer that can bring down God's blessing.

This is an invitation to daily prayer, to remind God of His promises and to pray for His blessing on His people and on this needy world. Regard it a privilege to pray on behalf of the saints for the working of the Holy Spirit, for the coming of His kingdom, and for His will to be done on earth as it is in heaven. Even those who already

Lord, let my first priority always be to pray for others and for the world.

pray for the work of certain groups should be encouraged to expand their vision, and their hearts, to include all God's saints and all the work of His kingdom. Let them pray for the abundant outpouring of the Holy Spirit, so that their hearts may be strengthened with a joy and a love and a faith that they have never known before.

One of Heart in Prayer

They were all together in one place....
All of them were filled with the Holy Spirit.
ACTS 2:1, 4

Our recent daily readings have opened to us wonderful thoughts of the solidarity of the whole body of Christ, and the need to deliberately cultivate our slumbering or buried talents of intercession. We may indeed thank God for the tens of thousands of His children who intercede for others. However, there is still a lack of that large-hearted and universal love that takes up all the saints of God and their service into its embrace.

We said that a wrestler in the games gathers up his entire strength and counts on every member of his body to do its best. A country's soldiers, though deployed all over the world, pledge their loyalty to one army and one leader. And this is what we need in the church of Christ—enthusiasm for the King and His kingdom and faith in His purpose! May our daily prayers therefore include the *entire* body of Christ, even to the very feeblest.

Thank You, Lord, that I may be a member of Your victorious army.

As we have seen, the strength unity provides is inconceivable. The power of each individual member is increased by the inspiration of fellowship with a large and conquering host. Nothing can so help us to an ever larger faith as knowing we are one body and one spirit in Christ Jesus. United prayer brings the answer to prayer!

A Personal Call

It is true that some preach Christ out of envy and rivalry,
but others out of goodwill. The latter do so in love, knowing that
I am put here for the defense of the gospel.
The former preach Christ out of selfish ambition, not sincerely.

PHILIPPIANS 1:15–17

When we plead with Christians to pray without ceasing, there are many who quietly decide that such a life is not possible for them. They do not have a special gift for prayer; they do not have an intense desire to glorify Christ by winning souls for Him; they have not yet learned what it is to live for Him who died for them and rose again. Such people only use Christ as a convenience to escape from hell and to secure a place in heaven.

It is to these people that we bring the call to surrender their lives entirely to Christ. We come to them with the assurance that God can change their lives and fill their hearts with Christ and His Holy Spirit. We plead with them to believe that with God all things are possible. He is able and willing, and even most anxious, to restore them to the Father's house, to the joy of His presence and service.

To attain this they must listen to the call for men and women who, in the power of Christ's abiding presence, will pray unceasingly for all saints. It is nothing less than the acknowledging of a duty, a sacrifice that Christ's love has a right to claim. Anyone who, despite his own shortcomings, accepts this call as coming from Christ and humbly prays for God's grace to do it, will have taken the first step toward fellowship with God.

Lord, I want to obey Your call. Please change my life and fill my heart with Your Holy Spirit.

The Secret of Brotherly Love

The subject of love is one of the most difficult and profound of themes. When one sees the hatred on earth that reached its climax in the rejection and the crucifixion of the Lord Jesus Christ, it is difficult to think of the heavenly glory as an ocean of holy, all-embracing love. Think of the state of the world at present, and then realize the power Satan wields to divide even God's children from each other in bitterest enmity.

And how shall we, above all, persuade God's children to believe that this life in the love of God is not only possible, but also a solemn duty and worth the sacrifice of all to possess and proclaim it? People will not believe that it is possible to be so filled with the love of God that love shall flow forth from them as streams of living water.

The reason so many Christians fail to live a life in the love of God is simply that we have no power in ourselves to love God or our fellow men or our enemies. Such love we can only receive from above when we cast ourselves down before God with a sense of our own impotence and unworthiness, that He may fill us with His Holy Spirit.

Love and Faith

*And this is his command: to believe in the name of his Son, Jesus Christ,
and to love one another as he commanded us.*

1 JOHN 3:23

At a conference the subject of brotherly love fell to the lot of a certain minister. But he demurred, saying, "I cannot speak on that subject, and I have never yet preached on it." In explanation he said, "You know that I studied in Holland, where the subject of love was left to the liberal section. They did not believe in God's stern justice or in the redemption through Christ. God is love; that is enough. The orthodox party was not allowed to suggest that their opponents should be put out of the church. No, all should be borne in love! And so it came to pass that the orthodox party were strong in preaching faith, but left the preaching of love to the liberal section."

The church must learn not only to preach the love of God in redemption. She must go further and teach Christians to show that the love of Christ is in their hearts, by love shown to their brothers. Our Lord called this command a badge by which the world could recognize His disciples!

There is great need for the preaching of love. God sometimes allows bitterness to arise between Christians, that they may view the terrible power of sin in their hearts and shrink back at the sight. How greatly a minister and his people should feel the importance of Christ's command to love one another. A life of great holiness will result, if we only but love each other as Christ loves us.

Help me to understand God's love for me, and the love the Holy Spirit works in me to love God and my fellow men.

Faith and Love

*The grace of our Lord was poured out on me abundantly,
along with the faith and love that are in Christ Jesus.*

1 TIMOTHY 1:14

These words of Paul show us the connection between faith and love in the life of the Christian. Faith always comes first; it roots itself deeply in the love of God and bears fruit in love to others. As in nature the root and the fruit are inseparable; so it is with faith and love in the realm of grace.

Too often the two are separated, though on the Day of Pentecost they were one. There was a powerful faith towards the Lord Jesus, along with a fervent love to others. The sum of the preaching on that day was simply, *Believe in the name of Jesus Christ and you shall receive the gift of the Holy Spirit.* The result was that the believers became one of heart and soul, and they shared all their possessions with one another.

Alas, that this should not have been wholly the case at the Reformation. A powerful reformation took place in regard to the doctrine of faith, but at the same time there was a lack of love between the preachers and the leaders in that faith! So the world was not taught the lesson that God's love was all-powerful to sanctify the entire life of a man.

Let this thought sink deep into our hearts: *The grace of our Lord abounds exceedingly with faith and love.* As we cultivate faith in God's love, our hearts will be filled with love toward others. The genuineness of our faith in the love of God must be shown by love in our daily lives at home.

May God help us by faith to be rooted in His love, that we may at all times be living examples of its truth and power, and so become a blessing to others.

The Love of God

God is love.
Whoever lives in love lives in God, and God in him.
1 JOHN 4:16

The God who wills nothing but good is a God of love. He does not seek His own. He does not live for Himself, but pours out His love on all living creatures.

The characteristic of love is that it does not seek its own. Love finds its happiness in giving to others; it sacrifices itself entirely for others. Even so, God offered Himself to people in the Person of His Son, and the Son offered Himself on the cross to bring that love to men and to win their hearts. The everlasting love with which the Father loved the Son is the same love with which the Son loves us. Christ has poured this love of God into our hearts through the Holy Spirit, so that our whole life may be permeated with its vital power.

The love of God to His Son, the love of the Son to us, the love with which we love the Son, the love with which we in obedience love others, the love with which we try to love all men and win them for Christ—all is the same eternal, incomprehensible, almighty love of God. Love is the power of God in the Father, Son, and Holy Spirit. This love is the possession of all who are members of the body of Christ, and it streams forth from them to the entire world.

Lord, I thank You for the love that You poured into my heart. Inspire me to radiate this love to the world around me.

The Love of Christ

For Christ's love compels us.
2 CORINTHIANS 5:14

God sent His Son to the world to reveal His everlasting love as it is known in heaven. God's desire was that this same love should take possession of the hearts of men.

And how did He fulfill this desire? By sending Christ to earth to reveal the love of the Father and win our hearts to Him. The Lord Jesus became man and in His dealings with the poor and needy, and with those who were unbelieving and rebellious, and through His miracles, He poured out His love into the hearts of sinful men.

With the same purpose our Lord chose the disciples to be always with Him and to be filled with His love. With this purpose He gave on the cross the greatest proof of love that the world has ever seen. He took our sins upon Him. He bore the suffering and the scorn of His enemies, so that friend and foe alike might know God's eternal love.

Lord, I yield my heart and life to You. Please fill it with Your love to such an extent that it will flow out to others around me.

And then, after He had ascended to heaven, He gave us the Holy Spirit to pour out His love into our hearts. Impelled by the love of Christ, the disciples in turn offered their lives to reveal His love to others.

God longs to have our hearts filled with His love. Open your heart and life for this love. Then He will be able to use you as a channel for His love to flow out to your fellow men.

Love of the Holy Spirit

God has poured out his love into our hearts by the Holy Spirit,
whom he has given us.
ROMANS 5:5

Many Christians have to confess to their heavenly Father that they lack a fervent, childlike love. They realize that they cannot keep Christ's great command to love their neighbors as themselves.

What is the cause of this failure? Has the heavenly Father made no provision for His children on earth, enabling them to prove their love to Him and to one another? Certainly He has. But God's children have not learned the lesson that there must be a constant renewal of faith in what God is able to do. One tries to stir up love toward God in one's heart, yet is conscious all the time that in one's own strength one cannot awaken the slightest love toward God.

Believe that the love of God will work in your heart as a vital power to enable you to love God and your fellow men. Cease to expect the least love in yourself. Believe in the power of God's love working within you, teaching you to love God, your fellow men, and even your enemies with the love of God.

Pray each day for the Holy Spirit to pour out the love of God into your heart and then let it stream forth to all around you!

Lord, in my own strength I am incapable of stirring up my heart. Thank You for giving me love as a fruit of Your Spirit.

The Power of Love

In all these things we are more than
conquerors through him who loved us.
ROMANS 8:37

In days of unrest and strong racial feeling, we need a new discovery of the love of God. Let us anchor our hope in the thought of God's love. God's power, by which He rules and guides the world, is the power of an undying, persistent love. He works through men and women wholly yielded to Him and His service. He waits for them to open their hearts to Him and then, full of courage, to become witnesses for Him.

When this has been achieved, Christ's kingdom is manifested and the reign of love on earth begins. Christ died in order to establish this kingdom. The only means He used to gain influence was through the manifestation of a serving, suffering love. He saw the possibility of redemption in the hearts of even the worst of men and women. He knew that our hearts could never resist the steady, continuous influence of love; that unbounded faith in God's love would be our strength and stay. It was this love that enabled the disciples to expect and do the impossible.

Arguments or reproaches can never overcome a spirit of hatred and bitterness. Our faith in love as the greatest power in the world should prepare us for a life in communion with God in prayer, and for a life of unselfish service amongst our fellow men.

Lord, I pray that others will be able to see Your love radiating from me. Your love is the strength in my life!

The Sign of a True Church

"By this all men will know that you are my disciples, if you love one another."
JOHN 13:35

We are taught that the true church is to be found where God's Word is rightly preached and the holy sacraments dispensed, as instituted by Christ. Christ Himself took a much broader view. To Him the distinguishing mark of His followers is a life lived in love to others. In God, love reaches its highest expression and is the culmination of His glory. Christ Jesus is the expression of this love.

We owe everything to this love. Love is the power that moved Christ to die for us. In love, God highly exalted Him as Lord. Love is the power that broke our hearts, and love is the power that heals them. Love is the power through which Christ dwells in us and works in us. Love can change my whole nature and enable me to surrender all to God. It gives me the strength to live a holy, joyous life, full of blessing to others. Every Christian should mirror the love of God.

Alas, Christians seldom realize this! They seek, in the power of human love, to love Christ and their fellow men. And when they fail, they stop desiring it or praying for it. They do not understand that we may, and can, love with God's own love that is poured into our hearts by the Holy Spirit. If we fully believe that the Holy Spirit will maintain this heavenly love from hour to hour, we shall be able to love God and Christ with all our heart. We shall also be able to love our fellow men and, yes, even our enemies.

Lord, I desire to be Your witness and win hearts for Your kingdom through the love that the Holy Spirit pours into my heart.

Race-Hatred

*At one time we too were foolish…. We lived in malice and envy,
being hated and hating one another.*
TITUS 3:3

What a dark picture of the state of human nature and of human society! But what caused this sad condition? Adam's Fall. Cain, the first child of Adam, was guilty of murdering his own brother and came under the power of the devil, who "was a murderer from the beginning" (John 8:44). When God saw how wicked the human species had become, He almost destroyed mankind by a flood. But soon after the flood there were signs that man was still under the power of sin.

No wonder that man's love of his own people, implanted in his heart by nature, soon changed to hatred. Love for the country became the fruitful source of race-hatred, war, and bloodshed. Note how, here in South Africa, God placed two groups side-by-side to see if our Christianity will enable us to overcome race-hatred and prove the text: "There is neither Jew nor Greek, slave nor free, male nor female, for you are all one in Christ Jesus" (Galatians 3:28).

Oh God, make known to us Your love in heavenly power, and let it take full possession of our lives!

What an opportunity for the church of Christ and her ministers to preach and proclaim the love of God, and to prove its might to change race-hatred into brotherly love! God has abundant power to bring this to pass.

What a call to every Christian to pray for himself and others, that we may not make the Word of God powerless by our unbelief!

Love Your Enemies

You have heard that it was said,
"Love your neighbor and hate your enemy."
MATTHEW 5:43

The Jewish teachers in Christ's earthly days used these words in reference to what was written in Leviticus: "Do not hate your brother in your heart" and "Do not seek revenge or bear a grudge against one of your people, but love your neighbor as yourself" (Leviticus 19:17–18).

From this text the rabbis drew the wrong conclusion that they only had to love their own people, but could hate their enemies. The Lord, however, said that we must love our enemies and bless those who curse us.

Of course, it is much easier for a Christian to follow the example of the Jewish teachers! The command of our Lord is too strict and narrow for us. We often do not yield ourselves to God in obedience to His commandment to love our fellow men with Christ's love. What if that love should flow out to all around, even to those who hate us? This would require much grace and cost us time and trouble and serious prayer.

When I was a minister in Cape Town, I experienced the wonder of a black man who at first found it impossible to love members of the Fingo tribe. After he had seriously prayed for the love of Christ to be poured out into his heart by the Holy Spirit, he was able to confess, "Me *now* love Fingo!" He had prayed about it, and God had heard his prayer. There is only one way to love our enemies: by the love of Christ, sought and found in prayer.

Lord, You know how difficult I find it to love some people. Please work within me until I can truthfully say that I love all human beings.

Forgive, Forget

"For I will forgive their wickedness and
will remember their sins no more."
JEREMIAH 31:34

At the unveiling of the Women's Monument at Bloemfontein in 1913, I was sitting in the front row of the platform at the foot of the monument. After a while the sun became very hot. Suddenly, I felt that someone behind me was holding an umbrella over my head. When the speaker had finished, I asked the man beside me, "Who was so friendly to hold an umbrella over my head?" His answer: "General De Wet." I was surprised and, turning round, thanked the general heartily. He answered, "I would gladly have paid for the privilege of doing it." What a generous nature to speak in this way!

Lord, enable me to forgive and forget.

Then the general's turn came to address the audience. I could agree with all that he said that day, except with his last words. Regarding the suffering of the Boers during the Boer War, he said, "Forgive—yes; but forget—never." When the ceremony was over, I shook hands with the general again and gave him a friendly warning: "Beware of the consequences that the words 'forget—never' may hold."

Many people have allowed themselves to be deceived by these words. I have often seen a dog come in at the front door, looking for shade. He would be driven out and the door closed. Then he would come through the back door and be in the house again. One wishes to put away all thoughts of hatred or ill feeling. But see how quickly and quietly these evil thoughts return through the back door. God forgives and forgets. "Forgive as the Lord forgave you" (Colossians 3:13). Whenever you find it difficult to forgive, go to the throne of grace and pray that the Lord will fill your heart with love.

As God Forgives

"But if you do not forgive men their sins,
your Father will not forgive your sins."
MATTHEW 6:15

God forgives sinners. He sets them free and receives them back into His love and favor. The forgiveness of sins gives us the confidence to approach God and is the source of our salvation. The forgiveness of sins gives us cause for thankfulness every day of our lives.

God desires that we should live as people who have been freely forgiven. And we can only prove our sincerity by forgiving those who have offended us, as freely and as willingly as God has forgiven us.

How clearly and urgently our Lord speaks of forgiveness in His Word! In the Lord's Prayer we are taught to pray, "Forgive us our debts, as we also have forgiven our debtors" (Matthew 6:12). Jesus then says, "But if you do not forgive men their sins, your Father will not forgive your sins" (Matthew 6:15).

In Matthew 18:21–22, we have the question of Peter: "Lord, how many times shall I forgive my brother when he sins against me? The Lord's answer: "I tell you, not seven times, but seventy-seven times."

Lord, give me the grace to forgive others as willingly and freely as You forgive me.

The parable of the servant who refused to forgive ends with this warning from our Lord: "This is how my heavenly Father will treat each of you unless you forgive your brother from your heart" (Matthew 18:35).

Let us remember to forgive others as God forgives us!

The Preaching of Love

But the greatest of these is love.
1 CORINTHIANS 13:13

During the Boer War, when there was much unrest in the country, a certain minister asked his colleague—a leader in the church—to do his best to calm the minds of those around him. His answer was, "I am not able to do it, as I am unsettled in my own mind." Many of our ministers today would most probably give the same answer if they were asked to preach about love. How can they preach love if they have no love in their hearts?

Yet there is a remedy. John Wesley's ministry was at first powerless and, according to him, without the joy and love that a Moravian colleague possessed. He asked the Moravian what he should do. The answer was, "Preach love because you believe it is what God's Word teaches, and you will soon find what you are seeking. Then you will be able to preach it because you possess it." Wesley took the advice and soon began to preach with such power that many were converted.

Lord, I pray for all preachers of the gospel. Give them the strength through Your Holy Spirit to preach about love, to live in love, and to act in love.

This has been my own experience. Often in preaching, or in writing, I have asked myself, *But do you possess what you preach to others?* And I have followed this advice: Preach it, because you believe it to be the teaching of God's Word and heartily desire it. Preach the truth by faith, and the experience will follow. Let the minister who feels impelled to preach about love not hesitate to do so, and he will soon be able to preach it because he has himself received that which he commends.

The Two Leaders

*I urge, then, first of all, that requests, prayers,
intercession and thanksgiving be made for everyone—
for kings and all those in authority, that we may live
peaceful and quiet lives in all godliness and holiness.*
1 TIMOTHY 2:1–2

At the time of the unveiling of the Women's Monument at Bloemfontein, I spoke a few words about the suffering, praying, and all-conquering love of these women, who prayed that God would keep them from hatred or want of love toward their enemies. I expressed the hope that their prayers might be ours, and that nothing would disturb the feeling of peace and unity. The danger existed that strife may ensue not only between the different races in the country, but also between brothers and fellow countrymen. Not long after, we heard that there had been a breach between the leaders of the two parties.

I felt compelled to write an article on the question "For whom do you pray?" Most of the readers were of the opinion that they should pray only for the party and the leader of their choice. But would it not be sad if we came into God's presence divided into two camps, praying one against the other? No, we must pray for both our leaders and for all those who are in authority. As leaders of the people, their influence for good or evil is inexpressible. Their hearts are in God's hands, and He has the power to change them according to His will.

Lord, the hearts of our leaders are in Your hands. Teach them to do Your will.

Let our prayers ascend to God in all sincerity, and He will hear and grant that which is good for the whole country.

Unfeigned Love of Others

Now that you have purified yourselves by obeying the truth so that you have sincere love for your brothers, love one another deeply, from the heart.
1 PETER 1:22

Peter speaks of love to the brethren. In the days of the early church it was clearly understood at conversion that in confessing Christ the new convert also promised unfeigned love to others. Unfeigned, fervent love for others through the Spirit should be the chief token of a true conversion.

Peter's letter lays much stress on love. He says, "All of you, live in harmony with one another; be sympathetic, love as brothers, be compassionate and humble" (1 Peter 3:8). He continues, "Above all, love each other deeply, because love covers over a multitude of sins" (1 Peter 4:8). These are all signs of the life of God in one's soul. Unfeigned, fervent love for others is the indispensable sign of true godliness.

Lord, purify my life from all hatred and selfishness and let Your Spirit of love rule in my heart.

God's Word is a mirror into which the church and each individual member must look to see whether we are truly Christian, showing by our conduct that we take God's Word as our rule of life. If our hearts condemn us, we must turn at once to God, confessing our sins. Let us believe that the Spirit of love does indeed dwell within us, that He will shed abroad God's love in our hearts and purify us from all hatred and selfishness, and that He will restore the image of Christ within us. Let us not rest content until we have surrendered ourselves wholly to God, that His Spirit of love may reign and rule within.

The Spirit of Love

This is love for God: to obey his commands.
And his commands are not burdensome.

1 JOHN 5:3

Our love, which is the fruit of the Spirit, does not consist merely in the knowledge of, and faith in, God's love as revealed in our redemption. No, the matter goes far deeper. Our love has its origin in the fact that the Holy Spirit has poured out the love of God in our hearts, not only as an experience or feeling, but as something that takes possession of us and directs, controls, and inspires us. This love becomes a heavenly life-power, a disposition of the soul, whereby man knows that God is good. The Spirit gives to love such a form that it contains the commands of the divine love within itself, and thus can keep His commandments without difficulty (see 1 John 5:3).

The sum total of God's law is love. It governs the life of the man wholly devoted to God and controls his thoughts and actions. The divine love in the heart of man is the source from which the child of God receives the power to live in the love of God. This divine love includes fellowship with God, union with Christ, and love to others.

Thank You, Lord, that Your Holy Spirit enables me to obey Your law of love.

This love can only be attained through faith, together with a deep sense of our own impotence. Love is a gift given to us by the Holy Spirit. We must thank God for this love. We can only love God and our fellow men in the power of the Holy Spirit.

A Song of Love

And now these three remain: faith, hope and love.
But the greatest of these is love.
1 CORINTHIANS 13:13

First Corinthians 13 is devoted to the praise of love. The first three verses speak of the importance of love in our religion. If I speak in the tongues of angels or have the gift of prophecy; if I have the faith to remove mountains or bestow all my goods on the poor and give my body to be burned, but have no love, then I am nothing.

Then follows the Song of Love (1 Corinthians 13:4–8). Here fifteen things are said about love—what it is and what it is not. Two sentences here sum up the whole nature of love: "It is not self-seeking" and "Love perseveres." Prophecies, tongues, and knowledge will pass away. Even faith and hope will disappear. But love abides to all eternity, as long as God endures. We should read this chapter more often, so that these words may be indelibly imprinted on our hearts. Let love rule in your life. God is love.

Lord, I confess that without love I am nothing. Please fill my heart with Your everlasting love.

We are living in a world that is uncharitable and selfish, full of bitterness and hatred. Therefore, take refuge under the wings of everlasting love. Let your heart be filled with it, so that by God's almighty power you may be a witness to the transforming power of love. Thus you will be a fountain of blessing to all around you.

Live each day in fellowship with the triune love of the Father, Son, and Holy Spirit, and you will learn the secret of how to love.

The Obedience of Love

If you love me, you will obey what I command.
JOHN 14:15

The Father loved His Son with a wonderful, everlasting love. The Father gave His Son all that He was and had. The Son responded to this love by giving His Father all. Cost what it might, He kept the Father's commands and abided in His love.

Christ, in His great love to us, sacrificed all: His life and death were wholly at our disposal. All He asks from us is that we, out of love, should keep His commands. "If you love me, you will obey what I command." These words lose their power because Christians believe it is impossible to always keep His commands. Yet our Lord really meant it, for in the last night with His disciples He promised them that the power of the Spirit would enable them to live a life of obedience.

But what becomes of man's sinful nature? The Holy Spirit is the power of God that works within us, both to will and to do, and so prevents the flesh from gaining the upper hand (see Philippians 2:13; Hebrews 13:20–21).

"If anyone loves me, he will obey my teaching...and we will come to him and make our home with him" (John 14:23). "He who loves me will be loved by my Father, and I too will love him and show myself to him" (John 14:21). These are no mere idle words. Believe it, and the Holy Spirit will give you the power to abide in the love of Jesus and to keep His commands with great joy.

Lord, I do love You and it is my greatest desire to obey Your commands. Please help me to do Your will.

Love and Prayer

The end of all things is near.
Therefore be clear minded and self-controlled so that you can pray.
Above all, love each other deeply, because love covers over a multitude of sins.
1 PETER 4:7–8

In the above text, prayer and love are closely linked. Love forces us to pray not only for ourselves, but also for those whom we love and even for those with whom we do not agree.

Prayer plays an important role in the life of love. These two fruits of the Spirit are inseparably connected. If you wish your love to grow and increase, forget yourself and seriously pray for God's children and His church. And if you want to increase in prayerfulness, give yourself in fervent love to the service of those around you, helping to bear their burdens.

Lord, forgive my selfishness to pray only for myself.

Help me to intercede for others and for a troubled world.

There is a great need of serious, powerful intercessors. If there is little love among Christians it can be ascribed to a lack of prayer for others. God desires His children, as members of one body, to pray down the power of the Spirit upon all believers. Unity is strength. Real spiritual unity will help us to forget ourselves, to live unselfishly, to live wholly for God and our fellow men. There can be no surer way of growing in the spirit of love than by uniting daily at the throne of grace.

When we meditate on love, we shall feel compelled to pray. And those who pray will be filled with the love of God.

The First and Great Command

*The LORD your God will circumcise your hearts
and the hearts of your descendants, so that you may love him
with all your heart and with all your soul, and live.*

DEUTERONOMY 30:6

God greatly desires our love. It is the nature of all love to long to be acceptable and to meet with response. Yes, God longs with a never-ending, fervent desire to have the love of our whole heart.

But how can we ever respond wholeheartedly to God's love? In the same way that we receive salvation—through faith alone. Paul says, "The life I live in the body, I live by faith in the Son of God, who loved me and gave himself for me" (Galatians 2:20).

When we take time to wait on God and remember with what burning desire He sought to win our love, through the gift of His Son, we shall realize how God longs for us to respond to His love. Ask God to let His light shine into your heart. God longs to give you the light and glow of His love. There is nothing on earth that can be compared to this experience!

In the Old Testament, God gave us the promise of a New Covenant: "I will give you a new heart and put a new spirit in you" (Ezekiel 36:26). And so He gave His Son to die for us, in order to win our love. God, who so greatly longs for my love, will work within me by His Spirit, granting my desire to love Him with my whole heart and enabling me to prove my love by obeying His commands.

Oh Lord, I bow before You; fulfill my longing desire, which is also Your desire, that my heart may be filled with Your love.

The Royal Law of Love

If you really keep the royal law found in Scripture,
"Love your neighbour as yourself," you are doing right.
JAMES 2:8

Our Lord asks us to love our neighbors as we love ourselves. This is the second great command. In heaven and on earth, love is the royal law—love is supreme.

The Christian's love for his fellow men has more than one purpose: It reveals to us our new nature which God implanted in us, and it implicates that we should love ourselves and love our neighbors with the same love.

Christianity teaches us to love our neighbor because God loves him. Every human being has a share in God's compassion and love, because he is made in God's image. We ought then to love our neighbors, not merely because they are fellow men, but because we can see God's likeness in them. As Christians we should love others with the same love that God has for us. Christ died on the cross for our sins; therefore, we who received this love should share it with others. We must learn from our Father in heaven how to love.

The Christian love for all human beings can always increase. This is the law for each child of God: He must love his brother with the same love with which Christ has loved him.

May God write the royal law of love deep in our hearts.

Thank You, Lord, for Your royal law of love in which I may share. Help me to show my gratitude with acts.

One in God's Hand

*I am going to take the stick of Joseph—which is in Ephraim's hand—
and of the Israelite tribes associated with him, and join it to Judah's stick,
making them a single stick of wood, and they will become one in my hand.*
EZEKIEL 37:19

When Ephraim and Judah became one in God's hand, the differences between the two did not disappear. Each kept his characteristics. But they were one in true unity and mutual love. "Ephraim shall not envy Judah, and Judah shall not vex Ephraim." God will fulfill this promise to us, too, but only on one condition: We must place our people in God's hand by praying for them.

At a certain stage in the history of South Africa, the mighty British Empire overpowered a small group of Afrikaners. Each of these nations had its own history, its own national characteristics, and its own virtues and shortcomings. In God's plan and council there was room for both of them.

Why then was there so much strife and discord between the two nations? Because people would not accept both viewpoints and accord to each its right; they wanted one or the other, exclusively, in the foreground. Ideally, people should be faithful in preserving their own nationality, and at the same time show love and appreciation for the second nationality with whom their lot has been cast.

In the South Africa of today, Afrikaners have the opportunity to show what it means to be true South Africans, and yet, at the same time, be faithful subjects of the present government. Let us, by means of intercession, place our people in God's hand. He can and will give the love and mutual endurance that is needed.

Lord, I pray for every nation in our land. Give us the love and mutual endurance to become one.

Pray for Love

*May the Lord make your love increase and overflow for each other
and for everyone else, just as ours does for you. May he strengthen your
hearts so that you will be blameless and holy in the presence of our
God and Father when our Lord Jesus comes with all his holy ones.*

1 THESSALONIANS 3:12–13

Paul regarded love for one another as a condition for growth in the
knowledge of God. Christians should not live for themselves, he said,
but be bound to one another in love. Paul often prayed that the love
of believers for others would increase:

In 1 Thessalonians 3:12–13, Paul said that believers' lives and
progress on the road to spiritual maturity would be strengthened if
they loved one another.

In 2 Thessalonians 3:5, he said that the Lord wanted to direct
believers' hearts into God's love and Christ's perseverance to give them purpose in life.

*Lord, by your
great love, grant
me a heart of love
and teach me
to pray.*

In Colossians 2:2, Paul wrote, "My purpose
is that they may be encouraged in heart and
united in love…in order that they may know the
mystery of God, namely, Christ, in whom are
hidden all the treasures of wisdom and knowledge."

Paul's prayer for the Philippians was that
their "love may abound more and more in knowledge and depth of insight" (Philippians 1:9).

As the sun gives its light and heat to plants
that they may grow and bear fruit, so God longs to give us His love
in ever-increasing measure. Take these words of divine love, and ponder them in your heart. You will gain a strong and joyous assurance of
what God is able to do for you. He will make you to abound in love.

Like Christ

"I have set you an example that you should do as I have done for you."
JOHN 13:15

The love of Christ, manifested in His death on the cross, is the only rule for our daily life and conduct. Our Lord clearly says, "You should do as I have done for you." The love of Christ is our only hope of salvation. A walk in that love is the way truly and fully to enjoy that salvation.

"Be imitators of God, therefore, as dearly loved children and live a life of love, just as Christ loved us and gave himself up for us as a fragrant offering and sacrifice to God" (Ephesians 5:1–2). Here again, love is everything. Christ loved us even unto death, and because of that we are now God's children. It follows naturally that we should walk in love. It is certain that those who keep close to Christ will walk in love.

Colossians 3:12–14 tells us we must be patient with one another and forgive whatever grievances we may have against one another. Romans 15:7 tells us God will work the power within us to accept one another as Christ accepted us. What a blessed life in the love and the power that we have in Christ! What a blessed life in His fellowship, when we are led by the Holy Spirit and strengthened for a life in His likeness!

"Whoever claims to live in him must walk as Jesus did" (1 John 2:6). Follow the example of Jesus Christ and live in His likeness.

Oh God, the Father of love, the Father of Christ, our Father, strengthen me each day to love my neighbor in Christ, just as you love me.

The Power of God's Word

The words I have spoken to you are spirit and they are life.
JOHN 6:63

The question constantly recurs: Why do God's children not realize the great value and absolute necessity of brotherly love? One answer is, because of unbelief. Without persevering faith there can be no thought of the power of love within us. But this is a different faith from what we usually mean when we say we believe in God's Word.

True faith bows before God in the deep realization of His greatness, of His power to work wonders in our hearts, and of His loving care for us. We must be convinced of our utter inability to produce on our own this love, which is holy and can conquer sin and unbelief. We need a burning desire to receive instead this heavenly love into our hearts, whatever the cost may be. Then we shall gain an insight into God's Word as a living power in our hearts. This supernatural power is a gift from God through the Holy Spirit living and working within us. It is not something that we can generate in our own strength.

Take time in God's presence to wait on Him in the confidence that His Word will work effectually in you as a seed of new life. Allow the Holy Spirit to take control of your life, so that you may experience the power of God's Word in your life. "I am not ashamed of the gospel, because it is the power of God for the salvation of everyone who believes" (Romans 1:16).

Lord, I wait on You in the firm belief that Your Word will powerfully work in me as the seed of a new life, so that I will love You and my fellow men just as You love me.

Perfect Love

Whoever loves his brother lives in the light,
and there is nothing in him to make him stumble.

1 JOHN 2:10

The main theme of John's letter is love:

"Anyone who does not do what is right is not a child of God; nor is anyone who does not love his brother" (1 John 3:10).

"This is how we know what love is: Jesus Christ laid down his life for us. And we ought to lay down our lives for our brothers" (1 John 3:16).

"Let us love one anther, for love comes from God. Everyone who loves has been born of God and knows God" (1 John 4:7).

"God is love. Whoever lives in love lives in God, and God in him" (1 John 4:16).

"If anyone says, 'I love God,' yet hates his brother, he is a liar. For anyone who does not love his brother, whom he has seen, cannot love God, whom he has not seen" (1 John 4:20).

Each of these words is a living seed and has within it a divine power that is able to take root, grow, and bear fruit in our hearts. But just as the seed requires that the soil in which it grows be kept free of all weeds, so the heart must be wholly surrendered to God and His service, so that the seed of the Word may bear heavenly fruit.

Read 1 John 3:23. Faith and love are both necessary for our salvation. Love to God and love to others are inseparable.

Lord, keep my heart free from weeds, so that the good seeds may bear heavenly fruit. I surrender myself to You.

The Love That Suffers

*Live a life of love, just as Christ loved us and gave himself up for us
as a fragrant offering and sacrifice to God.*
EPHESIANS 5:2

Is it not strange that love, which is the source of our greatest happiness, should also be the cause of our most intense suffering? Life on earth is such that suffering always follows when love seeks to save the object of its love. Yes, it is only by means of suffering that love can gain its end, and so attain the highest happiness. What a wonderful thought! Even the almighty power of God's love could not achieve its purpose without suffering that passes all understanding. By means of His suffering, Christ bore and overcame the sins of the entire world, and man was drawn closer to God.

Let no one, with such an example before Him, imagine that love is self-sufficient. True love manifests itself in a life of continual self-sacrifice. Love's strength lies in renunciation. Just think of what a mother suffers when a beloved child is ill, or when a son falls into evil ways—love gives her strength to endure, whatever the circumstances may be. Think of the suffering one who has yielded himself wholeheartedly to work and to pray for others, and what he must often endure—tears and heartache and wrestling in prayer. But love overcomes all obstacles.

Lord, thank You that You were prepared to give Your life to save us. Help me to live the life of love, whatever the cost may be.

Do you really long to know the love of Christ in all its fullness? Then yield yourself entirely to God and His service. Regard yourself as a channel through which His love can reach others. Suffer with others and intercede for them. Then you will realize that the life of love is to live for the welfare and happiness of others.

The Works of the Flesh

The acts of the sinful nature are obvious:
sexual immorality, impurity and debauchery;
idolatry and witchcraft; hatred, discord, jealousy,
fits of rage, selfish ambition, dissensions, factions and envy;
drunkenness, orgies, and the like.
GALATIANS 5:19–21

Here Paul mentions seventeen of the terrible works of the flesh; nine of these are sins against love. Even the most devoted Christians are guilty of these sins. Paul himself called out in despair, "I know that nothing good lives in me" (Romans 7:18).

Why is there so little love among Christians? And why is it so hard to arouse such love? Because of the works of the flesh. It is impossible for a Christian by his own efforts to lead a life of love. Only the Spirit of God will set us free from the law of sin and death. The fruit of the Spirit is the love of Christ that is poured out into our hearts as a fountain of love. The grace of God enables the Christian to walk not after the flesh, but after the Spirit.

Three lessons are to be learned from this:

The Christian cannot in his own strength love God and his fellow men.

The reason for so much bitterness and lack of love is that Christians often allow a sinful nature to control their lives.

The only sure way to abide in the life of love is an absolute surrender to the Holy Spirit and to be led and guided by Him each day of our lives.

Holy Spirit, take possession of me and work within me a life of love to Christ and all men.

Allow the Holy Spirit to take entire possession of you, and He will work continually within you a life of love to Christ and to all men.

The Love of a Woman

I grieve for you, Jonathan my brother; you were very dear to me.
Your love for me was wonderful, more wonderful than that of women.

2 SAMUEL 1:26

God created woman to demonstrate tenderness and quiet endurance—someone willing to sacrifice herself for the sake of others. During the first years of a child's life, he or she is dependent on the mother and learns to love her. In turn the mother learns through the child the meaning of self-sacrificing love: the beauty of the inner self and the unfading beauty of a gentle and quiet spirit (see 1 Peter 3:4).

Nowadays women are on an equal footing with men, and rightly so. One must remember, however, that a gentle and quiet spirit is of great worth in God's eyes. It is the suffering, prayerful, all-conquering love of women that secures the happiness of a people.

Lord, I pray for all the women of the world. May their lives be proof of how beautiful and powerful the love of women is!

Women should reflect the love of God in all its tenderness and sympathy. By doing so, they become living witnesses to what the love of God can do.

Think of Mary, the woman who loved much, and the other women to whom the Lord revealed Himself after His resurrection. It was the love of these women that gave them the right to be the first to meet the Lord, and to take the message to the disciples.

May God bless all the mothers and wives and daughters of the world!

Stewards of God's Love

*So then, men ought to regard us as servants of Christ
and as those entrusted with the secret things of God.*
1 CORINTHIANS 4:1

A steward is a servant to whom the king or master entrusts his treasures and goods to give to those who have a right to them. God in heaven needs men on earth to make the treasures of His love known to others, and to give love to those who need it. The minister of the gospel is a steward of the mystery of God and, above all, of the deep mystery of His everlasting love and all the blessings that flow from it.

Stewards are servants of God. They must be faithful and entirely devoted to their life's task. They must be faithful not only to God, but also to their fellow men, caring for their needs and sharing God's love with them. The divine love is a mystery and can only dwell in a heart set apart for God and filled with His love, which flows from Him as a stream of living water.

Take time to think what it really means to be a steward of God. Pray for your ministers that they may be faithful stewards of the mystery of God and of His divine love.

As servants to whom the love of God in heaven, and of Christ on the cross, has been entrusted, we must remember that the congregation, the church, and our fellow men are dependent on our faithfulness to live a heavenly life in fellowship with God. Then we will be able, with joy and in the power of the Holy Spirit, to pass on the love of God to those who so greatly need it.

*Lord, I pray for
the spiritual
leaders of our
church. Give them
the strength to be
worthy stewards
of Your
divine love.*

Faith Working Through Love

For in Christ Jesus neither circumcision nor uncircumcision has any value.
The only thing that counts is faith expressing itself through love.
GALATIANS 5:6

Faith is the root; love is the fruit. Faith becomes strong in the love of God and of Christ. Faith in God and love to our Christian brothers must always go hand in hand. Faith in the wonderful love that God gives us enables us to live in love. True faith gives us power for a life of fervent, all-embracing love.

Yet how little the church realizes of all this! How seldom does a preacher lay stress on a Christlike love to the brothers as the fruit and joy of a life of faith!

All our life—between father and mother, parents and children, brothers and sisters, friends and servants—should be a life in the love of Christ. Do not think it is impossible, for all things are possible to God. He will give us this love through His Holy Spirit.

Christians must realize that the message of salvation lies in these two words: faith and love. Let our faith each day take deeper root in God's eternal love, and the fruit of the Spirit will grow our love for others. May God imprint these words deeply in our hearts and make them a joy and strength to us.

Lord, deliver us from our blindness and our selfishness. Let Your love take full possession of us so that we may yield ourselves to live wholeheartedly in and for that love.

Abiding Presence

We know the promise of our Lord Jesus Christ, "Surely I am with you always, to the very end of the age" (Matthew 28:20). But do you experience the glorious presence of Jesus Christ in your life every moment of the day?

This month we are going to search the Bible for the blessings that God's abiding presence holds for us. We will search for ways to become more conscious of God's presence, and ways to remove the obstacles that prevent us from experiencing His presence.

Each one of us in the service of God's kingdom needs the assurance that God will accompany us on our way. We do not want to attempt in our own power to meet the challenges or resist the temptations that confront us daily. We also need the presence of God in our inner chamber when we pray.

God's presence is not reserved for a few of His children; it is for all those who love Him. As we are now preparing for Christmas, it is necessary to consider what God's abiding presence means to you and how you can live in a way that is pleasing to Him.

Abiding Presence

And surely I am with you always, to the very end of the age.
MATTHEW 28:20

When the Lord chose His twelve disciples, it was "that they might be with him and that he might send them out to preach" (Mark 3:14). A life in fellowship with Him was to be their preparation and fitness for the work of preaching. The disciples were so deeply conscious of this great privilege that when Christ spoke of His departure to the Father, their hearts were filled with great sorrow. The presence of Christ had become indispensable to them; they could not think of living without Him. To comfort them, Christ gave them the promise of the Holy Spirit, with the assurance that they would then have His heavenly presence in a sense far deeper and more intimate than they had ever known while He was on earth.

Their first vocation remained unchanged: to be with Christ and to live in unbroken fellowship with Him. Without His abiding presence, their preaching would have no power. The secret of their strength was the living testimony that Jesus Christ was with them, inspiring and directing and strengthening them. It was this that emboldened them to preach Him as the Crucified One in the midst of His enemies. They never for a moment regretted His bodily absence; He was with them, and in them, in the divine power of the Holy Spirit.

Thank You, Lord, for Your abiding presence in my life. Knowing that You are always with me inspires and strengthens me.

Everything depends on the living experience of the presence of Jesus as an essential element in preaching the gospel. Without it, work becomes a human effort, without the freshness and the power of the heavenly life. And nothing can bring back the power and the blessing but a return to the Master's feet to hear His blessed words, "I am with you always!"

The Omnipotence of Christ

All authority in heaven and on earth has been given to me.
MATTHEW 28:18

Before Christ gave His disciples their great commission, they had begun to know Jesus in that mighty resurrection power which had conquered sin and death; there was nothing too great for Him to command or for them to undertake.

Every disciple of Jesus Christ who would take part in conquering the world in His name must realize that they are doing this work as servants of the omnipotent Lord. We are to count literally upon the daily experience of being "strong in the Lord and in his mighty power" (Ephesians 6:10).

Just think of what the disciples saw of the power of Christ Jesus here on earth. And yet it was but little compared with the greater works that He will do in and through us. He has the power to work in the feeblest of His servants with the strength of the almighty God, even to use our apparent impotence to carry out His purposes. He has power over every enemy and every human heart, over every difficulty and danger.

But Christ never gives this power to be regarded as our own. It is only as He dwells and works in our hearts and lives that there can be power in our preaching and personal testimony. Only after God had said to Paul, "My power is made perfect in weakness," could Paul say, "When I am weak, then am I strong" (2 Corinthians 12:9–10).

Thank You, Lord Jesus, for the promise that You will be with me every day. Give me the strength to do whatever I have to do today.

The Omnipresence of Christ

I will be with you.
EXODUS 3:12

The first thought of man in his conception of a god is that of power, however limited. The first words with which the true God introduced Himself to Abram is, "I am God Almighty" (Genesis 17:1). The second thought in Scripture is His omnipresence. God gave His servants the promise of His unseen presence with them. To His "I am with you," their faith responded, "You are with me."

Psalm 139 speaks of God's omnipresence as something beyond comprehension: "Such knowledge is too wonderful for me, too lofty for me to attain" (v. 6). The revelation of God's omnipresence in the man Christ Jesus deepens the mystery. The grace that enables us to claim this presence as our strength and our joy is something inexpressibly blessed. And yet many of us find it difficult to understand all that is implied in this promise, and do not know how it can become the practical experience of our daily lives.

Here, as elsewhere in the spiritual life, everything depends upon our accepting Christ's Word as reality and trusting the Holy Spirit to make it true to us from moment to moment. There need not be a moment in which His presence cannot be our experience.

Our attitude must be that of a quiet, restful faith; of a humble, lowly dependence: "Be still before the LORD and wait patiently for him" (Psalm 37:7). The Lord wants to keep you in perfect peace, with all the light and the strength you will need for His service.

Lord, thank You that You are with me every moment of my life. Keep me in Your perfect peace and give me the strength to serve You faithfully.

The Savior of the World

Now we have heard for ourselves, and we know that this man really is the Savior of the world.
JOHN 4:42

Omnipotence and omnipresence are what are called natural attributes of God. They have their true worth only when linked to, and inspired by, His moral attributes, holiness and love. When our Lord spoke of His omnipotence and His omnipresence in Matthew 28, His words pointed to that which lies at the root of all—His divine glory as the Savior of the world and Redeemer of men. It was because He humbled Himself and became obedient to death, the death of the cross, that God so highly exalted Him.

It is this that gives meaning and worth to what Jesus says of Himself as the omnipotent and omnipresent One. Between His mention of these two attributes, He gives His command that His disciples should go out into the world and preach the gospel, and teach men to obey all that He has commanded. It follows as a matter of necessity that it is only when His servants obey His commands that they can expect the fullness of His power and His presence to be with them. It is only when they themselves are living witnesses to the reality of His power to save and to keep from sin that they can expect the full experience of His abiding presence, with the power to train others to the life of obedience.

The abiding presence of the Savior is promised to all who have accepted Him in the fullness of His redeeming power, and who preach by their lives as well as by their words what a wonderful Savior He is. We can say along with the psalmist, "I desire to do your will, O my God; your law is within my heart" (Psalm 40:8).

Thank You, Lord Jesus, for the assurance of Your power and presence in my life. Teach me to obey Your commands.

Christ the Crucified

May I never boast except in the cross of our Lord Jesus Christ,
through which the world has been crucified to me, and I to the world.
GALATIANS 6:14

Christ's highest glory is His cross. It was in this that He glorified the Father, and the Father glorified Him. It is as the slain Lamb in the center of the throne that He receives the worship of the ransomed and the angels and all creation (see Revelation 5). And it is of Christ the crucified that Paul writes the words of today's text—words that have been echoed by a multitude of believers. Is it not reasonable that Christ's highest glory should be your only glory, too?

When Jesus said to His disciples that He would be with them always, it was as the crucified One that He gave this promise. And each one who seeks to claim the promise should realize: It is the crucified Jesus who promises, who offers, to be with me every day.

Thank You, Lord Jesus, that You strengthen me with Your power and presence when I humble myself and obey Your commands.

Is it the fact that we do not glory in the cross by which we are crucified to the world, could that be why we find it so difficult to expect and enjoy the abiding presence of Jesus? How little we experience that we are dead to the world and that we are free from its power! How little we have learned to deny ourselves, to have the mind that was in Christ when He emptied Himself and took the form of a servant, humbling Himself and becoming obedient even to the death of the cross! (see Philippians 2:5–8).

Remember this: It is the crucified Christ who is with you every moment of the day, and in whose power you can confess, "I have been crucified with Christ, and He lives in me."

Christ Glorified

For the Lamb at the center of the throne will be their shepherd;
he will lead them to springs of living water.
They follow the Lamb wherever he goes.
REVELATION 7:17, 14:4

Who is it that says, "I will be with you always"? We must take time to know Him well if we are to understand what we may expect from Him when He offers to be with us all the day. Who is He?

He is none else than the slain Lamb at the center of the throne! The Lamb in His deepest humiliation, enthroned in the glory of God. It is He who invites you to the closest fellowship and likeness to Himself.

Time, deep reverence, and adoring worship are required to realize that He who lives in the glory of the Father, He before whom all heaven bows in prostrate adoration, is the One who offers to be your companion and your shepherd. Read Revelation 5 over and over until you can, with the elders, cast your crown before the throne and join in the praises of all creation.

The Lamb in the center of the throne is indeed the embodiment of the omnipotent glory of the everlasting God and of His love. To have this Lamb of God as your almighty Shepherd and your faithful Keeper does indeed make it possible that the thoughts and the cares of earth shall not separate you from His love for a single moment.

Lord, I bow before
You in adoration
and pray that You
will accept my
humble praise.

The Great Question

[Jesus] asked [the blind men], "Do you believe that I am able to do this?"
"Yes, Lord," they replied.
MATTHEW 9:28

Jesus often spoke about the power of faith. To the father of a boy who was possessed by an evil spirit, Jesus said, "Everything is possible for him who believes." Immediately the father exclaimed, "I do believe; help me overcome my unbelief!" (Mark 9:23–24).

To Martha, Jesus said, "He who believes in me will live, even though He dies. Do you believe this?" She answered, "Yes, Lord, I believe." (John 11:25–27).

Are you ready to say with the father and Martha, " Yes, Lord, I believe that you are the Christ, the Son of God"? It is not such a difficult question to answer. It is, however, more difficult to believe Christ's promises of the power of the resurrection life and of His abiding presence. It seems almost too much to venture. And yet it is this faith that Christ expects from us and is waiting to work within us.

Lord, I do believe that You will be with me every day.

God will never force His blessings on you against your will. He seeks in every possible way to convince you that He is able and most willing to keep His promises. The resurrection of Christ from the dead is His great plea, His all-prevailing argument to convince us. If He could raise Christ from the dead, surely God can fulfill His promise that Christ will be with you every moment of every day.

Are you prepared to take His Word when He says that He will be with you always? Let us not rest until we have bowed before Him in adoration and said, "Yes, Lord, I do believe."

Christ Manifested

"Whoever has my commands and obeys them, he is the one who loves me.
He who loves me will be loved by my Father,
and I too will love him and show myself to him."

JOHN 14:21

When the Spirit came upon them, the disciples would learn to know Christ in a new way: In the power of the Spirit they would know Him far more intimately than they ever had on earth, and He would be with them unceasingly.

The condition of this revelation of Himself is comprised in the one word—*love*. The love with which Christ had loved His disciples had taken possession of their hearts, and would show itself in the love of a full and absolute obedience. The Father would see this, and His love would rest upon their souls; Christ would love them with the special love drawn out by their loving hearts and would manifest Himself. The love of heaven shed abroad in their hearts would be met by the new and blessed revelation of Christ Himself.

But this is not all. When the question was asked, "But, Lord, why do you intend to show yourself to us and not to the world?" the answer came, "If anyone loves me, he will obey my teaching. My Father will love him, and we will come to him and make our home with him" (John 14:22–23). In the heart thus prepared by the Holy Spirit, showing itself in the obedience of love in a fully surrendered heart, the Father and the Son will take up their abode.

Holy Spirit, I thank You for making Christ Jesus a glorious reality in my life.

Has your heart been so prepared that Christ's abiding presence is your strength and joy every moment of the day?

The Morning Watch

Early on the first day of the week, while it was still dark, Mary Magdalene went to the tomb.... Jesus said to her, "Mary." She turned toward him and cried out in Aramaic, "Rabboni!" (which means Teacher).
JOHN 20:1, 16

Here we have the first appearance of the risen Savior after His resurrection from the dead. The person who had the privilege of seeing Him first was Mary Magdalene, the woman whose many sins had been forgiven and who therefore showed much love (see Luke 7:47).

Think of what the morning watch meant to Mary. She isolated herself from all else in her longing to find Christ. In fear and doubt, and yet with a burning love and strong hope, she waited for Jesus to manifest Himself as the Lord of Glory. Her love was met by the love of Jesus, and she found Him, the living Lord, in all the power of His resurrection life.

Lord, when I plan my day, my interests usually come first. Inspire me and give me the strength to devote time to You in the early morning.

On that first morning watch a woman waited for Jesus to manifest Himself. What a prophecy and pledge of what believers experience when the risen Lord reveals Himself to those who love Him! During this meeting Mary Magdalene learned, not in words or thought, but in the reality of a divine experience, what it meant that He, to whom all power had been given on earth and in heaven, had taken her into the keeping of His abiding presence.

There is nothing that can prove a greater attraction to our Lord than the love that sacrifices everything and rests satisfied with nothing less than Himself. It is to such a love that Christ manifests Himself. He loved us and gave Himself for us. Christ's love needs our love in which to reveal itself.

The Evening Prayer

But they urged him strongly, "Stay with us." So he went in to stay with them.
When he was at the table with them...their eyes were opened
and they recognized him.
LUKE 24:29–31

If Mary Magdalene teaches us what the morning watch can mean for the revelation of Jesus *to* the soul, Emmaus reminds us of the place that the evening prayer may have in preparing for the full manifestation of Christ *in* the soul.

For two of the disciples the day started in darkness. When they received the first messages that Jesus was alive, they did not know what to think. They were discussing what had happened, when Jesus Himself came up and walked along with them. "But they were kept from recognizing him" (Luke 24:16). Jesus often comes near to us with the purpose of manifesting Himself, but is hindered because we are slow of heart to believe what the Word has spoken. While the Lord was speaking, their hearts began to burn within them, and yet they never even thought that this could be Jesus. This happens even today. In the fellowship of the saints our hearts are stirred with the new vision of what Christ's presence may be, and yet we do not see Him.

Lord Jesus, thank You that You want to reveal Yourself to me. I desire nothing more than that.

When they neared the village, the disciples begged Jesus to stay. That night Jesus gave new meaning to the word *abide*. The disciples got far more than they expected: They received a foretaste of the abiding presence that Christ's resurrection had made possible.

What convinced Jesus to reveal Himself to these two men? Despite their ignorance and unbelief it was surely their intense longing for the Lord, their constraining prayer, and the divine inspiration of the Scriptures that Jesus opened to them (see Luke 24:32).

The Divine Mission

On the evening of that first day of the week, when the disciples were together,
with the doors locked for fear of the Jews,
Jesus came and stood among them and said, "Peace be with you!"
JOHN 20:19

When Jesus suddenly stood among them and said, "Peace be with you," the disciples were startled and frightened, thinking He was a ghost. He then showed them His hands and His feet. This was not only a sign of recognition, but also the deep eternal mystery of heaven: Jesus on the throne as the Lamb that was slain. The disciples were filled with joy and amazement.

With Mary, Jesus revealed Himself to a fervent love that could not rest without Him. With the men at Emmaus, it was their constraining prayer that received the revelation. Here He meets the willing servants whom He has trained for His service and hands over to them the work He has done on earth. By breathing the Spirit upon them, He changes their fear into the boldness of peace and gladness. The mighty power of God, by which He raised Christ from the dead, will henceforth work in them.

Thank You, Lord Jesus, that You will reveal Yourself to me and strengthen me with Your presence and the power of the Holy Spirit.

What Jesus said to the disciples applies to all believers: "As the Father has sent me, I am sending you" (John 20:21). For us, too, is the promise of the Holy Spirit. For us, too, is the personal manifestation of Jesus as the living One, with the pierced hands and feet. If our hearts are set on nothing less than the presence of the living Lord, we may confidently count on receiving it. Jesus never sends His servants out without the promise of His abiding presence and His almighty power.

The Blessedness
of Believing

Then Jesus told him, "Because you have seen me, you have believed;
blessed are those who have not seen and yet have believed."
JOHN 20:29

Many think that Thomas was exceptionally privileged because Christ manifested Himself by allowing Thomas to touch His hands and His side. No wonder he could find no words but those of holy adoration: "My Lord and my God!" (John 20:28). Has there ever been higher expression of the overwhelming nearness and glory of God?

And yet Christ said, "Because you have seen me, you have believed; blessed are those who have not seen and yet have believed." True living faith gives a sense of Christ's nearness far deeper and more intimate than the joy that filled the heart of Thomas. Even after all these centuries, we may experience the presence and power of Christ on a far deeper level than Thomas did. To those who do not see, yet truly believe, Christ has promised that He will manifest Himself, and that He and the Father will come and dwell in them. We must never think of this as something beyond our reach.

How can we attain this childlike faith? The answer is very simple: Where Jesus Christ is the one object of our desire and our confidence, He will manifest Himself in divine power. He will make His holy promise a reality in our conscious experience. Pray for this kind of faith in His blessed Word, in His divine power, and in His abiding presence. Christ will indeed manifest Himself, abide with you, and dwell in your heart as His home.

Thank You, Lord, that I have the privilege to believe and experience, although I have not seen.

The Greatness of Love

Peter was hurt because Jesus asked him the third time, "Do you love me?"
He said, "Lord, you know all things; you know that I love you."
JOHN 21:17

We can easily understand why Christ asked Peter whether he loved Him three times. It was to remind Peter of the self-confidence with which Peter had said, "Even if I have to die with you, I will never disown you" (Matthew 26:35).

Peter's new task would be to feed the Lord's sheep and to care for His lambs. And for that task he would need much love.

God is love. Christ is the Son of His love. And because He loved His people to the end, He asked them to prove their love to Him by obeying His commands, and by loving one another with the love with which He loves them. In heaven and on earth, and in all our work for Christ and our care for the world, the greatest thing is love.

To everyone who longs to have Jesus manifest Himself in their life, the essential requisite is love. Peter teaches us that man does not have the power to offer such love. We become partakers of this love through the power of Christ's resurrection life. Thank God, if Peter the self-confident could be so changed, Christ will work in us the wondrous change, too. It is to love that Christ will manifest Himself, as the only fitness for feeding His sheep and tending His lambs.

Thank You, Lord, for the power of Your Holy Spirit working within me, and for the love He pours out into my heart like a stream of living water that flows out to those around me.

Life from the Dead

When I saw him, I fell at his feet as though dead. Then he placed his right hand on me and said, "Do not be afraid. I am the First and the Last. I am the Living One; I was dead, and behold I am alive for ever and ever!"
REVELATION 1:17–18

John fell down as dead at the feet of Jesus, more or less sixty years after the resurrection. Moses once asked God, "Show me your glory." God answered, "You cannot see my face, for no one may see me and live" (Exodus 33:18–20). Man's sinful nature cannot live in the presence of God's divine glory. When John fell as dead at Christ's feet, it proved how little he could endure the wonderful heavenly vision.

When Christ placed His right hand on John, He reminded him that He Himself had passed through death before He could rise to the life and the glory of God. For the Master Himself and for every disciple, for Moses and for John, there is only one way to the glory of God: through death.

The lesson is a deep and most needful one to all who long for Jesus to manifest Himself to them. The knowledge of Jesus, fellowship with Him, and the experience of His power are not possible without the sacrifice of all there is in us of the world and its spirit. The old Adam must die, just as a grain of wheat must die if it wants to yield a crop. If we desire the abiding presence of Christ with us every moment of every day, we will have to accept this lesson—through death to life.

If you have been crucified with Christ, you can be sure that you have risen from the dead with Him. You can also be certain that He will place His right hand on you to assure you of His presence.

Thank You, Lord, for the assurance of Your abiding presence with me. It is by Your grace alone, for I have nothing to boast about.

Christ Revealed in Paul

[God] who…called me by his grace,
was pleased to reveal his Son in me.
GALATIANS 1:15–16

All our study and worship of Christ are focused on five points: Christ incarnate, the crucified Christ, the enthroned Christ, the indwelling Christ, and Christ coming in glory. If the first is the seed, the second is the seed cast into the ground, with the third the seed growing up to heaven. The fourth is the fruit through the Holy Spirit, and the fifth is the gathering of the fruit when Christ appears.

Paul tells us that it pleased God to reveal His Son in him. The result of that revelation is that Christ lives in him. And the distinguishing mark of this new life is that he is crucified with Christ. It is this that enables Paul to say that he no longer lives. In Christ he has found the death of self. Just as the cross is the chief characteristic of Christ Himself, so the life of Christ in Paul made him inseparably one with his crucified Lord.

Lord, give me the strength of Your Holy Spirit to die of self and this sinful world, so that You can live in me always.

If Christ so actually lived in Paul that Paul no longer lived, what became of his responsibility? Paul's answer is ready and clear: "I live by faith in the Son of God, who loved me and gave himself for me" (Galatians 2:20).

This was the sum and substance of all Paul's preaching. He asks for intercession that he might speak the mystery of Christ (see Colossians 1:26–29). The indwelling Christ was the secret of his life of faith, the one power, the one aim of all his life and work, the hope of glory. Let us believe in the abiding presence of Christ as the sure gift to each one who trusts Him fully.

Why Could We Not?

Then the disciples came to Jesus in private and asked,
"Why couldn't we drive it out?" He replied, "Because you have so little faith."
MATTHEW 17:19–20

The disciples had often cast out devils, but here they had been impotent. They asked the Lord what the reason might be. His answer was very simple: "Because you have so little faith."

We have here the reply to the great question so often asked: "How is it that we cannot live the life of unbroken fellowship with Christ, which the Scripture promises?" Simply because of our unbelief. We do not realize that faith must accept and expect that God will, by His almighty power, fulfill every promise He has made. We do not live in that utter helplessness and dependence on God alone which is the very essence of faith. We are not strong in the faith, fully persuaded that what God has promised He is able and willing to perform. We do not give ourselves with our whole heart simply to believe that God, by His almighty power, will work wonders in our hearts.

But what can be the reason that this faith is so often lacking? According to Mark, Jesus said that there is not enough prayer and fasting. To have a strong faith in God requires that we keep in close touch with Him by persistent prayer. We cannot call up faith at our bidding; it needs close communion with God. To gain the prizes of the heavenly life here on earth requires that we sacrifice all that earth can offer. Just as God is needed to satisfy the human heart and work His mighty miracles in it, faith requires the whole man to be utterly given up to God. And to have the power of that faith which can cast out every evil spirit, prayer and fasting are essential.

Lord, I am totally dependent on You. I believe with all my heart that You will work wonders in my heart and cast out every evil spirit.

The Power of Obedience

*"The one who sent me is with me; he has not left me alone,
for I always do what pleases him."*
JOHN 8:29

In these words Christ not only describes the quality of His life with the Father, but also reveals the law of communion with God: simple obedience.

How strongly He insisted upon it we see in the Farewell Discourse. In John 14, Jesus says three times that if the disciples love Him, they will obey His commands. Then He will ask His Father to send them the Holy Spirit to reveal Christ to them and to dwell in them. In John 15 obedience is also mentioned three times.

Obedience is the proof and the exercise of the love of God that the Holy Spirit has poured out into our hearts. It comes from love and leads to love—a deeper and a fuller experience of God's love and indwelling. It assures us that what we ask will be given us. It assures us that we are abiding in the love of Christ. It seals our claim to be called the friends of Christ. And so it is not only proof of love but also of faith, assuring us that we ask and receive because we obey His commands and do the things that are pleasing in His sight.

Obedience enables us to abide in the Lord's love and gives the full experience of His unbroken presence. Christ did not speak of impossibility; He saw what we might confidently expect in the power of the Spirit. Let the thought take deep hold of us. It is to the obedient that His Word comes, "I am always with you."

Lord, through Your Holy Spirit make me obedient to Your commands, so that I can abide in Your presence all day long.

The Power of Intercession

So Peter was kept in prison,
but the church was earnestly praying to God for him.
ACTS 12:5

Missionaries often speak of the imperative need of more intercession—above all, of more united intercession. We can serve the deepest interests of the church in no better way than by multiplying the number of real intercessors, and by focusing the prayers of Christendom on those situations that demand the almighty working of the Spirit of God. It is far more important and vital than any other service we can render to missions. We must unite the true intercessors of all countries and release the superhuman energy of prayer to help the ushering in of a new era abounding in signs and wonders characteristic of the working of the living Christ. Immeasurably more important than any other work is the linking of all we do to the fountain of divine life.

There is no greater need than focusing the united intercession of Christendom on the great army of missionaries. They confess the need of the presence and the power of God's Spirit in their life and work. They long for the experience of the abiding presence and power of Christ every day. They need it and they have a right to it.

Shall we not be part of that great army that pleads with God for the endowment of power that is so absolutely necessary for effective work? Shall we not, like the early apostles, "continue steadfastly in prayer" until God sends an abundant answer? As we give ourselves continually to prayer, the power of the promise "I will always be with you" will be proved in our lives.

Lord, I pray that every missionary will experience the power of Your abiding presence. Bless their work so that the world can be won.

The Power of Time

My times are in your hands.
PSALM 31:15

The plural implies the singular: My *time* is in your hand. It belongs to you, Lord. You alone have the right to command it. I yield it wholly and gladly to your disposal. What mighty power time can exert if wholly given up to God!

Time is lord of all things. What is all the history of the world but a proof of how, slowly but surely, time has made man what he is today? All around us we see the proofs. In the growth of the child to manhood, both physically and mentally, in all our labors and all our attainments, it is under the law of time and its inconceivable power that we spend our lives.

This is especially true in the intercourse with God. Time here, too, is master. What fellowship with God! What holiness and blessedness! What likeness to His image, and what power in His service for blessing to men! All on the one condition: that we have sufficient time with God for His holiness to shine on us with its light and its heat, to make us partakers of His Spirit and His life. The very essence of religion lies in this thought: *time with God.*

And yet many of God's servants frankly confess that they do not spend enough time in daily communion with God. What can be the cause of such a sad confession? Nothing but a lack of faith in the God-given assurance that time spent alone with God will indeed bring into the lives of His servants the power to enable them to experience His abiding presence with them all the day.

Stop looking for petty excuses as to why you cannot have daily communion with God. Put your time in His hands!

Lord, nothing is more important than spending time in Your glorious presence. Thank You for Your blessing on the time that I spend with You.

The Power of Faith

"Everything is possible for him who believes."
MARK 9:23

There is not one truth on which Christ insisted more frequently, both with His disciples and with those who came seeking His help, than the absolute necessity of faith and its unlimited possibilities. And experience has taught us that there is nothing in which we fall so short as the simple and absolute trust in God to fulfill literally in us all that He has promised. A life in the abiding presence of God must of necessity be a life of unceasing faith.

Think for a moment of the marks of a true faith. First of all, faith counts upon God to do all He has promised as the only measure of its expectation. It does not rest content with taking *some* of the promises; it seeks nothing less than to claim every promise that God has made, in its largest and fullest meaning. Under a sense of its own nothingness and utter impotence, faith trusts the power of an almighty God to work wonders in the heart in which He dwells.

Faith also recognizes the inseparable link that unites God's promises and His commands, and yields itself to do the one as fully as it trusts the other. In the pursuit of the power that such a life of faith can give, there is often a faith that seeks and strives but cannot grasp. This is followed by a faith that begins to see that waiting on God is needed, and therefore quietly rests in the hope of what God will do.

The life of faith to which the abiding presence will be granted must be disciplined. If you want to experience God's presence in your life all day long, you will have to part with much that you formerly thought lawful. Then He will become your blessed friend, the joy and light of your life.

Lord, please strengthen my faith. Open my eyes to see what I have to part with to make Your presence a greater reality to me.

John's Missionary Message

We proclaim to you what we have seen and heard,
so that you also may have fellowship with us.
And our fellowship is with the Father and with his Son, Jesus Christ.

1 JOHN 1:3

What a revelation of the calling of the preacher of the gospel! His message is nothing less than to proclaim that Christ has opened the way for us simple men to have, day by day, living, loving fellowship with the holy God. He is to preach this as a witness to the life He Himself lives in all its blessed experience. In the power of that testimony, He is to prove its reality and to show how a sinful man on earth can indeed live in fellowship with the Father and the Son.

The very first duty of the minister or the missionary every day of his life is to maintain such close communion with God that he can preach the truth in the fullness of joy, so that his words appeal with power to the heart. It is such teaching, revealing the infinite claim and power of Christ's love as maintained by the power of the Holy Spirit, that will encourage and compel men to make the measure of Christ's surrender for them the only measure of *their* surrender to Him and His service.

It is this intimate fellowship with Christ as the secret of daily service and testimony that has power to make Christ known as our deliverer from sin and the inspiration of a life of wholehearted devotion to His service.

We need this intimate and abiding fellowship with Christ in order to maintain a spiritual efficiency that will influence everybody we come into contact with.

Lord, give me the power through Your Holy Spirit to live in such a way that my life will glorify Your name.

Paul's Missionary Message

Devote yourselves to prayer, being watchful and thankful.
And pray for us, too, that God may open a door for our message,
so that we may proclaim the mystery of Christ, for which I am in chains.
Pray that I may proclaim it clearly, as I should.
COLOSSIANS 4:2–4

To Paul's mind the very center and substance of His preaching was the indwelling Christ. He spoke of the riches of the glory of the mystery of Christ in us. Though he had been a preacher of this gospel for many years, he still asked for prayer, that he might make known this mystery, as he should.

The complaint is often made that churches stagnate—that after a time there appears to be no further growth, and that the members show little joy and power for bearing witness to Christ Jesus. It is as though these churches have lost the truth of the indwelling Christ.

We often speak of Paul's missionary methods, but is there not a greater need of Paul's missionary message, as expressed in his letter to the Colossians? In Colossians 1:27, Paul said, "Christ in you, the hope of glory."

Paul felt the need of much prayer to enable him to give this message, as he should. Is this not a call to all of us, to make it a matter of first importance? It is, after all, the rightful heritage of each believer to live in daily communion with Christ and to experience His abiding presence.

Lord, keep me from being so busy with other things that I neglect my daily communion with You.

May the church and all of us share in the blessing, the restoration to its right place, of this truth: "Christ is in you. He is your hope of glory."

The Missionary's Life

You are witnesses, and so is God, of how holy,
righteous and blameless we were among you who believed.
1 THESSALONIANS 2:10

Christ taught His disciples as much by His life as by His teaching. Paul more than once appealed to what his converts had seen of his own life. Paul desired to be a living witness to the truth of all that he had preached about Christ: that He is able to save and to keep us from sin, renewing our whole nature by the power of His Holy Spirit, Himself becoming the life of those who believe in Him.

We must be careful not to hide the Christ we try to proclaim behind a lifestyle that is unworthy of Him. Only to the extent that we reveal the lifestyle of Christ in our own lives, shall we be able to touch people's hearts with our words. We must be living examples of what we preach. Only then will people regard our message as true and understand it.

Heavenly Father,

give me the

strength to

practice what

I preach.

Paul's appeal to his life as holy and blameless placed a high standard before his converts, and he called upon his readers to follow his example (see Acts 20:25; 1 Corinthians 4:16, 11:1; Philippians 3:17; 1 Timothy 1:16). Paul did not boast about Himself. He spoke of an actual, divine, unceasing abiding of Christ in him, working in him all that was well-pleasing to the Father.

Take time to seriously think about your lifestyle and what others can read from your life and actions. Do you have the courage to ask people to follow your example? Let us not rest until we can say, "Christ lives and He dwells in me!

The Holy Spirit

*"He will bring glory to me by taking from what is mine
and making it known to you."*
JOHN 16:14

When our Lord said, "I will be with you always," His disciples did not at first understand or experience the full meaning of His words. It was only at Pentecost when they were filled with the Holy Spirit, who brought into their hearts the glorified Lord Jesus, that they began a new life in the joy of His abiding presence.

All our attempts to live that life of continuous, unbroken communion with Jesus will be in vain unless we yield ourselves wholly to the power and the indwelling of the Holy Spirit.

Our faith in the fulfillment of Christ's glorious promises of the Father and Son making their abode in us is subject to one essential and indispensable condition—a life utterly and unceasingly yielded to the rule and leading of the Spirit of Christ.

Let no one say, "The experience of Christ's being with us every day and all the day is impossible." Christ meant His Word to be a simple and eternal reality. He meant the promises to be accepted as absolute divine truth. But this truth could only be experienced where the Spirit, in His power as God, was known and believed in and obeyed.

We need to understand that the Spirit as God claims absolute subjection, and is willing to take possession of our whole being and enable us to fulfill all that Christ asks of us. It is the Spirit who can deliver us from the power of the flesh. It is He who can conquer the power of the world. It is the Spirit through whom Christ Jesus will manifest Himself to us in nothing less than His abiding presence.

Lord, I yield my life to the rule and leading of Your Holy Spirit. I long for Your presence in my life all day long.

Like Jesus

Your attitude should be the same as that of Christ Jesus.
PHILIPPIANS 2:5

And what was the attitude that was in Christ Jesus? Being in the form of God, He emptied Himself, taking the form of a servant; being made in the likeness of men, He humbled Himself, becoming obedient even unto death, the death of the cross.

Self-emptying and self-sacrifice, obedience to God's will, and love to men, even unto the death of the cross—such was the character of Christ for which God so highly exalted Him. Such is the character of Christ that we are to imitate. On Christmas day Jesus came to the earth in the likeness of a man, that we might be conformed into the likeness of God.

Let no one say that this is impossible. Just as impossible as the thought of the Son of God as a helpless baby in a manger, so real is it. "What is impossible with men is possible with God" (Luke 18:27).

Thank You, Father, that Jesus came to us in the form of a man to show us what it means to live a life totally devoted to You.

It has been said that the missionary who is to commend the gospel must first embody it in a character fully conformed to the likeness of Jesus Christ. It is only as far as he can live Christ before the eyes of the converts that he can help them to understand His message. As the church aims at making some marked degree of likeness to Christ's character the standard for Christian teachers, our missionaries will be able to pass this on to their converts and say to them, "Be our followers as we are followers of Christ."

Let us not rest until our faith lays hold of the promise that God works in us to fulfill our high and holy calling. Receive this promise as your own Christmas gift.

Christt Life

Christ ... is your life.
COLOSSIANS 3:4

Christ's life was more than His teaching, more than His work, more even than His death. It was His life in the presence of God and man that gave value to what He said and did and suffered. And it is this life, glorified in the resurrection, that He imparts to His people and enables them to live out before men.

It was life in the new brotherhood of the Holy Spirit that made both Jews and Greeks feel that there was some superhuman power about Christ's disciples. His followers gave living proof of the truth of what they said, that God's love had come down and taken possession of them.

Spiritual leaders agree that the life of Christians is either the greatest asset or the greatest obstacle in the winning of souls for Christ. Too many miss the deepest secret of power and success in their work because they do not live out the Christ life on an entirely different level from where other men live. When Christ sent out His disciples it was with this command: "But stay in the city until you have been clothed with power from on high" (Luke 24:49).

Thank You, Lord, for being my life, my strength, and my joy. I pray that my words and deeds will be proof of this.

Everything depends upon this life with God in Christ being right. The simplicity and intensity of your life in Christ, and of the life of Christ in you, make you conqueror over self and everything that could hinder the Christ life. The Christ life will give you victory over the powers of evil, and over the hearts from which evil spirits must be cast out.

Christ is life! And when He lives in you—every moment of every day, as He promised—you can live your life to the fullest. He is your life, your strength, and your joy.

The Nearness of God

Come near to God and he will come near to you.
JAMES 4:8

It has been said that the holiness of God is the union of God's infinite distance from sinful man with God's infinite nearness in His redeeming grace. Faith must ever seek to realize both His distance and His nearness.

In Christ, God has come near, so very near to man, and now the command comes: *Come near to God and He will come near to you.* The nearness of Christ Jesus can only be experienced as we draw near to Him.

This means that we must yield ourselves to Him every day, so that His holy presence can rest on us. This also means a voluntary, intentional, and wholehearted turning away from the world, to wait on God to make Himself known to us. It means giving time and all our heart and strength to allow Him to reveal Himself. We cannot possibly expect the abiding presence of Christ with us throughout the day unless we engage in the definite daily exercise of strong desire and childlike trust in His promise, *Come near to God and He will come near to you.*

Then comes the quiet assurance of faith—even if there is not much feeling or sense of His presence—that God is with us when we go out to do His will. He will watch over us and keep us and strengthen our inner man with divine strength for the work we are to do for Him.

Wait patiently on the Lord when you pray to Him…and you will hear Him say, "Remember, I am with you always."

Thank You, Lord, that I am never alone; that You are walking with me every step of the way. Thank You for strengthening me with the power of Your Holy Spirit.

Love

*Having loved his own who were in the world,
he now showed them the full extent of his love.*
JOHN 13:1

These are the opening words of that holy, confidential talk of Christ with His disciples, as out of the depths of eternity He spoke to them in the last hours before He went to Gethsemane. They are the revelation and full display of that divine love which was manifested in His death on the cross.

The word He used most in this conversation was the word *love*. Jesus spoke of His love for His Father and His Father's love for Him. He spoke of His love for the disciples and of their love for Him that could be lived out in obedience to His commands. He also spoke about love to others. Read chapters 13–17 again and note how many times love is mentioned. There can be no misunderstanding.

God's love to Christ is given to pass into us and to become our life. In this way the love with which the Father loved the Son lives in our hearts. If the Lord Jesus is to manifest Himself to us, it can only be to the loving heart. If we are to claim His daily presence with us, it can only be in a relationship of infinite tender love between Him and us. Only in the atmosphere of a holy living love can the abiding presence of the loving Christ be known.

*Lord, as the year
is nearing its end,
I humbly kneel
before You. Keep
me in Your love.*

In the early church their first love was forsaken after a time, and they placed their confidence in all the activities of service. And they were told in no uncertain terms, "You have forsaken your first love" (Revelation 2:4).

And this is the tragedy: We keep ourselves busy with the things of the Lord and not with the Lord of the things.

Trial and Triumph

[Jesus said] "Everything is possible for him who believes."
Immediately the boy's father exclaimed, "I do believe;
help me overcome my unbelief!"

MARK 9:23–24

What a glorious promise: *Everything is possible for him who believes.* And yet it is the greatness of the promise that constitutes the trial of faith. At first we do not really believe its truth. And when we have grasped it, we think that the faith needed is utterly beyond our reach.

When Christ said to the father of the child, "Everything is possible for him who believes," the man was cast into deeper despair. How could his meager faith be able to work a miracle? But when he looked into the face of Christ, and he saw the love in those tender eyes, he felt sure that this Man not only had the power to heal his child, but also could inspire in him the faith he needed. Jesus' presence made possible both a miracle of healing and the miracle that this man should have so great a faith. And with tears the father cried, "I do believe; help me overcome my unbelief!" The very greatness of faith's trial was the greatness of its triumph.

Lord, I do believe, but please help me to overcome my unbelief.

What a lesson! Of all things that are possible to faith, the most impossible is that I should be able to exercise such faith. The abiding presence of Christ is possible to faith, and this faith is possible to the soul that clings to Christ and trusts Him. You are entirely dependent on Christ for the faith as well as the blessing. And when you become conscious of the unbelief that is still struggling within, cast yourself on the power and the love of Jesus, saying, "Help me overcome my unbelief!"

Filled with the Holy Spirit

*Instead, be filled with the Spirit. Speak to one another with psalms,
hymns and spiritual songs. Sing and make music in your heart to the Lord,
always giving thanks to God the Father for everything,
in the name of our Lord Jesus Christ.*
EPHESIANS 5:18–20

If the expression "filled with the Spirit" were used only in the story of Pentecost, we might naturally think that it was something special and not meant for ordinary life. But the New Testament teaches us that to be filled with the Spirit is meant for every Christian, every day.

To understand this more fully, think of the Holy Spirit in Christ Jesus. The Spirit led Jesus all through His life on earth until He, by the eternal Spirit, offered Himself unblemished to God. In Christ, the Spirit meant prayer, obedience, and sacrifice.

If we are to follow Christ, to have His mind in us, and to live out His life, we must regard the fullness of the Spirit as a daily provision to live the life of obedience, of joy, of self-sacrifice, and of power for service. There may be occasions when that fullness of the Spirit will become especially manifest. But every day and all the day it is only as we are led by the Spirit that we can abide in Christ Jesus, conquer the flesh and the world, and live a life with God in prayer and with our fellow men in humble, fruitful service.

Our faith in Christ will be the measure of our fullness of the Spirit. The measure of the power of the Spirit in us will be the measure of our experience of the presence of Christ.

*Lord, Your abiding
presence made
this a very special
year for me.
I praise You for
Your abundant
grace I received
so undeservedly.*

Immeasurably More

Now to him who is able to do immeasurably more than all we ask or imagine, according to his power that is at work within us, to him be glory in the church and in Christ Jesus throughout all generations, for ever and ever! Amen.

EPHESIANS 3:20–21

Paul had apparently reached the highest expression possible of the life to which God's mighty power could bring the believer. But Paul is not content. In this doxology he rises still higher and lifts us up to give glory to God as "able to do immeasurably more than all we ask or imagine." Pause for a moment to think what that *immeasurably more* really means, and how everything we receive is the fruit of the abiding presence of Jesus in the life of the believer.

While you are kneeling before God in adoration, you are reminded of the greatness of His power that is working in you. When you realize it is the same power that raised Jesus from the dead and forgave your sins, you will feel like falling down before the Lamb to join the crowds in the universal chorus that John describes so vividly in Revelation 5. The Lamb is indeed worthy of your adoration!

Give glory to God, until your heart learns to believe, *The prayer will be fulfilled, Jesus Christ will dwell in my heart by faith.* Faith in this almighty God, and the exceeding abundance of His grace and power, will teach us that the indwelling of Christ in our heart is the secret of His abiding presence.

To him who sits on the throne and to the Lamb be praise and honor and glory and power, for ever and ever!

REVELATION 5:13

Scripture Index

Are You Living Your Dream?
Or Just Living Your Life?

1-59052-201-X $16.99

Your life dream is the key to God's greatest glory and your greatest fulfillment. There's no limit to what He can accomplish if you wholeheartedly pursue your created purpose! Let Bruce Wilkinson show you how to rise above the ordinary, conquer your fears, and overcome the obstacles that keep you from living your Big Dream.

THE DREAM GIVER SERIES

THE DREAM GIVER FOR COUPLES
Let Bruce and Darlene Marie Wilkinson take you on a journey that will give you hope as you discover the seven principles to experiencing the marriage you've always dreamed of.

ISBN 1-59052-460-8

THE DREAM GIVER FOR TEENS
It's time to begin the journey of your life. Let Bruce and Jessica Wilkinson help you find your dream and pursue it on a quest to discover the life you've always dreamed of.

ISBN 1-59052-459-4

THE DREAM GIVER FOR PARENTS
In this practical guide, Bruce and Darlene Marie share with you the seven secrets for guiding your children to discover and pursue their Dreams.

ISBN 1-59052-455-1